Hidden Resources

Classical Perspectives

On Subjectivity

Edited by

Dan Zahavi

IMPRINT ACADEMIC

OF RELATED INTEREST FROM IMPRINT ACADEMIC
Full details on: http://www.imprint-academic.com

Series Editor: Professor J.A. Goguen
Department of Computer Science and Engineering, UCSD

Francisco J. Varela and Jonathan Shear, ed.
The View From Within:
First-Person Approaches to the Study of Consciousness

Evan Thompson, ed.
Between Ourselves:
Second-Person Issues In the Study of Consciousness

Michel Ferrari, ed.
The Varieties of Religious Experience: Centenary Essays

Anthony Jack and Andreas Roepstorff, ed.
Trusting the Subject? Volumes 1 & 2

Published in the UK by Imprint Academic
PO Box 200, Exeter EX5 5YX, UK

Published in the USA by Imprint Academic
Philosophy Documentation Center,
PO Box 7147, Charlottesville, VA 22906-7147 , USA

ISBN 0 907845 96 7 (paperback)

ISSN 1355 8250 (*Journal of Consciousness Studies*, **11**, number 10–11, 2004)

British Library Cataloguing in Publication Data
A catalogue record for this book is available from the British Library
Library of Congress Card Number: 2003102065

Cover Art: Karen Sutherland

Contents

Contributors

Andrew Brook (Department of Philosophy, Carleton University, Ottawa, Ontario, Canada. *Email: abrook@ccs.carleton.ca*) is professor of philosophy and Director of the Institute of Cognitive Science at Carleton University. His books include *Kant and the Mind* (1994) and *Self-Reference and Self-Awareness* (co-edited 2001).

John J. Drummond (Department of Philosophy, Fordham University, Bronx, NY 10458, USA. *Email: drummond@fordham.edu*) is professor of philosophy and Director of Graduate Studies at Fordham University in New York City. He is the author of *Husserlian Intentionality and Non-Foundational Realism: Noema and Object*. He has edited or coedited four collections on Husserl's phenomenology and has published numerous articles on Husserl's theory of intentionality and his ethics.

Shaun Gallagher (Department of Philosophy, Colbourn Hall 411, University of Central Florida, Orlando, FL 32816-1352, USA. *Email: gallaghr@mail.ucf.edu*) is professor of philosophy and cognitive science at the University of Central Florida. His research and teaching interests include phenomenology and philosophy of mind, cognitive science, hermeneutics, and theories of the self and personal identity. He co-edits the interdisciplinary journal *Phenomenology and the Cognitive Sciences* and has authored three books, *Hermeneutics and Education* (1992), *The Inordinance of Time* (1998) and *How the Body Shapes the Mind* (2004). He has edited and co-edited several volumes, including *Models of the Self* with Jonathan Shear (1999).

Arne Grøn (Danish National Research Foundation, Center for Subjectivity Research, University of Copenhagen Købmagergade 46, DK-1150 Copenhagen K, Denmark. *Email: ag@cfs.ku.dk*) is professor of ethics and philosophy of religion at the University of Copenhagen and an editor of *Kiekegaardiana*, issued more under the auspices of the Søren Kierkegaard Society. He is also engaged at the Danish National Research Foundation's Center for Subjectivity Research at the University of Copenhagen.

Josef Parnas (The Danish National Research Foundation: Center for Subjectivity Research, University of Copenhagen, Købmagergade 46, DK-1150 Copenhagen K, Denmark. *Email: jpa@cfs.ku.dk*) received his MD (1974) and Dr. Med. Sci. (1986) from the University of Copenhagen, where he is now based at the Danish National Research Foundation's Center for Subjectivity Research. He has extensive clinical experience and also holds a position in the University Department of Psychiatry, Hvidovre Hospital, Denmark. He has conducted epidemiological, genetic, and psychopathalogical research in the realm of schizophrenia, collaborating with many centres in the US and Europe.

Peter Poellner (Department of Philosophy, University of Warwick, Coventry CV4 7AL, UK. *Email: Peter.Poellner@warwick.ac.uk*) is Senior Lecturer in the Philosophy Department, University of Warwick. His main research interests lie in the philosophy of consciousness and of thought, in value theory, and in the methodological resources of phenomenology, broadly conceived.

Sonja Rinofner-Kreidl (Institut für Philosophie/Karl Franzens-Universität Graz, A-8010 Graz, Heinrichstraße 26/VI, Austria. *Email: sonja.rinofner@uni-graz.at*) was born in 1965 in Salzburg and studied philosophy and art history at the Karl-Franzens-University, Graz, Austria, where she is now assistant professor. From 1994 to 1998 she was a member of the interdisciplinary research programme *Modernity: Vienna and Central Europe Around 1900*, gaining her PhD in 1997 and habilitation in 2002. Publications include *Edmund Husserl: Zeitlichkeit und Intentionalität* (2000) and *Mediane Phänomenologie* (2003).

Louis A. Sass (GSAPP—Busch Campus, Rutgers University, 152 Frelinghuysen Rd, Piscataway, NJ 08854–0819, USA. *Email: lsass@rci.rutgers.edu*) is professor of clinical psychology at the Graduate School of Applied and Professional Psychology at Rutgers University. He has strong interdisciplinary interests involving the intersection of clinical psychology with philosophy, the arts, and literary studies. His publications include *Madness and Modernism: Insanity in the Light of Modern Art, Literature, and Thought* (1992) and *The Paradoxes of Delusion: Wittgenstein, Schreber, and the Schizophrenic Mind* (1994).

Dieter Teichert (Department of Philosophy, University of Konstanz, D-78457 Konstanz, Germany. *Email: Dieter.Teichert@uni-konstanz.de*) studied at the University of Tübingen, University of Paris (Sorbonne) and University of Konstanz. He teaches philosophy at the department of philosophy at the University of Konstanz. His research areas are philosophical hermeneutics, philosophy of mind, and aesthetics. His publications include *Erfahrung, Erinnerung, Erkenntnis – Untersuchungen zum Wahrheitsbegriff der Hermeneutik Gadamers* (1991) and *Personen und Identitäten* (1999).

Dan Zahavi (Danish National Research Foundation: Center for Subjectivity Research, University of Copenhagen, Købmagergade 46, DK-1150 Copenhagen K, Denmark. *Email: zahavi@cfs.ku.dk*) is professor at and Director of the Danish National Research Foundation: *Center for Subjectivity Research*, University of Copenhagen. He has published widely in phenomenology and philosophy of mind, and is the author or editor of more that 15 books, including *Self-Awareness and Alterity* (1999), *Exploring the Self* (2000) and *Husserl's Phenomenology* (2003). He is currently completing a new book entitled *Subjectivity and Selfhood: Investigating the First-Person Perspective*.

Dan Zahavi

Editorial Introduction

The Study of Consciousness and the Reinvention of the Wheel

Many scientists have until recently considered consciousness to be unsuitable for scientific research. As Damasio remarks, 'studying consciousness was simply not the thing to do before you made tenure, and even after you did it was looked upon with suspicion' (Damasio, 1999, p. 7). Prompted by technological developments as well as conceptual changes, this attitude has changed within the last decade or so, and an explanation of consciousness is currently seen by many as one of the few remaining major unsolved problems of modern science. It has become customary to describe this change in terms of an ongoing 'Consciousness Boom'. What is occasionally forgotten, however, is that although contemporary main stream neuroscience might only recently have started to investigate consciousness, the topic is by no means a *terra incognita* for those familiar with the philosophical tradition. Since the beginning of the modern era, consciousness has been subjected to intense investigations by such diverse thinkers as Descartes, Locke, Leibniz, Hume, Kant, Hegel, Kierkegaard, Nietzsche, James, Dilthey, Bergson and many others. As for more recent times, consciousness and subjectivity have been of main concern to phenomenologists throughout the twentieth century, whereas the interest in these issues in analytical philosophy has only been particularly evident in the last ten to fifteen years. The majority of the systematic investigations in analytical philosophy have moreover been conducted in a rather ahistorical manner, with no particular attention being paid to the possible resources of the tradition. But by ignoring the tradition one might miss out on important insights that in the best of circumstances end up being rediscovered decades or centuries later (cf. Zahavi, 2002).

Much current research aims at locating and identifying particular neural correlates of consciousness. It might appear obvious that, say, German Idealism or phenomenology have little if anything to offer to this specific enterprise. But one should not forget that we will not get very far in giving an account of the relationship between consciousness and the brain if we do not have a clear conception of what it is that we are trying to relate. To put it differently, any assessment of the possibility of reducing consciousness to more fundamental neuronal structures, any appraisal of whether a naturalization of consciousness is possible, will not only involve metaphysical and epistemological clarifications, it will also call for a detailed analysis and description of consciousness. As Nagel once pointed out, a necessary requirement for any coherent reductionism is that the entity to be reduced is properly understood (Nagel, 1974, p. 437). In other words, although much current research focuses on questions concerned with the precise relation between brain and consciousness, questions of this kind by no means exhaust the challenges currently facing the study of consciousness. To mention just a few quite different urgent questions:

What is the relation between intentionality and self-consciousness?

What is the temporal structure of the stream of consciousness?

What is it like to think abstract thoughts?

How does social interaction influence the structures of experience?

Is it possible to conceptualize experiential life?

What is the cognitive function of affective experiences?

Is self-experience always embedded and embodied?

What does it at all mean to be a subject, to be a self?

But questions like these are not new, and have been explored for centuries. To think that the contemporary study of consciousness, as a result of the last ten to fifteen years impressive achievements, is already on top of things and that it has superseded whatever insights the tradition might have had to offer merely expresses a too optimistic confidence in the progress of science.

To put it bluntly, it would be folly for any systematic investigation of consciousness to proceed as if its subject-matter had only been discovered in the last fifteen years. Given recent developments within cognitive science, given the increased tendency to actually investigate the structure of consciousness (the status of the first-person perspective, the nature of selfhood, the significance of embodiment, etc.) it is counterproductive to continue to ignore the rich insights that can be found in the tradition. The danger of spending precious resources on rediscoveries is too great.

It is of course impossible to do justice to the entire philosophical tradition in a single volume. But hopefully the contributions contained in this special issue of *Journal of Consciousness Studies* can serve as appetizers. They all address the following issue: To what extent can the current discussion of consciousness in mainstream cognitive science and analytical philosophy of mind profit from the resources found in the Kantian and post-Kantian tradition, in phenomenology and in hermeneutics.

Why this specific focus? The focus of the volume reflects the kind of work done at the Center for Subjectivity Research, where three of the contributors reside. This is a centre of excellence funded by the Danish National Research Foundation and located at the University of Copenhagen. The research at the Center is based on an unorthodox collaboration between researchers coming from philosophy of mind, comparative literature, philosophy of religion, psychology, and psychiatry, and aims at clarifying and analysing three fundamental structures of consciousness: Intentionality, self-consciousness, and intersubjectivity (i.e., consciousness in its relation to the world, to itself, and to others). In working on these topics, the center explicitly seeks to further the dialogue between philosophy and empirical research and to encourage the integration of different philosophical traditions (Kant, Hegel, Kierkegaard, phenomenology, hermeneutics and analytical philosophy).[1]

In the first of the contributions, 'Kant, cognitive science and contemporary neo-Kantianism', **Andrew Brook** argues that Kant should be considered the intellectual godfather of cognitive science, and that many of Kant's ideas — in particular his views on consciousness of self, on the unity of mind, and on the structure of conscious experience — far from having been superseded by more recent cognitive research, has not even been assimilated by it. To exemplify the contemporary relevance of Kant, Brook then compares Kant's own views with recent neo-Kantian proposals by Cassam and Hurley.

In his article 'The embodied self: Reformulating the existential difference in Kierkegaard', **Arne Grøn** argues that one can find a sophisticated conception of embodiment in Kierkegaard. According to Kierkegaard, the human mind exteriorizes itself in history and language, in action and speech. It is embedded and embodied in a social, historical, and cultural context. Grøn points to some of the affinities between this conception and ideas in contemporary cognitive science, and then argues that Kierkegaard's investigation might be particularly pertinent for those interested in an enactive approach to consciousness and cognition.

The contribution by **Peter Poellner**, 'Self-deception, consciousness, and value: The Nietzschean contribution', contains a discussion of Nietzsche's analysis of self-opacity and self-deception. Poellner argues that none of the three main contemporary models of self-deception (split mind, nonintentional motivated error, and bad faith) can satisfactorily accommodate the kind of phenomenon Nietzsche claimed to have discovered and which he called *ressentiment*: a subject's intentional misinterpretation of her own current affective experiences. Poellner points to certain limitations in Nietzsche's own model, but then argues that it can be improved by means of an incorporation of insights found in Husserl and Sartre concerning pre-reflective self-awareness, and that it thereby remains relevant for any contemporary attempt to do justice to the complexity of affective experience.

In his paper 'Back to Brentano?', **Dan Zahavi** starts out by discussing some of the objections that have recently been raised against the higher-order theories of consciousness. Within the last few years, a number of authors have suggested that a Brentanian or neo-Brentanian theory of consciousness might provide a better one-level alternative. Zahavi presents this alternative in detail, and argues that although it might contribute important insights to our understanding of the

---

[1] More information about the research activities of the center can be found at www.cfs.ku.dk.

relation between consciousness and self-awareness, it ultimately remains beset with problems. He then suggests that it would make more sense to take a closer look at the work of Sartre, Husserl, and Heidegger, if one is on the lookout for promising alternatives to the higher-order theories, than to return all the way to Brentano.

In her contribution, 'Representationalism and beyond: A phenomenological critique of Thomas Metzinger's self-model theory', **Sonja Rinofner-Kreidl** subjects Metzinger's recent analysis of the first-person perspective to a phenomenological criticism. Rinofner-Kreidl discusses the differences between Metzinger's neurophenomenology and classical Husserlian phenomenology, and argues that Metzinger on a number of points misrepresents the latter. She then takes particular issue with Metzinger's representationalism and naturalism, and makes the case that phenomenology as a form of transcendental philosophy must remain non-naturalistic.

In his article '"Cognitive impenetrability" and the complex intentionality of the emotions', **John Drummond** focuses on the issue of 'cognitive impenetrability', a phrase introduced by Goldie to designate the fact that emotional reactions are often impervious to what we know. Certain emotions continue to be experienced even though we recognize that the beliefs belonging to them are false. This fact speaks against the exaggerated cognitivism of recent 'belief-desire' accounts of emotions, which deny to the feeling component of emotions any element of intentionality. Drummond does not challenge Goldie's findings, but argues that only a phenomenological account — which analyses the fundamental presentational character of the experiences — can fully illuminate the complexity of emotional intentionality.

The contribution by **Louis Sass**, 'Affectivity in schizophrenia: A phenomenological view', contains an analysis of the affective or emotional disturbances in schizophrenia. Focusing on three distinct modes of schizophrenic experience: body alienation, 'un-worlding' and inner fantasy, Sass suggests that a phenomenological approach can explain why schizophrenic individuals display at one and the same time both an exaggerated and a diminished level of emotional response; an apparent paradox that was first discussed in the work of the German psychiatrist Kretschmer.

In his article 'Belief and pathology of self-awareness: A phenomenological contribution to the classification of delusions', **Josef Parnas** argues that the phenomenon of delusion — typically defined as a false, incorrigible belief about the world — is, in fact, quite heterogeneous, and that it from a phenomenological perspective makes good sense to distinguish two importantly different types of delusion: empirical delusions and autistic-solipsistic delusions. Whereas empirical delusions involve something close to normal forms of belief, even though these beliefs are incorrect, autistic-solipsistic delusions, which are frequent in schizophrenia, derive from and express radically altered structures of experience. They do not involve truth claims about the world in the same sense as do empirical delusions and normal beliefs. For the very same reason, they are not explicable by means of the standard way of accounting for delusions, namely in terms of a defective 'reality testing'.

In his contribution 'Hermeneutics and the cognitive sciences', **Shaun Gallagher** examines the relationship between philosophical hermeneutics, i.e., the theory of interpretation which was developed by thinkers like Schleiermacher, Dilthey and Gadamer, and contemporary cognitive science. By considering three questions: How do we know objects? How do we know situations? How do we understand other people? Gallagher argues that what hermeneutics discovers is not in opposition to what cognitive science discovers, and that the two sides can learn from each other.

In the final article of the volume, 'Narrative, identity and the self', **Dieter Teichert** examines Ricoeur's hermeneutical concept of narrative identity. Teichert first shows how Ricoeur develops his concept in the context of an encompassing reflection on time and narrative. He then accounts for Ricoeur's distinction between identity as sameness and identity as selfhood and contrast Ricoeur's view of the self with current neo-Lockean theories of personal identity. In the final section of his paper, Teichert then compares Ricoeur's conception with Dennett's well known notion of the self as a centre of narrative gravity.

References

Damasio, A. (1999), *The Feeling of What Happens* (San Diego, CA: Harcourt).
Nagel, T. (1974), 'What is it like to be a bat?', *The Philosophical Review,* **83**, pp. 435–50.
Zahavi, D. (2002), 'First-person thoughts and embodied self-awareness: Some reflections on the relation between recent analytical philosophy and phenomenology', *Phenomenology and the Cognitive Sciences,* **1**, pp. 7–26.

Andrew Brook

Kant, Cognitive Science and Contemporary Neo-Kantianism

Through nineteenth-century intermediaries, the model of the mind developed by Immanuel Kant (1724–1804) has had an enormous influence on contemporary cognitive research. Indeed, Kant could be viewed as the intellectual godfather of cognitive science. In general structure, Kant's model of the mind shaped nineteenth-century empirical psychology (Herbart, Helmholtz and Wundt all viewed themselves as Kantians) and, after a hiatus during which behaviourism reigned supreme (roughly 1910 to 1965), became influential again toward the end of the twentieth century, especially in cognitive science. Kantian elements are central to the models of the mind of thinkers otherwise as different as Sigmund Freud and Jerry Fodor, for example.[1]

Some of the most characteristic elements of Kant's model of the mind have been taken up into cognitive science. Kant held that cognition requires application of concepts as well as sensory input, and that cognition proceeds by way of synthesis, indeed by way of three kinds of synthesis. He advanced a functionalist model of the mind almost 200 years before functionalism was officially articulated. And he developed a distinctive form of inference to the best explanation as the central method for studying the mind. All these things are now orthodox in cognitive science.

It is also true that some of Kant's most important ideas about the mind have not be taken up into cognitive science or even into contemporary philosophy of mind. In addition to the general model of the mind just sketched, Kant

1. had penetrating insights into consciousness of self,

---

[1] That Kant's view of the mind has been so influential is a bit ironic. He himself saw his remarks on the mind as 'not . . . an essential part' of his 'chief purpose' and 'somewhat hypothetical in character' (1781/7, Axvii; further references to this work will be by page number only, using the pagination of the first (A) and/or second (B) editions).

2. viewed the unity of consciousness as central to cognition and held that it requires a special form of synthesis, and
3. developed a striking argument that for synthesis to produce unified consciousness, the contents of conscious experience must have a certain structure.

Far from these ideas having been superseded by more recent cognitive research, not one of them has even been assimilated by it.[2]

The three ideas have had different fates. A few philosophers have recovered some of the ideas that Kant was the first to articulate about consciousness of self, usually without recognizing that they have Kantian roots. (Also, these philosophers seldom know that Kant had the makings of a theory to explain these features, despite the fact that they don't have one.) As to the unity of consciousness, after decades of neglect, it has reappeared in contemporary cognitive research in a major way. However, the kind of synthesis that Kant connected to it, indeed its cognitive underpinnings in general, are still seriously underexplored. Kant's argument that for consciousness to be unified, the content of conscious experience must have a certain structure has had a more complicated fate.

It has not been ignored but it has received a curious reading and spawned curious offspring. The curious reading attributes to Kant a stronger notion of objectivity than any that he would have embraced and tries to link objectivity in this strong sense to unity. (We will see how this goes later.) The arguments that this reading has spawned are called neo-Kantian, though, as we will see, how Kantian they in fact are is a real question. Though of interest to some philosophers, neither Kant's original argument, nor the strong reading of it, nor the offshoot arguments have played any role in cognitive science (though the offshoots relate to some issues that have, the situatedness of cognition in particular).

Our agenda. After a sketch of Kant's life and central project and some remarks about his immediate influence, we will sketch his model of the mind, his views on consciousness of self, and his view of unified consciousness and the special form of synthesis and structure in the contents of consciousness that it requires. With this overview of his ideas in place, we will then examine what in these ideas has become the foundation of contemporary cognitive research, namely, his model of the mind, and what has not been thus taken up, namely, the three items on the list. Since I have written elsewhere about Kant's influence on cognitive science (Brook, 1994), views on consciousness of self (Brook, 2001a) and views on synthesis and the unity of consciousness (Brook, 2004), I will spend more time on unified consciousness and the structure of conscious experience than on the other topics. On this score, we will look at a couple of recent neo-Kantian arguments and check them against what Kant actually said, one by Quassim Cassam and one by Susan Hurley, both representatives of recent neo- Kantianism.

---

[2] The three points just mentioned are, or should be, congenial to cognitive science. Some of Kant's other ideas about the mind are not at all congenial to cognitive science, his deep hostility to materialism about the mind and his extreme innatism about central cognitive capacities of the mind, for example. That these views have played no role in cognitive science is less surprising.

Life and Influence: A Sketch

Kant was the last great thinker of the German Enlightenment (which among other things means that he focussed more on the human individual than on state, society or culture) and overall one of the most influential philosophers of all time. Philosophy of mind and knowledge were by no means the only areas in which Kant made seminal contributions. He founded physical geography. His work on social ethics grounds modern liberal democratic theory. His deontological approach to the justification of ethical beliefs put ethics on a new footing, one that remains influential to this day. In the lecture hall, he taught metaphysics, ethics, anthropology, physical geography, logic, mechanics, theoretical physics, algebra, calculus, trigonometry, and history, an almost unimaginable range of topics for anyone now.

Kant's life was as unremarkable as his work was epoch-making. He lived his whole life in Königsberg (now Kaliningrad), just below Lithuania. His father was a saddle maker. He was deeply engaged with religion but hostile to both the official Lutheranism of his time and the stricter pietistic offshoot in which he was raised. Though he started his academic career late (he tutored privately for many years), he became an important figure in the University of Königsberg and late in life served terms at different times as rector of the University, though he hated the work. (One story about the extent of his hostility to official religion is well-known: as Rector, he had to lead the church parade of students and instructors to the main church in Königsberg each Sunday. He refused to enter the church. Instead, he would step out on the church steps and go home.) By the time of his death, he was virtually the official philosopher of the German-speaking world. Though viewed as a quintessentially German philosopher, he is said to have been one-quarter Scottish. Some people even say that 'Kant' is a Germanization of the Scottish name 'Candt'. (Scottish philosophers are particularly fond of this idea; many others reject it.)

Kant's most important work on the mind is to be found in the *Critique of Pure Reason (CPR)* of 1781/7 (two editions), even though the topic is far from being Kant's main interest in the work (see note 1 and the next section). He was already fifty-seven when he wrote the first edition, yet he went on to write two further *Critiques,* the *Critique of Practical Reason* (1788) on moral reasoning and the *Critique of Judgment* (1790), a work devoted to a number of topics including reasoning about ends, the nature of judgment, and aesthetics. He also wrote books on natural science, cosmology, history, physical geography, logic, anthropology — the list is long. For our purposes, *CPR* and a small book worked up from lecture notes late in his life, *Anthropology from a Pragmatic Point of View* (1798), are his most important works.

After Kant, and drawing on his work, German philosophy went off in two directions. One we have already seen: into empirical (broadly, scientific) work on the mind. The other was into what we know as German romanticism (Hegel, Schelling, Schopenhauer). The romantics were interested in units much larger than individual minds (all that exists through all of history in the case of Hegel, a foundation of all that exists, Will, in the case of Schopenhauer).

Main philosophical views

Until middle age, Kant was a conventional rationalist. (To over-simplify and sticking to the official line on the topic, rationalists hold that the mind can discover truths just by thinking about things, without need of observation or experience.) Then memories of reading David Hume 'interrupted my dogmatic slumbers', as he put it (1783, Ak IV:260). He called the new approach that ensued Critical Philosophy.

In the part of the critical philosophy of interest to us, Kant aimed among other things to,

> Justify our conviction that physics, like mathematics, is a body of necessary and universal truth (B19–21),

and,

> Insulate religion and morality, including the possibility of immortality and of free will, from the corrosive effects of this very same science (Bxxx).

Kant had not the slightest doubt that 'God, freedom and immortality' (Bxxx) exist but feared that, if science were relevant to the question of their existence at all, it would provide reason to doubt their existence. Fortunately, as he saw it, science is quite irrelevant to these questions.

Model of the mind

In the course of his attempt to put knowledge in general and physics in particular on a secure foundation, Kant asked the following question: What must the mind be like for our knowledge to be as it is (A96–7)? Put simply, he held that for our experience, and therefore our minds, to be as they are, our experience must be tied together in the way that physics says it is. So physics is vindicated. But this also tells us a lot about what our minds must be like. Though, as we saw, Kant said that the ensuing model of the mind was inessential to his chief purpose and somewhat hypothetical (Axvii), it became the framework of most subsequent cognitive research.

Interestingly, Kant held that psychology (by which he meant the introspective study of the mind) could never be a science. Of course, he is notorious for saying the same thing about chemistry (in his defence, it should be said that there was nothing resembling a single unified theory of chemical reactions in his time). Once, after stating this view of chemistry, he went on, 'the empirical doctrine of the soul . . . must remain even further removed than chemistry from the rank of what may be called a natural science proper' (1786, Ak. IV:471). So how should we study the mind? By thinking through what the mind *must* be like and what capacities it *must* have to represent things as it does (A96–7). This is his famous *transcendental method*.

1. To study the mind, examine the necessary conditions of experience being as it is.

The arguments that result from this examination are called transcendental arguments. The core of a transcendental argument is what we now call inference to the best explanation: postulate unobservable mental mechanisms to explain observed behaviour. To be sure, Kant thought that he could get more out of his arguments than just 'best explanations'. He had a tripartite doctrine of the *a priori*. He held that some features of the mind and its knowledge had *a priori* origins, i.e., must be in the mind prior to experience (because using them is necessary to have experience). That mind and knowledge has these features are *a priori* truths, i.e., 'necessary' and 'universal' (B3/4). And we can come to know these truths, or that they are *a priori* at any rate, only by using *a priori* methods, i.e., we cannot learn these things from experience (B3). Kant thought that transcendental arguments were *a priori* or yielded the *a priori* in all three ways (Brook, 1993). Nonetheless, at the heart of this method is inference to the best explanation. The latter was just the approach taken up by researchers when introspection fell out of favour about 100 years ago. Its nonempirical roots in Kant notwithstanding, it is now the major method used by experimental cognitive scientists.

Kant's application of this method led him to a number of substantive claims about the mind. The most famous is his claim that representation requires concepts as well as percepts — rule-guided acts of cognition as well as deliverances of the senses. As he put it in one of his most famous sayings, 'Concepts without intuitions are empty, intuitions without concepts are blind' (A51–B75). In more contemporary terms,

2. The functions crucial for knowledge-generating activity are processing of sensory inputs and application of concepts to sensory inputs.

Cognition requires concepts and percepts. As we might say now, to discriminate, we need information; but for information to be of any use to us, we must organize the information. Next,

3. The functions that organize sensory and conceptual raw materials into experiences are different abilities to synthesize.

Kant postulated three kinds of synthesis (A98–110; the three have a more diffuse presence in the second edition, though all of them are still there). Synthesis of Apprehension in Intuition locates the raw materials of experience temporally (and presumably also spatially, though Kant does not say so). Synthesis of Reproduction in the Imagination associates spatio-temporally structured items with other spatio-temporally structured items. And Synthesis of Recognition in a Concept recognizes items using concepts, the Categories in particular. This threefold doctrine of synthesis is one of the cornerstones of Kant's model of the mind.

In fact, Kant held that to organize information as we do, we require two kinds of Synthesis of Recognition in Concepts. The first ties the raw material of sensible experience together into objects (A105). This is now called binding. Put in contemporary terms, initially colours, lines, shapes, textures, etc., are represented separately. For an object to be represented, the contents of these representations have to be integrated.

The second kind of synthesis ties the contents of these individual representations and the representations themselves together so as to produce what might be called a *global representation* (Kant's general experience, A114). A global representation connects individual representations and their contents to one another in such a way that to be conscious of anything thus tied together is to be conscious of other things thus tied, too, and of the group of them as a single group. Kant thought that the capacity to form global representations is essential to both the kind of cognition that we have and the kind of consciousness that we have. As we will see, the two kinds of synthesis of recognition in a concept have had very different fates in contemporary cognitive research.

Kant's model of the mind is a model of cognitive function, not underlying mechanisms or whatever. This is an effective way to approach the mind, as cognitive science has shown, but Kant had a special reason for adopting it. One of his most deeply held general convictions was that we know nothing of anything as it is. We know things only as they appear to us — including the mind, even our own mind. But things he said imply that we *do* know things about the mind — that it must apply concepts, synthesize, and so on. He never addressed the tension squarely but a natural way out for him would have been to distinguish the mind's functions from its composition, what makes it up, and then maintain that what we can know are its functions and what we lack all knowledge of are its composition and makeup.

This would be a version of the functionalist idea that function does not dictate form — a given function could be implemented by systems having very different forms (multiple realizability). This thought was what led many cognitive scientists until about fifteen years ago to believe that you could study cognitive function without knowing anything about the neural structures that implemented these functions. Kant's view that we know *nothing* of the structure and composition of the mind is just a radical version of this idea. At any rate, in his model, cognitive functions are central.

4.   The mind is a complex set of cognitive functions (cognitive abilities).

As Meerbote (1989) and many others have observed, Kant held a functionalist view of the mind almost 200 years before functionalism was officially articulated in the 1960s by Hilary Putnam and others. Kant even shared functionalists' lack of enthusiasm for introspection, as we have seen, and their belief that we can model cognitive function without knowing anything very much about underlying structure, as we have also seen.

Of course, Kant did not even articulate, let alone advocate, many key features of contemporary functionalism. For example, he never explicitly mentioned anything like multiple realizability. Equally, given his personal hostility to materialism about the mind, he would have found the naturalizing tendencies of much contemporary functionalism repugnant. However, because the unknowability of things as they are in themselves entails that one must be utterly neutral about what the underlying composition of the mind might be like, he would have had to allow that multiple realizability and even naturalism are open *intellectual* possibilities, however repugnant they might be to him or dangerous to things of the deepest importance to him, namely, that we have free will and that personal immortality is possible (for a fine discussion of these issues, see Ameriks, 2000, postscript).

The four ideas just laid out are the core of Kant's model. He also had subtle and penetrating insights into consciousness of self.

Consciousness of Self

Kant made his remarks about consciousness of self in the course of pursing his second objective, to insulate immortality (and God and free will but only immortality is relevant here) from the corrosive threat of science. His rationalist predecessors thought that they could prove that the mind is substantial, simple (without parts), and persists in a special way. Descartes and Leibniz both took this approach. (Thomas Reid did, too, even though he wasn't in other respects a rationalist.[3]) Well, if something is open to proof, it is also open to disproof — and, as Kant saw it, given the course of science, disproof would be a more likely fate than proof for doctrines such as immortality if they are susceptible to proof or disproof at all.

In Kant's view, the best hope was to insulate such matters from all argument and evidence. That way, God, freedom and immortality could be accepted on the basis of faith (and Kant did so accept them) without being at risk from science. The positive model of the mind (and many other things) was the topic of the first big part of *CPR*, which Kant called the Analytic. The work of insulation comes in the second big part of *CPR*, which Kant called the Dialectic and which consists of a series of attacks on, as he saw it, unjustifiably grand aspirations of rationalism. The attack on rationalist conclusions about the mind comes in a chapter called 'The Paralogisms of Pure Reason'.

The rationalist conclusions that Kant attacked were that the mind is substantial (a thing), simple (has no parts or components), and persists through time in an especially strong way. Since at least the second conclusion and arguably the first have seemed to many philosophers to follow from the fact that our consciousness is unified (and therefore from his own claims in the first, positive part of *CPR*) he has powerful motives to resist rationalism's conclusions.

In addition to rationalist arguments, Kant considers certain appeals to introspection in that chapter. As he saw it, introspection provides strong *prima facie* support for the rationalist conclusions about what we can know about the mind. In particular, in introspection one appears to be substantial, simple and persisting, just as rational psychology held ('rational psychology' was Kant's name for

---

[3]   The relationship of Kant to Reid is interesting. Among other things, they were near-contemporaries and some of the phrasing of views that Kant attacks is very similar to phrasing that Reid used. I explore the matter briefly in Brook, 1994, pp. 191–2.

these views). If so, it was incumbent upon him to show that introspection reveals nothing of the sort.

   In the course of this deflationary attack on the implications of consciousness being unified and the deliverances of introspection, Kant advanced a number of remarkable theses about consciousness of self:

1. There are two quite different kinds of self-consciousness, consciousness of one's states and consciousness of oneself as the subject of these states.
2. The cognitive and semantic machinery used to obtain consciousness of self as subject is quite unusual. In it, we 'denote' but do not 'represent' ourselves (A382). Put otherwise, we designate ourselves without noting 'any quality whatsoever' in ourselves (A355).
3. When one is conscious of oneself as subject, one is conscious of oneself in a way that does not provide consciousness of features of oneself, a way in which 'nothing manifold is given.' (B135).

As we saw, Kant also had to insist that,

4. One is conscious even of oneself only as one appears to oneself, not as one is.

As he put it,

> inner sense . . . represents to consciousness ever our own selves only as we appear to ourselves, not as we are in ourselves. For we intuit ourselves only as we are inwardly *affected* [by ourselves] [B153].

Now Kant faces a problem. It is not plausible to say that we are conscious only of an appearance of the self, not the self itself, when we are conscious of ourselves as subject of our experience. On the other hand, he cannot allow that one has knowledge of oneself as one is. Kant avoided this implausible outcome by distinguishing between consciousness of self as subject or (in one use of the term) *transcendental apperception* and consciousness of one's ever-fluctuating state in inner sense or *empirical apperception* (A107). By thesis 3,

5. When one is conscious of oneself as subject (transcendental), the bare consciousness of self that we have, a consciousness that has no manifold, yields no knowledge of self.

Here we are closely paraphrasing Kant's own words. We have, he tells us, a 'bare . . . consciousness of self [that is] very far from being a knowledge of the self' (B158). Thesis 4 is then about empirical apperception — where the idea that we are aware merely of our states as they appear to us is not only acceptable but actually quite plausible.

   Finally, Kant has the rudiments of a theory to explain 1–5. It starts from a further thesis about consciousness of self:

6. The representational base of consciousness of self as subject is not a special experience of self but any experience of anything whatsoever.

Here is how the basis of consciousness of oneself can be provided by representations of things in the world. Consider the sentence:

> I am puzzled by what Kant says about apperception on A107.

Kant claimed (to be sure, with less than perfect clarity) that the representation of words such as this is all the experience that one needs to be conscious not just of the words, the page, etc., but also of the act of seeing them, and of *who* is seeing them, namely, oneself. A single representation can do all three jobs. In Kant's words, consciousness of representation and self is given 'not indeed in, but with . . . intuitions' (B161). Here is how Kant's story goes.

For Kant, we come to represent the world as a result of performing acts of synthesis. He held that it is the doing of acts of synthesis that is the representational base of consciousness of oneself and one's acts of representing. The activity that performs synthesis he called apperception (though he used the latter term for consciousness of self, too). In the *Anthropology,* he put the point this way: 'apperception [is] . . . consciousness of what we are doing' (1798, Ak. VII:161). The way in which one becomes conscious of an act of representing and of oneself is by doing that act: 'synthesis . . ., as an act, . . . is conscious to itself, even without sensibility' (B153); '. . .this representation is an act of *spontaneity*, that is, it cannot be regarded as belonging to sensibility' (B132). This point was of fundamental importance to Kant because, when one is conscious of oneself by doing cognitive and perceptual acts, one is conscious of oneself as spontaneous, rational, self-legislating, free — as the doer of deeds, not just as a passive receptacle for representations: 'I exist as an intelligence which is conscious solely of its power of combination' (B158–9), of 'the activity of the self' (B68) (Sellars, 1970–1; Pippin, 1987). Let us call an act of representing that can make one conscious of its object, itself and oneself as its subject the *representational base* of consciousness of these three items.[4]

So far we have focussed on individual representations. For Kant, however, the acts of representation that serve as the representational base of consciousness of oneself as subject are usually much 'bigger' than that, i.e., contain multiple objects and often multiple representations tied together into what Kant called 'general experience'.

> When we speak of different experiences, we can refer only to the various perceptions, all of which belong to one and the same general experience. This thoroughgoing synthetic unity of perceptions is the form of experience; it is nothing less than the synthetic unity of appearances in accordance with concepts [A110].

This general experience is the *global representation* introduced earlier. When I am conscious of many objects and/or representations of them as the single object of a single global representation, the latter representation is all the representation

---

[4] This idea that representations can represent themselves and the thing that has them may seem fairly unremarkable but in fact it has some far-reaching implications. If right, we have, *pace* Rosenthal (1991), no need of a higher-order thought in order to be conscious of our own psychological states, for example (Brook & Raymont, 2005, Ch. 6).

I need to be conscious not just of the global object but also of myself as the common subject of all the constituent representations.

If so, then, to use a phrase of Wittgenstein's, a global representation has no neighbour; there will not be other, simultaneous global representations of which one is conscious in the same way (namely, by having them, though Kant never says this explicitly) from which to distinguish one from another. And this in turn will allow the resulting consciousness of self to have the special features delineated earlier: reference that does not denote, manifoldlessness, a consciousness of self that yields no knowledge of self. In this, Kant goes further than any theorist since (for the details, see Brook, 2001a).

Unity of Consciousness and Synthesis

Let us turn now to what Kant had to say about the unity of consciousness. Though by no means everything in a global representation need be consciously accessible to us (Kant is widely misunderstood on this point), Kant thought we must be conscious of some of what they represent and for this, our consciousness must have a distinctive kind of unity.

Indeed, two kinds of unity are required:

1.   The experiences must have a single common subject (A350); and,
2.   The consciousness that this subject has of represented objects and/or representations must be unified.

Kant said little about what a 'single common subject' is like, so we won't say anything more about it. He never said what he meant by 'unified consciousness', either, but he did use the notion often enough for us to be able to see what he had in mind. One plausible articulation of the notion at work in his writings goes as follows,

> The unity of consciousness = *df* (i) a single act of consciousness, which (ii) makes one consciousness of a number of representations and/or objects of representation in such a way that to be conscious of any of them is also to be conscious of others of them and of at least some of them as a group.

As this definition makes clear, consciousness being unified is more than just being one act of consciousness. The act of consciousness in question is not just singular, it is unified. This 'is to be' relationship will need some further attention, however.

In Kant's view, moreover, to have unified global representations, we must unify them. We must synthesize them using unifying acts of synthesis. (Kant called this special kind of synthesis *transcendental* apperception, though he used the term for consciousness of self as subject, too.) It takes a unified consciousness to perform unified acts of synthesis.

Relationship between Unified Consciousness and Structure in Content

Unified consciousness is also central to Kant's most famous argument, his 'transcendental deduction of the categories', at any rate to the version of it found in

CPR. In this argument, boiled down to its essentials, Kant claims that in order to be conscious of the array of things that one is experiencing as aspects of a single global experience and to be aware of oneself as the single common subject of such an experience, one must tie the various things that one is experiencing into a single unified representation of the world. In order to do the latter, one must be able to apply certain concepts to the items in question, namely, concepts from each of what he saw as the four fundamental categories of concept: quantitative, qualitative, relational, and what he called 'modal' concepts. Modal concepts are concepts for whether an item might exist, does exist, or must exist. Thus, the four kinds of concept are concepts for how many units are represented in an experience and what features, what relationships, and what existence status these units have.

It was the relational concepts that most interested Kant and of the relational concepts, he thought the concept of cause-and-effect to be by far the most important. Once we see why, we will immediately see why this argument that unified consciousness requires a special structure in the contents of consciousness was so important to him. Kant wanted to show why natural science (which for him meant Newtonian physics) was genuine knowledge (he thought that Hume's sceptical treatment of relationships of cause and effect challenged this status). He believed that if he could prove that we must tie items in our experience together causally if we are to have a unified consciousness of them, then he would have shown how physics can be what he thought that it manifestly is, namely, a science, a body of necessary and universal truth.

The details of his argument have exercised philosophers for over two hundred years and we will not go into them here (Brook, 1994, Ch. 6:II explores some of the twists and turns). But the general idea is this. To have a single, unified consciousness of an array of represented items, the items themselves must be related to one another in some stable, regular way. (Kant once put this by saying that such items must have an *affinity* for connection with one another [A113].) Kant thought that the only relationships up to the job are causal relationships. So unified consciousness requires that the items of which we are conscious be related to one another causally. QED.[5]

Where Kant's Ideas Have — and Have Not — Influenced Cognitive Research

We have laid out Kant's ideas about the mind in four areas:
model of the mind as a whole,
consciousness of self,
unity of consciousness and synthesis, and,
relation of unity of consciousness to structure in conscious contents.

---

[5] Or so Kant seems to have thought. However, even if his argument is sound, it is a long way from 'we must find causal relations among items' to 'items must be causally related' and a further long way from there to 'items must be related to one another as Newton says they are'. These vexed issues are beyond our scope. However, we should note that even Kant himself thought of Newtonian physics as only one of the physics compatible with 'general metaphysics' (Ak 4:478). Clearly, this argument linking unity of consciousness to structure in conscious content would have to have been of the greatest importance to him. We will return to it.

The fate of these four sets of ideas in recent cognitive research is interesting. As we said, most of the ideas in Kant's general model are now part of the very foundations of cognitive science: transcendental method, the claim that most representation requires concepts as well as percepts, the doctrine of synthesis (half of it, anyway; see below), and the functionalist conception of the mind. By contrast, his ideas on consciousness of self, and unified consciousness and synthesis have been largely ignored. As we said, his ideas about the relationship of unified consciousness to structure in the contents of consciousness have had a more complicated fate, a matter to which we will return. Let us start with his ideas on consciousness of self.

Fate of Kant's Ideas on Consciousness of Self

Contrary to what is often said, Kant did not consider consciousness of self to be essential to all forms of unified cognition but, as we saw, he did make a number of penetrating discoveries about it. In particular, he seems to have anticipated at least two important theses about reference to self that next saw the light of day only about four decades ago.

1. *Self-reference without identification.* In certain kinds of consciousness of self, one can be conscious of something as oneself without identifying it (or anything) as oneself via properties that one has ascribed to the thing (Shoemaker, 1968).
2. *The essential indexical.* In such cases, first-person indexicals (I, me, my, mine) cannot be analysed out in favour of anything else, in particular anything description-like (Perry, 1979).[6]

One standard argument for (1), that certain references to self do not require descriptive identification, goes as follows:

> My use of the word 'I' as the subject of [statements such as 'I feel pain' or 'I see a canary'] is not due to my having identified as myself something [otherwise recognized] of which I know, or believe, or wish to say, that the predicate of my statement applies to it [Shoemaker, 1968, p. 558].

The standard argument for (2), that certain indexicals are essential, goes as follows. To know that *I* wrote a certain book a few years ago, it is not enough to know that someone over six feet tall wrote that book, or that someone who teaches philosophy at a particular university wrote that book, or ... or ... or ... , for I could know all these things without knowing that it was *me* who has these properties (and I could know that it *was* me who wrote that book and not know that any of these things are properties of me). Nor would it help to add details of a more identifying kind — the person whose office number is 123 in building ABC, the person whose office phone number is . . . . If I don't know that that

---

[6] (1) and (2) are often linked to another putative peculiarity of consciousness of self, what Shoemaker calls immunity to error through misidentification with respect to the first person (Shoemaker, 1970, who claims to have found the core of the idea in Wittgenstein, 1933-4, pp.66–70). We will not explore this issue here (see Brook, 2001a).

office is my office, that that phone number is my phone number, I could know all these things and still not know that it was me who wrote the book. And vice-versa — through bizarre selective amnesia, I could *cease* to know all such things about myself and yet continue to know that it was *me* who wrote the book. As Shoemaker puts it,

> . . . no matter how detailed a token-reflexive-free description of a person is, . . . it cannot possibly entail that I am that person [1968, p. 560].

Kant clearly articulated (1):

> In attaching 'I' to our thoughts, we designate the subject . . . only transcendentally, without noting in it any quality whatsoever — in fact, without knowing anything of it either directly or by inference [A355].

The idea behind Kant's 'transcendental designation' is that one can refer to oneself using 'I' without 'noting any quality' in oneself. One can refer to oneself in a variety of ways, of course: as the person in the mirror, as the person born on such and such a date in such and such a place, as the first person to do X, and so on, but one way of referring to oneself is special: it does not require identifying or indeed any ascription to oneself. So Kant tells us. Whether Kant also discovered (2) is a more complicated question, too complicated to go into here (see Brook, 2001a). Note that if reference to self takes place without 'noting any properties' of oneself, the consciousness that results will have special features, including the ones noted earlier.

The ideas of Kant's on consciousness of self that we have just laid out next appeared in a small, relatively isolated line of investigation of self-consciousness and self-reference beginning in the 1960s (Brook & DeVidi, 2001). One aspect of this situation was a bit surprising. Almost no one at the time seems to have known that Kant had arrived at them nearly 200 years earlier. If philosophers have rediscovered some of these ideas of Kant's in the past few decades, neither the ideas nor Kant's original articulation of them has had any impact in cognitive science. This is regrettable. If consciousness of oneself has distinctive features, they would be well worth investigating. Thus far, however, cognitive science has had little to say about consciousness of oneself as subject, focussing instead on consciousness of psychological states.

Fate of Kant's Ideas on the Unity of Consciousness and Synthesis[7]

As to the unity of consciousness, after both philosophy and cognitive science neglecting consciousness in general and the unity of consciousness in particular for decades, consciousness and the unity of consciousness are back. The new interest in them dates from the mid-1980s. In the past twenty years, there have been hundreds of books and papers on consciousness. However, their cognitive underpinnings are still underexplored and Kant's claim that one kind of synthesis is central to these underpinnings deserves more attention than it is receiving.

---

[7] Discussions with Paul Raymont have played a central role in shaping my views on the unity of consciousness.

To understand what in Kant's doctrine of synthesis has and what has not played a role in contemporary cognitive research, recall the two forms of Synthesis of Recognition in a Concept that we distinguished earlier. One form, generation of individual objects using concepts, has received enormous attention in cognitive science, though now called binding. Indeed, one model, Anne Treisman's (1980) three-stage model, is similar to Kant's whole threefold doctrine of synthesis. According to Treisman, object recognition proceeds in three stages: feature detection, location of features on a map of locations, and integration and identification of objects under concepts. These compare closely to Kant's three-stage model of apprehension of features, association of features in something like clusters (Kant called this stage 'reproduction'), and recognition of these 'clusters' as objects falling under concepts (A98–A106).

But what of the second form of Synthesis of Recognition in a Concept, namely, the tying of individual represented objects and individual representations together in a global representation (A107–14)? Here we find a very different story. Cognitive science has paid little attention to this kind of synthesis. This neglect is a bit surprising. The ability to relate represented objects to other represented objects consciously, the ability to be conscious of representing things in a variety of sensible modalities, and so on, are fundamental to comparison, to seeing relationships, in short, to all human thinking of any complexity.

Fate of Kant's Argument Linking Unity of Consciousness to Conscious Contents

Now Kant's claim that unity in consciousness requires structure in the contents of consciousness and specifically that the contents of consciousness must be tied together causally. This claim has certainly not been assimilated into contemporary cognitive research any more than the others have. However, it has not been entirely ignored, either. Its fate has been more complicated — and a bit curious. First it was being read as a different argument. This different argument then spawned some further, roughly parallel arguments — for which their authors then claim Kantian roots.

P. F. Strawson (1966) started it all. The details of Strawson's reading of how Kant connects unity of consciousness and content are complicated and subtle but the general idea is this: Strawson thinks that Kant is trying to argue from unity to objectivity or for an interdependence of unity and objectivity. So far, so good. But what Strawson had in mind by objectivity is different from what Kant had in mind. Strawson had in mind consciousness (knowledge) of something independent of oneself and one's states, something that many can be conscious of in the same way — i.e., objective knowledge in the usual sense. However, for Kant, all that one is directly aware of is states of oneself. 'Matter is . . . only a species of representation . . .' (A370).[8] If the term 'objectivity' is to get a purchase at all in his work, it has to be on such states.

And Kant does give it such purchase. He mounts arguments that for consciousness, experiences must have objects and these objects must be tied together in various ways. When judgments are 'united in consciousness in general [i.e., in all conscious beings], that is to say, necessarily', they are objective (1783, Ak. IV: 305). (As DeVidi, in progress, notes, these ideas by themselves take him beyond Berkeley.) This gets him at least some common knowledge.[9] However, necessary structure in experience is necessary structure in intentional objects — the things that experiences are about (A104). For consciousness to be unified, it is objects of this sort that have to be tied together according to causal laws. So far as I can see, there is no argument in Kant linking unity, or anything, to objectivity *in the sense of true or at least warranted beliefs about things other than oneself,* or to causal connectedness in such objects (Brook, 1994, pp. 97–8). The German term *objective Gültigkeit* is often translated 'objective validity' in English. *As Kant used the term,* however, it frequently means something more like 'valid of [intentional] objects'. Often the term has nothing to do with objectivity in the usual sense.[10]

A number of philosophers who think of themselves as Kantians have followed Strawson in thinking that Kant had to be attempting to link unity (or whatever) to objectivity in the usual sense. Two leading examples are Cassam (1997) and Hurley (1994; 1998; 2003). Though different from each other in many ways, they both link unity to something objective in the usual sense and they both view the endeavour as broadly Kantian.[11] Consider Hurley (1998, Essay 3). While she says that the options before her are not directly attributable to Kant, she says that they are: 1. arguments that unity requires something objective; 2. arguments that unity requires content that is about the objective; and, 3. arguments that something about the objective requires the unity of consciousness, and tells us that these options are neo-Kantian (1994, p. 60; see 1998, p. 61).

Cassam's neo-Kantian claim is this:

> Consciousness of self as subject requires consciousness of self as a physical object [1997, p. 25; all references to Cassam are to this work],

where by 'consciousness of the self as a physical object', he has two things in mind: thinking of oneself as a physical object and appearing to oneself as a physical object. To be a physical object is to have shape, be located in space, and be

---

[8] Statements like this one in the first edition led to a charge that Kant was a Berkeleyan idealist. Kant repudiated the charge and tried in the second edition to block the interpretation (Refutation of Idealism, B274–9). However, he seems never to have abandoned the notion at the heart of the charge, that we are directly aware only of our own representations, though he says things in the Refutation of Idealism and elsewhere that are difficult to reconcile with this notion.

[9] Only of necessary truths, of course; this move does not help at all with *a posteriori* knowledge.

[10] Thanks to Rick DeVidi for helpful discussions of Kant and objectivity.

[11] Strawson's reading of Kant has had an overwhelming influence on especially British students of Kant. It is the source of a lot of contemporary neo-Kantianism, especially in the UK.

solid (p. 30). So when one is conscious of oneself as subject of one's own experience, one must be conscious *of that subject* as shaped, located and solid.

Cassam on Consciousness of Self as Subject and as a Physical Object

Cassam's claim is carefully limited in at least two ways. It takes up only consciousness of oneself as subject, not unified consciousness in general, and it tries to forge a link only to objective knowledge of oneself as physical, not to knowledge of the physical world in general. In fact, it is not much like anything actually to be found in Kant. However, it is a transcendental argument, so in that one respect it is broadly Kantian.

Abstracting away a lot of detail (see Brook, 2001b), Cassam supports his claim with two main arguments. One, the Objectivity Argument, argues that perception of 'weighty objects' requires consciousness of oneself *qua* subject as a physical object. The other, the Identity Argument, argues that consciousness of oneself as numerically identical over time requires consciousness of oneself as a physical object. Let us examine them.

The Objectivity Argument contains two moves. First, Cassam argues that to think of one's experience as of weighty objects that can exist unperceived, one must 'regard oneself as located in the world in the sense required to sustain the idea that one's experience is subject to spatio-temporal enabling conditions', then he urges that this 'self-location' condition can be met only if 'one regards oneself, *qua* subject of experience, as a physical object' (p. 44). Let us accept the self-location condition and focus on the second move.

The most promising sense of 'regards oneself' is 'experiences oneself' — *qua* subject as a physical object. Cassam cites two considerations that appear to favour the idea: spatial perception 'carries with it a sense' of the perceiver as a physical object (what the quoted phrase means is not clear) and touch involves experiencing oneself as solid. Cassam also points to the intimate connections between perception of objects and our sense of ourselves as solid, located objects in goal-directed causal interaction with the world. Cassam himself sees that these considerations establish at most that one must perceive one's *body* as solid, not oneself (p. 54) — but advances no further considerations in favour of his two-part argument.

Yet there is a powerful objection to it. Weighty objects are 'particular items that are capable of being perceived and of existing unperceived' (p. 25). The idea that perception of weighty objects of this sort requires consciousness of oneself as subject of any kind is not plausible. As early as the first few months of life, human children show a clear expectation that the objects they perceive will continue to exist when unperceived. For example, if they are shown an object moving behind a screen and then, when the screen is moved, there is nothing behind it, they are startled. Nonhuman animals display the same kind of effect (Pinker, 1997). In the case of children, these ways of experiencing objects develop long before there is any reason to think that they are conscious of themselves as subject of their experiences at all, let alone as a subject that is physical. In the case of the nonhuman animals just mentioned, such consciousness of self as subject probably never develops.

In response to this objection, Cassam (private communication) has said that he had in mind not simple perception of objects as weighty but a more complex cognitive state, namely, being able *to think of* at least some of one's perceptions *as* perceptions of objects in the weighty sense, 'someone who can *think* of her experience as experience of objects which can exist unperceived' (his emphasis), and that it is this that requires consciousness of oneself as a physical object. But it is hard to see why he believes that this link exists.

So let us turn to the Identity Argument, that 'conceiving of oneself as a physical object is a necessary condition . . . of consciousness of self-identity.' (p. 26) The claim is that discriminating oneself from other things requires consciousness of oneself as a physical object (p. 135). Unfortunately, it is hard to find an argument for this claim, too, and there seems to be a decisive objection to it.

When I am conscious of myself as subject, I am conscious of myself *as* myself. Now this is not a terribly exciting bit of information but it does allow me to do one thing: it allows me to distinguish states and events that are properties of me from states and events that are not. Further, because autobiographical memory provides temporally unified consciousness, my being conscious of myself as myself in the present allows me to distinguish which earlier states are within the temporally unified consciousness that is me now from all other earlier states. No consciousness of myself as an object is needed! (Note that whether the earlier states were actually mine is not crucial, for reasons articulated first by Kant (A363n): in consciousness of self over time, *unity of consciousness* and *identity of bearer,* i.e., one or the same person having all the different temporal stages of what is unified in current consciousness, can come apart.)

In addition to these particular problems, Cassam's analysis faces two general problems. First, it would seem that consciousness of merely intentional objects would give us all the consciousness of objects that we need in the cases he considers. Or even something weaker: a mere *ability to judge* or *resources to grasp* that objects are weighty would do the trick. If so, Cassam's argument does not establish that we must be conscious of any objects as physical, let alone oneself.

Second, there is an argument that when we are conscious of ourselves as subject, we are not conscious of ourselves as an object at all. This was Kant's view. It is backed by Shoemaker's claim that reference to self can take place without identification, that when one is conscious of oneself as oneself, it is not via any identifying description of the thing in question. If it follows from this, as it seems to do (see Brook, 2001a), that when I appear to myself as subject, I can appear to myself *nonascriptively,* i.e., as not characterised *as* anything at all, then it would also follow that in such cases when I am conscious of myself as subject, I am not conscious of myself as an object at all, let alone as physical object.

In short, Cassam's argument from consciousness of self as subject to consciousness of self as a physical object seems not to work. Before we look at whether it is even Kantian, let us examine Hurley's argument.

Hurley on Self-consciousness and Objectivity[12]

In contrast to Cassam, Hurley does focus on the unity of consciousness. Hurley's project is to understand in virtue of what a number of experiences of objects are co-conscious, i.e., elements of a single unified consciousness. Her central claim is that some basic questions about unified consciousness cannot be answered on a 'subjective' basis (by reference to how it is for the conscious subject) and so must make reference to something 'objective' (something equally available to any number of subjects). Two such questions are:

- In virtue of what are two conscious contents part of a single unified consciousness (in the terms she uses, in virtue of what are they co-conscious)?
- Is partial unity possible and, if it is, do we have it in some particular cases?

The second first. Partial unity is what we would have if, for three conscious states, p, q, and r, p and q are co-conscious, part of a single unified consciousness, q and r are co-conscious, but p and r are not. If partial unity were possible, then co-consciousness would not be a transitive relationship and no combination of p, q, and r together would make up a unitary state of the kind that we expect to typify unified consciousness (Hurley, 1994, p. 65). Under laboratory conditions (see Nagel, 1971 for the details), commissurotomy (brain bisection) patients display *prima facie* evidence of partial unity. In them, there seem to be some conscious experiences in each lobe not available to the other lobe and also some conscious experiences, probably related to the lower, non-bisected part of the brain, available to both lobes. (Whether there actually is partial unity here is an issue to which we will return.)

Hurley thinks that subjective, first-person approaches cannot settle such questions because of what she calls the *just-more-content argument* (see, for example, Hurley, 1998, p. 101). Suppose we say that what unifies a number of co-conscious items is itself presented alongside them as a content of the same unified experience. We would then face the question of what makes *this* item co-conscious with the items that it supposedly unifies. In general, any attempt to account for co-consciousness in terms of something that is itself a relatum of co-consciousness will just reproduce the original puzzle. So whatever unifies contents cannot itself be a content.

In particular, appeals to content cannot resolve the putative partial unity case that we just introduced. The problem is that while both the unit conscious of p and the unit conscious of r would be conscious of experiencing an item of type q (in addition to p or r), neither would have any basis, going purely by what it is conscious of, for deciding whether two instances of type q are in play or just one. But two instances would yield two transitive instances of unified consciousness, not partial unity.

If appeals to 'more content' cannot do the job, what should we do? If partial unity is possible, we need a two-level account to determine whether it is present in any particular case. Normative coherence, i.e., a certain kind of structure

---

[12] Discussions with Paul Raymont and Kris Liljefors shaped my thoughts in this section.

within content, is necessary (as of course is being conscious in the first place). But normative coherence is not sufficient; separate centres of consciousness could have duplicate contents. So what she calls by 1998 a subpersonal element is also necessary (1998, pp. 214–18).

Hurley's thinking about the additional subpersonal element has evolved. In 1994, she may have been leaning toward proposing something neurobiological (p. 70). By 1998, she maintained that appeal to neurobiological factors (neural structure, neural activity as revealed by fMRI scans) could *not* do the job by itself. The reason is that there is no general or even local but type-stable isomorphism between the presence or absence of unity (which Hurley takes to be a functional matter) and the presence or absence of any given neural structure or activity. Neural isomorphism with unity isn't required and variable neural realizations are possible. An example: one gets breakdown in unity under laboratory conditions when the corpus callosum is cut (commissurotomies) but one also gets it in Dissociative Identity Disorder (DID) patients in whom the corpus callosum is intact. Then there are callosal agenesis people (people born with no corpus callosum) who seem to achieve and maintain unified consciousness. However, about what could do the job, in 1994 she said, 'What that something else is remains open.' (1994, p. 62). By 1998, she had developed a way to close this question.

Hurley's new analysis grows out of her examination of putative cases of partial unity. Justine Sergent (1990), for example, had commissurotomy patients with respect to whom it seemed that when a sign '6' was sent to one hemisphere of the brain and a sign '7' was sent to the other in such a way that crossover of information from one hemisphere to the other was extremely unlikely, they could say that one number was smaller than the other but could not say whether the signs were the same or different. (Researchers have had trouble replicating Sergent's findings, however.)

Colwyn Trevarthen (1984) reported cases in which commissurotomy patients are conscious of some object seen in the right side of the visual field by the left hemisphere until they form an intention to reach for it with the left hand, which is controlled by the right hemisphere. Somehow the act of reaching for it seems to obliterate the consciousness of it. However, if the object is slid over to the left visual field, then they can see it again.

When Anthony Marcel (1994) asked subjects to indicate when they see a light flash in three ways at the same time — say, by blinking, pushing a button, and saying, 'I see it' — under time constraints, any of these acts could occur without the other two.

These cases all feel a bit spooky. How could a subject consciously compare one kind of property of two representations while being conscious of a closely related and equally obvious property in only one of them (which one depending on which lobe is being considered)? How could something disappear from unified consciousness as soon as one forms an intention with respect to it? How could a subject push the button but not blink nor say anything when he or she receives a visual impression of a light flashing? Is the hand-controller conscious of the flash while the blink-controller and the speech-controller are not? How could the conscious system be fragmented in this way? And the general question is, what account can we give of what is going on with respect to unified consciousness in these cases?

Hurley's response is ingenious. Rather than developing an apparatus to sort out when partial unity is present and when it is not, she urges that as soon as we add the appropriate element of motor dependence of consciousness, in Marcel's case with an additional element of time-dependence, all motivation to think of any of them as cases of partial unity disappears (1998, p. 214). In the terms she uses, people are dynamic singularities in which perception and action are in complex two-way interactions. Put the personal level of normative coherence (and features of consciousness in general such as perspective and access) together with the subpersonal level, dynamic singularity, and you get a two-level interdependence account of unity of consciousness. Apply this account to the puzzling cases and all motivation to think of any of them as cases of partial unity evaporates.

So far, so good. Notice, however, that Hurley has not shown that partial unity is impossible. To be sure, showing that it is not to be found in standard putative cases of it removes a lot of the motivation to worry about the question but the question itself remains open. In 1994, Hurley held that partial unity is possible, because of the type-token problem described earlier. What does she think now? She does not say explicitly. However, unless it is possible, there would be nothing to which to apply an appeal to something objective and so no room for a neo-Kantian argument. So she must continue to think that partial unity is at least possible, whether or not it ever actually occurs.

Earlier we suggested that the strong putative cases of partial unity are commissurotomy patients appropriately manipulated. Partial unity here would require the following. First, that to be conscious of p is to be conscious of q and to be conscious of r is to be conscious of q, but to be conscious of p is not to be conscious of r. Then, that there is only one token of q in play here, not two. And Hurley's claim would have to be that to determine whether we have just one token of q in play here or two, we would have to appeal to something objective. Could anything objective help us here?

By her own lights, nothing neurological is going to help us. And because occurrences of experiences like q (whether one such or two) will always in fact be quite rare, it is unlikely that they would ever make a big enough difference to any dynamic singularity for appeal to such singularities to help us. Normative coherence could easily be present whether there is one token of q or two. So it is unlikely that appeal to anything objective is going to help us. Is there somewhere else to turn?

Recall our earlier explication of the notion of the unity of consciousness:

The unity of consciousness = *df* (i) a single act of consciousness, which (ii) makes one consciousness of a number of representations and/or objects of representation in such a way that to be conscious of any of them is also to be conscious of others of them and of at least some of them as a group.

Now go back to why scientists thought of commissurotomy patients as having two 'centres of consciousness' (Roger Sperry's term). It was because, via one mode of expression (say, speech), consciousness of having certain experiences, a, b, c, and either no consciousness of having others, e, f, g, is expressed or in some cases consciousness of having any of e, f, or g is actively denied. At the same time, via another mode (hand movements, for example), consciousness of e, f, g is expressed with no sign of consciousness of a, b, c. These patterns of co-consciousness of certain experiences in a body together with lack of consciousness of other experiences being expressed by the very same body are what led scientists to postulate two centres of consciousness.

Notice, what individuates centres of consciousness here are 'pools' of co-consciousness. And what determines whether a given experience is 'in' a given centre of consciousness is whether that centre is conscious of having it. Now think of a further experience, d. If the a, b, c pool is also aware of having d, d is one of the a, b, c pool's experiences. And if the e, f, g pool is not aware of having it? Then (assuming no behavioural manifestation), we have no reason to think that a second token of d might be lurking around somewhere. If so, were the e, f, g pool *also* conscious of having d, what reason could we possibly have for wondering if we might be dealing with only one token of d here? The answer can only be, no reason. That is because, having eliminated the objective possibilities, we have nothing with which to individuate experience-tokens except by number of occurrences in distinct centres of consciousness. If d occurs in two such centres, there are two tokens of it. This is the case in commissurotomy patients. If so, we would once again have no need to invoke partial unity.

Note that this resolution of the case would also fit behaviour. If the subject talked about being conscious of d but not e, f, g with a, b, and c in one modality and expressed consciousness of d with consciousness of e, f, and g but not a, b, c in another modality, our natural inclination would be to postulate that two tokens of d are at work.

This analysis does not deny that partial unity is *possible* any more than Hurley did. However, it leaves us with no putative cases. Moreover, the analysis proceeds entirely by reference to subjectively available properties, i.e., by what Hurley calls a 'just-more-content' approach (plus an observation about what conditions of individuation of token experiences would be available). We did not use anything objective, so the analysis is not neo-Kantian. And we get a bonus: our way of handling the partial unity question about commissurotomy patients also tells us in virtue of what two or more experiences are co-conscious. They are co-conscious when to be conscious of having one of them *simply is* to be conscious of having others of them and of the group of them as a group.[13]

Moreover, this notion has some teeth. For example, it renders doubtful Hurley's suggestion that callosal agenesis people, people born without a corpus

---

[13] This 'simply is' relationship is more than just another description of the target phenomenon. It asserts that you have co-consciousness when to be conscious of a representation or its contents by having it *is to be* conscious of other representations or contents by having them. More needs to be said about the meaning of 'simply is' and 'is to be' here — is this a causal relationship, a part-whole relationship, or what? — but the notions are clearly more than redescription.

callosum, have unified consciousness ranging over experiences realized in both halves of the upper brain, their prodigious feats of behavioural coordination not-withstanding (1998, p. 189). The answer is not entirely clear but at least we have identified the right question: In these people, is it the case that to be conscious of having experiences realized in one lobe by having them is to be conscious (at least some of the time) of having experiences realized in the other lobe by having them? Moreover, the question could be tested empirically. We could get acallosal subjects to do tasks requiring the conscious integration of a number of kinds of information, for example, and set up the experimental situation so that some of the information was available only to one lobe, some only to the other. If acallosal subjects failed to integrate the information, this would be evidence (far from conclusive evidence but still evidence) that in them no unified conscious-ness ranges over all the relevant information. A huge literature on callosal agenesis and its effects now exists (just do a Google search of 'callosal agenesis'). Researchers from Diamond's early (1972, p. 64) to the present (Bogen, undated; Temple & Ilsley, 1994; Agliotti *et al.*, 1998; Finlay *et al.* 2000) agree that there are relevant deficits in at least most cases. Some researchers speak of what they call 'asymptomatic' cases, by which they seem to mean cases where no deficits are apparent. Such cases are at best rare; in fact, one wonders if the researchers looked in the right places. (As Bogen notes, p. 9, not everyone goes looking for dysgraphia of the left hand or hemialexia in the left half-field.)

How Kantian are These Neo-Kantian Arguments?

Whether the just-more-content analysis that we gave is neo-Kantian, it is clearly Kantian, drawing as it does on exactly the notion of unity of consciousness at work in his writings. Whether or not Kant ever tried to link unity to anything objective (in the standard, not his special sense), his approach still has things to teach us about unity itself. How Kantian are Cassam's and Hurley's 'neo-Kantian' accounts?

As we saw, Kant thought that certain relationships *within* content are a necessary condition of unified consciousness, but Cassam's and Hurley's arguments are dif-ferent from this. Cassam argues and Hurley at least once argued (1994) that con-sciousness or settling questions about it requires consciousness or knowledge of something *outside* the conscious subject. As we saw, Kant's more limited argument dealt entirely with states *within* the conscious subject: co-consciousness, properties of representations, the contents of representations, and the subject of representa-tions. Linking anything in the subject to anything not-subject would have been to reject his claim that things as they are in themselves are unknowable. If so, Cassam's and Hurley's arguments may be Strawsonian but they are not very Kantian. (To be sure, Hurley does not, as we saw earlier, attribute her alternatives to Kant. However, she does say that her analysis is Kantian — repeatedly.)

Because trying to forge links of necessity between the contents of experience and the non-experiential is notoriously trouble-prone, Kant's strategy has more promise, *prima facie,* than Cassam's or Hurley's. Does it work? Alas, probably not. A single, unified group of experiences of which one is conscious can be related one to another in almost any way imaginable. I can be conscious in a single act of consciousness of: a siren that I am hearing, the average grade that I am calculating, and a fictitious landscape that I just read about. There seems to be nothing much tying these three experiences together except their relationship(s) to me. Unified consciousness *of* the contents of experience does not require connectedness *within* them, as great a philosopher as Kant to the contrary.[14]

Certainly order, if any, in the flow of experience need not reflect order in what is being experienced. In this regard, a certain change blindness experiment is telling. In this experiment, the subject sits in front of a computer screen wearing an eye tracker visor.[15] There is a paragraph of text on the screen. The subject is asked to read the text. When the subject's eyes are focussed on a particular word or phrase, all appears to her as it should. However, everything around the word or phrase at fixation beyond about 5° of arc immediately goes chaotic: words are out of order, some items are gibberish or just shapes that look vaguely like words, and so on. Each time the subject's eyes shift to a new bit of text, it pops into correct form just before the eyes get to it — and the word or phrase just left goes strange. What is remarkable about this experiment is that, while to observers all appears chaotic except for a succession of words or phrases, the subject is marching to a different saccadic drummer and has seamless perception and memory of a perfect paragraph. The subject may even have no idea that the experiment has begun (Dennett, 1991, pp. 361–2)! Clearly, unified consciousness of (in this case a series of) items is compatible with astonishingly little organization in the experienced items, the items experienced outside of foveal attention at any rate. The moral of the story is that if unified consciousness is to be tied to anything else, features of experience are the only plausible candidates.

Altogether, this section has been rather gloomy. Cassam's and Hurley's arguments linking unity and objectivity are neither very Kantian nor successful and Kant's own argument is not successful.

Concluding Remarks

The topics that we have discussed do not exhaust Kant's ideas about cognition, not by a long way. He also had a complex model of representation in space and time, holding that the spatial and the temporal matrices are properties of the mind, not the world, properties that we impose on the raw materials of our experience. Coordinate with these views, he had something (though not very much) to say about the raw materials of experience themselves. And, as we have seen,

---

[14] The examples just given of how diverse and unconnected a group of items can be and still enter unified consciousness also put some pressure on Hurley's normative condition on unified consciousness, the claim that the contents of consciousness have to cohere in certain ways.

[15] An eye tracker tracks the movements of the eyes as they move, particularly during the movements called saccades. In saccadic movement, the eye shifts to take a new bit of the scene in front of it into central, foveal vision 10 to 30 times or more a second. This movement is vital to forming a sharp representation of any significant part of a scene in front of us because, kept still, the eye can form a focused image of only about 6° arc where it is currently looking.

he had strong views on what we can and cannot know about the mind. None of these views has had much impact on contemporary cognitive science but it could be argued that this is the fate they deserve. By contrast, the ideas that we have considered in this paper, ideas about the consciousness, the synthesis of objects in global representations, and the peculiarities of consciousness of self, all continue to have value. Where cognitive researchers have not taken them up, they should do so.

References

Relevant books by Kant

Kant, I. (1781/7), *Critique of Pure Reason*, trans. P. Guyer and A. Woods (Cambridge and New York: Cambridge University Press, 1997). (Translations of all quoted passages have been checked. References to *CPR* are in the standard pagination of the 1st (A) and 2nd (B) editions, the two editions prepared by Kant and published in his lifetime. A reference to only one edition means that the passage appeared only in that edition. All other references to Kant are in the pagination of the *Gesammelte Schriften,* ed. Koniglichen Preussischen Academie der Wissenschaften, 29 Vols. Berlin: Walter de Gruyter et al., 1902– in the format, [Ak.XX:yy].
Kant, I. (1783), *Prolegomena to Any Future Metaphysics*, trans. P. Carus, rev. with intro. by James Ellington (Indianapolis, IN: Hackett Publishers, 1977).
Kant, I. (1786), *The Metaphysical Foundations of Natural Science*, trans. with intro. by James Ellington (Indianapolis, IN: Library of Liberal Arts, 1970).
Kant, I. (1798), *Anthropology from a Pragmatic Point of View*, trans. Mary Gregor (The Hague: Martinus Nijhoff, 1974).

Significant works about Kant on the mind

Ameriks, K. (2000), *Kant's Theory of Mind: An Analysis of the Paralogisms of Pure Reason*, 2nd ed. (Oxford: Clarendon Press).
Brook, A. (1994), *Kant and the Mind* (Cambridge and New York: Cambridge University Press).
Guyer, P. (1987), *Kant and the Claims of Knowledge* (Cambridge and New York: Cambridge University Press).
Kitcher, P. (1990), *Kant's Transcendental Psychology* (New York: Oxford University Press).
Meerbote, R. (1989), Kant's functionalism, in *Historical Foundations of Cognitive Science*, ed. J.C. Smith (Dordrecht, Holland: Reidel).
Pippin, R. (1987), 'Kant on the spontaneity of mind', *Canadian Journal of Philosophy* **17**, pp. 449–76.
Sellars, W. (1970), '. . . this I or he or it (the thing) which thinks . . .', *Proceedings of the American Philosophical Association* **44**.
Strawson, P.F. (1966), *The Bounds of Sense* (London: Methuen).

Other references

Aglioti, S., Beltramello, A., Tassinari, G., & Berlucchi, G. (1998), 'Paradoxially greater interhemispheric transfer deficits in partial than complete callosal agenesis', *Neuropsychologia* **36**, pp. 1015–24.
Bogen, J. (undated), 'The callosal syndromes', http://www.caltech.edu/~jbogen/text/callosal.htm
Brook, A. (1993), 'Kant's *a priori* methods for recognizing necessary truths', in *Return of the A Priori*, ed. P. Hanson and B. Hunter. *Canadian Journal of Philosophy* Supp. **18**, pp. 215–52.
Brook, A. (1994), 'Kant and cognitive science', in *Proceedings of the 16th Annual Conference of the Cognitive Science Society*, ed. A. Ram and K. Geissler (New York: Ablex).
Brook, A. (2001a), 'Kant, self-reference and self-consciousness', In Brook and DeVidi, eds. 2001.
Brook, A. (2001b), 'Review of Quassim Cassam, *Self and World* (Oxford, 1997)', *Mind* **110** (437), pp. 190–96
Brook, A. (2004), 'Kant's view of the mind and consciousness of Self', *Stanford Encyclopaedia of Philosophy.*
Brook, A. & DeVidi, R., eds. (2001), *Self-Reference and Self-Awareness* (Amsterdam: John Benjamins).
Brook. A. & Raymont. P. (2005), *A Unified Theory of Consciousness.*
Cassam, Q. (1997), *Self and World.* (Oxford: Oxford University Press).
Dennett, D. (1991), *Consciousness Explained* (New York: Little, Brown).
Diamond, S. (1972), *The Double Brain* (Edinburgh: Churchill Livingstone*).*

Finlay, D.C., Peto, T., Payling, J., Hunter, M., Fulham, W.R., Wilkinson, I. (2000), 'A Study of Three Cases of Familial Related Agenesis of the Corpus Callosum', *Journal of Clinical and Experimental Neuropsychology* (Neuropsychology, Development and Cognition: Section A) **22** (6), pp. 731–42.

Hurley, S. (1994), 'Unity and Objectivity', In Peacocke, C. (1994).

Hurley, S. (1998), *Consciousness in Action* (Cambridge, MA: Harvard University Press).

Hurley, S. (2003), 'Action and the unity of consciousness', in *The Unity of Consciousness: Binding, Integration, and Dissociation*, ed. Axel Cleeremans (Oxford: Oxford University Press).

Marcel, A. (1994), 'What is relevant to the unity of consciousness?', In Peacocke, C. (1994).

Nagel, T. (1971), 'Brain bisection and the unity of consciousness', *Synthese* **22**, pp. 396–413.

Peacocke, C., ed., (1994), *Objectivity, Simulation, and the Unity of Consciousness* (Oxford: Oxford University Press (for the British Academy)).

Perry, J. (1979), 'The essential indexical', in Brook and DeVidi, 2001.

Pinker, S. (1997), *How the Mind Works* (New York: Norton).

Rosenthal, D. (1991), 'The independence of consciousness and sensory quality', *Philosophical Issues* **1**, pp. 15–36.

Sergent, S. (1990), 'Furtive excursions into bicameral minds: integrative and coordinating role of subcortical structures', *Brain* **113**, pp. 537–68.

Shoemaker, S. (1968), 'Self-reference and self-awareness', in Brook and DeVidi, 2001.

Shoemaker, S. (1970), 'Persons and their pasts', *American Philosophical Quarterly* **7**, pp. 269–85.

Stawson, P.F. (1966), *The Bounds of Sense* (London: Methuen & Co. Ltd).

Temple, C.M. & Ilsley, J. (1994), 'Sounds and shapes: Language and spatial cognition in callosal agenesis', in *Callosal Agenesis: A Natural Split-Brain?*, ed. M. Lassonde & M.A. Jeeves (New York: Plenum Press).

Treisman, A., & Glade, G. (1980), 'A feature-integration theory of attention', *Cognitive Psychology* **12**, pp. 97–136.

Trevarthen, C. (1984), 'Biodynamic structures: cognitive correlates of motive sets and the development of motives in infants', in *Cognition and Motor Processes*, ed. W. Prinz & A.F. Sanders (Berlin: Springer-Verlag).

Arne Grøn

The Embodied Self

Reformulating the Existential Difference in Kierkegaard

This article argues for the notion of the embodied self in reformulating insights in Kierkegaard that point to the existential difference in being embodied. The main arguments are: 1. Kierkegaard uses a Hegelian model: the human mind exteriorizes itself, in history and language, in actions and speech. Human being is being (out) there. 2. This does not make the notions of self and interiority obsolete. On the contrary, in order to understand human exteriority, we need to re-define what a human self is. 3. The crucial point in this re-definition is that self is to be understood as self-relation. Self is to relate oneself to others and to a world in between, and, in these relations, to relate to oneself. 4. Human consciousness is embodied in being embedded in a social, historical and cultural context. A human being relates to itself as being corporeally and temporally determined. 5. Human embodiment, with its intrinsic history, is a matter of concern: how humans take themselves in being embodied. In this there is a critical difference between being present and not being present. Our embodied existence is to be taken over or to be appropriated by ourselves as embodied beings.

Embodiment has become an increasingly important issue in cognitive science during the last decade, in particular in the enactive approach that views cognition as embodied action (Varela *et al.*, 1991, esp. chapters 8 and 9; Clark, 1997). The focus on embodiment (of mind) and enactment (of world), however, seems to question the status of the self or the cognizing subject. If cognition takes place in interactions between mind and environment, if mind is being embodied in being out there, embedded in its environment, and extended beyond what seems to be its own boundaries, if the brain as the controller of the body, or embodied action, is itself without a centre and instead distributed in systems of networks, if biological aggregates are emergent, self-organizing processes without selves, where then should we look for the self? In this situation, however, we should also question the notion of self we bring along — self as a controlling centre or as an ultimate ground. What is meant by the self when we take ourselves and other human beings to be selves? In particular, what is the relation between embodiment and self?

In *The Embodied Mind*, Francisco Varela, Evan Thompson and Eleanor Rosch, following Merleau-Ponty, understand human embodiment in the double sense of being both observed and lived. But they also indicate that there is a critical difference in lived embodiment between being present and not being present. To be mindless is to be as if one was disembodied. When we ask what embodiment means we must therefore include ourselves, the asker of the question. Reflection can be theoretical, disembodied, but it can also be embodied, that is, it can take the embodiment of the one asking into account (Varela *et al.*, 1991, pp. 23–30). This argument is important in seeking to bridge the gap between science and experience — a problem which most acutely concerns the notion of the self. Thus, cognitivism can be taken as implying that the notion of a self is not needed for cognition; cognitivist theories are, Daniel Dennett claims, theories of the sub-personal level. But still, we experience ourselves as selves. In order to bridge this gap, we must, Varela *et al.* argue, enlarge our horizon and include non-Western traditions, in particular Buddhist pragmatic reflections and doctrines of no-self. The problem that seems to come out of, first, a cognitivist approach, and then the enactive approach to cognition, namely that we are ourselves not only disunified or fragmented, but also groundless, living in a world without ultimate grounds, finds an answer, they claim, in Buddhist transformative reflections on groundlessness as non-egocentric responsiveness. The existential concern is how we live in a world that science at the same time explains (cf. Varela *et al.*, 1991, e.g. pp. xvii, 127).

In the following I am not going to discuss in detail the stimulating suggestions put forward by Varela *et al.* Instead, I will argue that we should also enlarge our horizon in (re)discovering hidden resources in Western traditions in response to the problem of embodiment and self. Western traditions are often pictured in simplistic terms, especially as far as the issue of embodiment (e.g. dualism of mind and body) and self (e.g. the self as some substance or centre, or as the hidden true or inner self) is concerned. To be more specific, what I will do is to argue for a notion of the embodied *self* in reformulating some insights in Søren Kierkegaard that point to the existential difference in being embodied.

Let me briefly indicate the main arguments in the following:

1. Kierkegaard uses a Hegelian model: the human mind exteriorizes itself, in history and language, in actions and speech. Human being is being (out) there.
2. This does not make the notions of self and interiority obsolete. On the contrary, in order to understand human exteriority, we need to re-define what a human self is. Exteriority can also be a matter of inwardness, as inwardness in action and understanding.
3. The crucial point in this re-definition is that self is to be understood as self-relation. Self is to relate oneself to others and to a world in between, and, in these relations, to relate to oneself.

4. The human self is embodied and embedded. It is a synthesis of body and consciousness, being corporeally and temporally determined.

5. Human embodiment, with its intrinsic history, is also a matter of how humans take their embodiment. In this there is a critical difference that could be called a difference between being present and not being present (actually, Kierkegaard uses the term: to be simultaneous with oneself). Our embodied existence is to be taken over or to be appropriated by ourselves as embodied beings. This is the existential reformulated.

Thus, my argument concerning embodiment and self will be twofold. First, in order to understand human embodiment we need a notion of the critical difference as to how humans take their embodiment. Second, in order to account for this character of human embodiment we need to re-define what it means to be a self. Self is not a centre or a ground (this would already imply a self taking itself as centre or ground), but self-relation.

Consciousness in Context

In reconsidering the issue of embodiment, the link between being embodied and being embedded is of central importance. Human consciousness is embodied, but it is also embedded in a social, cultural and historical context. These two conditions are not separate, but go together as aspects of the human condition. Humans are embodied *in* being embedded, socially, culturally and historically. If we only understand embodiment as the fact that human consciousness is always instantiated bodily, located in the brain, we do not understand *consciousness* as being embodied. It is embodied *as* consciousness. Thus, we relate bodily to the world, to others, and to ourselves, and we can be aware of ourselves *as* being embodied.

Likewise, the fact that human consciousness is embedded socially, historically and culturally affects how it functions *as* consciousness. Human consciousness is a matter of context. It situates itself. The question is what it means *for* human consciousness to be situated bodily in a historical, social and cultural context. We relate to others in social settings and participate in a history as embodied beings. Our embodiment is expressed and reflected culturally. We form images of the body. When we take something in a spiritual or metaphorical sense, we do so as embodied beings, drawing upon our bodily experiences. For example, when we seek to orient ourselves in terms of the course of our lives, we can ask where we are going, or talk about finding one's way (in choosing education, job etc.). These ways of speaking, including talking about the course of our lives, draw upon experiences of orienting ourselves in actually walking or travelling.

Rich resources for understanding these two basic features of human consciousness (being embodied and being embedded) can be found in twentieth-century existential philosophy, phenomenology and hermeneutics, in particular, but also in, for example, German Idealism and its critics in the first half of the nineteenth century. Thus, Kierkegaard (1813–55) has, primarily as the inaugurator of modern existential philosophy, profoundly influenced modern philosophy and, increasingly, also non-Western traditions. He is one of the most prominent figures in post-Hegelian philosophy, critically transforming motives in German Idealism in ways that have been not only formative for existential philosophy, but also have become, as a background, part of modern philosophy.

Kierkegaard's reputation as the father of existentialism, however, has caused some misunderstandings. His theory of subjectivity has been taken as subjectivism, or even as implying some sort of a-cosmism. But the resources to be found in Kierkegaard go in the opposite direction. His existential approach implies, I will argue, a strong notion of human being as being *situated*. Therefore, we should reformulate what the key notion of the existential means, and we should do so in view of the issue of self and embodiment. Arguing along this line, for a notion of the embodied self, might seem unorthodox, given traditional views on Kierkegaard's thought. In a sense, then, the resources to be found in Kierkegaard are hidden behind pictures formed by Kierkegaard receptions in the twentieth century.

In the following I will not go into a detailed interpretation of Kierkegaard's texts, but will only take some key passages in order to give a more systematic presentation of what I consider to be some of the important potentials and resources in his approach.

History of Consciousness

Let us follow the lead given above and focus on the historical context of consciousness. If we are to understand human embodment we must take into account that humans are bodily embedded in histories. How is human consciousness *as* consciousness historically embedded? In what sense does it have a history?

In Kierkegaard we find a strong claim about the historicity of consciousness. The secret of spirit pertains to its history, he says in *The Concept of Anxiety*.[1] In making this claim, Kierkegaard transforms a key motive found in Hegel. Let us briefly see how the notion of the intrinsic history of consciousness is developed in Hegel's *Phenomenology of Spirit*.

In his *Phenomenology*, Hegel elaborates in highly sophisticated ways the interplay between relating to an object, relating to oneself and relating to others. The relation to an *object* seems to be given with the object being given. Consciousness, however, only relates to an object in distinguishing the object from itself. It is itself not the object, but *relates to* the object, as something other than itself. The object is *for* consciousness.[2] This implies that consciousness is part of its relation to the object. The implication will be clearer when we realize that we relate to an object in a *context*. Even when we think we can pick the particular object out by pointing at it (saying it is *this* object we mean) it only makes sense in a context in which we are able to distinguish this particular object (it is this and not that, or that kind of, object). We already understand the context

---

[1] Speaking about 'the history of spirit' Kierkegaard notes: 'and it is precisely the secret of spirit that it has history' (Kierkegaard, 1844/1980, p. 66).

[2] In German: 'Dieses [consciousness] *unterscheidet* nämlich etwas von sich, worauf es sich zugleich *bezieht*; oder wie dies ausgedrückt wird: es ist etwas *für dasselbe*' (Hegel, 1807/1952, p. 70). Consciousness distinguishes from itself that to which it relates.

in orienting ourselves towards the object in question. But we can also relate to the context itself; we can even question what the context is (what are we looking for?). Thus, implied in relating to an object is a context which has various layers and thus is open for further moves taken by us (we can redirect our attention, we can move ourselves in other directions). What is ultimately implied in relating to the object is a notion of the *world* in which we relate to the object. But this is *our* notion. We come to understand ourselves in seeking to understand our world.

The interplay between our notion of the object (context and world) and our notion of ourselves is at work in making an *experience* (cf. Hegel, 1807/1952, p. 73). When we really experience something, in the sense that we come to think differently, our view of the world will be changed, and in this we are ourselves changed. I have here only sketched the initial step in Hegel's *Phenomenology*. Crucial further steps in the book are first the theory of recognition where the interplay between relating to oneself and relating to the other self is brought into focus, and second, the notion of the world of spirit or mind (*Geist*) which both offers the context or framework for unfolding the interrelation between self-relation, relation to others and relation to a shared world, and explicates that consciousness is embedded in a social, cultural and historical world.[3] Thus language is, according to Hegel, the embodiment of spirit or mind.[4]

Let this suffice as a background, in order to give a preliminary answer to our question: in what sense is consciousness historical? *First*, we should note that the historical character of human consciousness has to do with the *interplay* between relating to an object, relating to oneself and relating to others (the dimensions of subjectivity). This can be indicated by questions such as: what happens to us when we come to understand something, what happens between ourselves, and what happens to the way we see the world? In experiencing something, our notions of the world and ourselves are not only presupposed, but also at stake. Our consciousness, defined both by the notion of the object and by the notion of the self implied, can be *changed*. *Second*, that consciousness can be changed should be understood as something intrinsic to consciousness. Human consciousness *takes place* in a history. In a sense, consciousness happens to us. We are ourselves, as subjects, changed, or changing, in *becoming* conscious of something that matters to us. The importance of what we come to understand is measured by the fact that our views of the world and ourselves are changed. But this change of consciousness makes a difference in our history. Thus, consciousness is also intrinsically historical in the sense that if it is changed, our *history* is changed. Experiences can be epoch-making in the sense that time is not the same after the event as it was before; experiences make a cut in time in that our consciousness is changed. This is to be seen from the fact that we can only go

---

[3] The connection between the two steps is indicated by Hegel when he calls the first a 'turning point' which in nuce gives the notion of spirit (cf. Hegel, 1807/1952, p. 140).

[4] Language is 'das Dasein des Geistes' (Hegel, 1807/1952, p. 458). Charles Taylor takes the embodiment of spirit as a key point in his interpretation of Hegel (Taylor, 1975). Embodiment here also implies being embedded. Hegel draws on and re-interprets a Christian understanding of spirit as incarnated.

backwards in time, trying to remember how things were before, *with* this changed consciousness, carrying it with us.

The insight that embodiment involves history is also formulated in the enactive approach. Living beings are embedded in their environments. An organism is not parachuted into its environment, but has become what it is in interacting with it. In a sense, this helps also to understand that humans, as embodied beings, have history. But how far does it account for the way humans have history? Human cognition is enactive, but how are humans embodied in being embedded in a history they also enact?

We will take these questions with us in the following. The moves to be taken can be seen as steps towards an answer, but they will, I think, only give an idea of what an answer could be. Before taking the next step, let me make just one point concerning the embedded nature of the human mind. A crucial insight in Hegel's model is that mind exteriorizes itself.[5] Mind makes itself exterior to itself — in language, artefacts and institutions. Its activity is self-exteriorization and self-appropriation. Spirit or mind (*Geist*) takes place *between* a subject and its world, and *between* subjects in a more or less shared world. This model could be a fruitful resource for exploring the relation between mind and world in cognitive science. For example, when Andy Clark defines mind as being extended beyond itself (or beyond the brain) into external, physical and social, scaffolding structures (artefacts, institutions, etc.) that, on the one hand, inform and guide the daily actions of individuals and that, on the other hand, are themselves informed and structured by their communicative acts (Clark, 1997, e.g. pp. 180, 186 f., 215), it would be obvious to take the Hegelian model into account. This goes in particular for the role of language as 'the ultimate artefact' (*ibid.*, chapter 10). In Hegel, as noted and quoted, language is the embodiment of spirit or mind.

Kierkegaard's critical transformation of key motives in Hegel applies especially to the model of self-exteriorization and self-appropriation. Also in Kierkegaard, mind makes itself exterior to itself. What he calls interiority or inwardness is inwardness *in* relating to others and to the world, or inwardness *in* understanding and acting. But Kierkegaard transforms this relational model in that he defines self as relational in a strong sense, as self-relation. This will be the point we are heading for.

Existence

The move from Hegel to Kierkegaard is often described as a move from a philosophy of the infinite to a philosophy of human finitude. In a sense this is also what the following is about, but we need to see how radical this move is.

Let us first have a look at the key notion of existence. While existence in philosophical traditions up to Kierkegaard meant the existence of something, irrespective of what it is, Kierkegaard coins the concept of existence anew in order to capture what *human* existence is. This step has been influential, not only giving rise to philosophies of existence, but also in becoming a manner of speaking in a broader cultural perspective.

[5]   The German expression is: 'sich entäussert'.

In Kierkegaard, existence means an *intermediate* being in a twofold sense (cf.
in particular Kierkegaard, 1846/1992). First, to exist is to be in a process of
becoming. A human being exists between past and future. It is on life's way, but
this is ultimately a way between birth and death. We are situated *between* a
beginning that is our own and yet out of reach of our consciousness and an end
that is, in an enigmatic sense, our own but also an ultimate limit to our consciousness. This double limit of consciousness forms what is in between: existence. The fact that our existence is an existence in-between means that it is in a
radical sense *finite*.

Second, human existence is an intermediate being in the sense that a human
being *relates to itself* in past and future. Existence thus not only implies being in
a process of becoming, but also relating to oneself in this process. To push the
point even further, to exist is to relate to one's existence. This means that humans
are not simply finite; they are finite beings in that they also relate to their being
finite (e.g. in being concerned about aging). Finitude is not only mortality (that
we are all going to die), but to exist between an ultimate beginning and end. It is a
reflected finitude in the sense that human consciousness itself is both finite
(limited or conditioned) and consciousness of being finite. Human consciousness is embodied, as consciousness *in* time, but also as consciousness *of* time.
Thus, what is implied in the notion of existence is, to put it briefly, that a human
being is *being situated* and that it is so *in relating to itself*. It is a situated self.

Existence thus understood implies an exteriority of the self. In existing, we
'stand out'[6] in the sense that we are living in time, in a world that demands us to
respond in taking action. Kierkegaard's emphasis on the temporality of human
existence accentuates human embodiment, and it does so in a twofold direction.
First, it implies that acting interferes with perception and thinking. We do not
step outside ourselves in order to take action, but are ourselves involved in
acting, under the pressure of time. Relating to time can already be a kind of
action. Thus, Kierkegaard emphasizes that one can become guilty in letting time
go and not acting. Second, as existing beings, something matters to us. We do not
exist in a detached mode. Both points help understanding what human embodiment means. Being embodied implies that we cannot escape ourselves as existing
beings. As embodied beings we are situated, and this is, to use a Kierkegaardian
key phrase, a serious matter. It matters to us. The further implication is that
embodiment itself is a matter of how we take our embodied existence.

Although the context is quite different, it might be fruitful to compare this
notion of the exteriority of the existing self to the insistence of an enactive
approach on embodiment as living in real time, as 'being there', and on the relation between cognition, perception and action.[7] 'Being there' is a translation of
Heidegger's *Dasein* (cf. Clark, 1997, p. 171). Actually, the notion of *Dasein* or
being-there has Kierkegaardian roots. Human being as being-there relates to its

---

[6] Cf. latin *existere*: to appear, to stand out.

[7] Cf. the emphasis in Clark on time, action and embodiment, 'real-world, real-time action taking' in
     contrast to 'timeless, disembodied reason' (Clark, 1997, e.g. pp. 7 f, 67).

existence, as the being it has to be, or to take as its own being.[8] This means that it is a concerned being.[9] Re-translated into the Kierkegaardian notion of the existential: to be embodied, being-there, is a matter of concern for the one existing.

Finitude of Perspective

Kierkegaard's existential approach thus transforms the motive of the historical character of consciousness that we found in Hegel. In this, Kierkegaard insists on the finitude of a human perspective. The insight into the perspective nature of human consciousness comes to the fore in Nietzsche's perspectivism, but is already part of Kierkegaard's transformation of the Hegelian motive.

One of the main assets of an existential approach is to focus on the *double character of the situated self*: a human self is *situated*, but it is situated *as a self*. This is reflected in the notion of the finitude of human existence. To exist is to be situated between past and future, to be in a process of becoming, and in this sense to be on one's way. The further implication is that a human being cannot escape its own perspective. As humans, we are not able to see from a nowhere point. We exist in perspectives; we *embody* our own perspectives. To see from a nowhere point of view would require a subject that could detach itself from its own perspective. The very act, however, of placing oneself in (what one takes to be) an absolute, detached perspective presupposes a subject, oneself, that is already situated in a perspective. The fact that a human being is embodied, in the sense of being in a process of becoming, affects its perspective. The notion of existence thus implies a notion of human embedded embodiment: to be embodied is to be part of a history that one has to take part in, also in seeking to come to terms with it. Understanding one's existence becomes part of this existence.

The Human Synthesis

The double aspect of the human condition (to be embodied in being embedded) is implied in Kierkegaard's basic definition of a human being as a synthesis. Let us first see how the definition of a human being as a synthesis is introduced in *The Concept of Anxiety*: 'That anxiety makes its appearance is the pivot upon which everything turns. Man is a synthesis of the psychical and the physical; however, a synthesis is unthinkable if the two are not united in a third. This third is spirit' (Kierkegaard, 1844/1980, p. 43). In summary form it reads: '. . . man is a synthesis of psyche and body that is constituted and sustained by spirit' (*ibid.*, p. 81). This suggestive definition is in need of interpretation, not only as to the content, but also as to the very form. So before focusing on the synthesis *of* psyche and body constituted by spirit we should ask what is implied in defining a human being as a *synthesis*.

As a synthesis, a human being is heterogeneous with herself; she is 'strangely put together' or 'wondrously constituted' (Kierkegaard, 1846/1992, p. 176). The

---

[8] Cf. Heidegger, 1927/1972, e.g. § 4. Existence is the being to which we already relate, in the mode of concern.

[9] Cf. *Ibid.*, esp. § 41 ('Das Sein des Daseins als Sorge') and § 42.

implication is that personal identity is not simply something given, but also something to be achieved; but it is to be achieved in the sense of becoming what one is, that is: acknowledging oneself to be 'this individual human being' (cf. *ibid.*, e.g. p. 329). The critical point is that it is possible to *forget* that one is a finite existing human being (cf. *ibid.*, e.g. p. 120), but the very attempt to forget this is already a way of relating to oneself.

Let us then consider the content of the definition, that is, the bodily and temporal nature of the situated self. When the synthesis of psyche and body is described more fully, it turns out to be a process. The synthesis is posited as a task in the moment the individual is estranged to herself. This happens especially at the age of puberty. The critical point in the synthesis definition is that a human being relates to herself *as* body and *as* psyche or consciousness. This can be called an internal alterity. The individual relates to herself as an other, but not in the same way as she relates to another person, because she is herself the other in question. She relates to *herself* as an other. A human being is in a strange way determined by herself. She relates to her body and she is in that sense other than the body, but this other than the body is precisely bodily determined.[10]

In this account of the human synthesis Kierkegaard links body and history together from within. When the individual discovers herself as bodily determined, at that moment her history begins. She is, as a synthesis, given to herself, but given to herself as a task. The question is what she does to herself and what she makes out of herself. The further implication is that a human being's identity with herself is fragile or vulnerable. She has a history in which her identity with herself is at stake.

Consequently, the synthesis definition harbours a critical difference. A human being has identity, as this individual. She is given to herself, as a synthesis of body and consciousness. Yet she also has to achieve identity with herself, in appropriating herself, her own acts and thoughts. This could be seen as a difference between being present to oneself and not being present to oneself. The synthesis definition is, also in this sense, a definition of human embodiment, as the embodiment of the self. We are *ourselves* embodied, which implies that we *take* our embodiment in various ways, but also that in our bodies *we* carry the history we take part in.

Embodiment and History

In order to further unfold the implications of being embodied in being embedded in a history, let us take, as point of departure, the following quote from *The Concept of Anxiety* to which I have already alluded. 'First in sexuality is the synthesis posited as a contradiction, but like every contradiction it is also a task, the history of which begins at that same moment' (Kierkegaard, 1844/1980, p. 49). The link between being embodied and being embedded in a history is implied in formulations such as: 'without sexuality, no history' (*ibid.*). At the

---

[10] Spirit or mind, the third making the synthesis a synthesis, is — so *The Concept of Anxiety* states — 'determined as *genus*' (Kierkegaard, 1844/1980, p. 69).

moment one experiences oneself as 'strangely put together', as body and as consciousness, one's individual history begins. One is situated in a process of becoming, but situated as a self, relating to oneself in this process: what do I make out of myself? We are subjects of our history in the double sense that we, as agents, should make something out of ourselves, but also are subjected to our own history. I live my history with a consciousness of it as mine, but this is also a consciousness of myself being subjected to my history. One can feel and fall victim of one's own history.

This complicated issue of *history* and *identity* pervades Kierkegaard's authorship, both in form of philosophical reflections and as embedded in narratives. One of the most important passages is the following in *Either/Or*: The individual that chooses himself

> discovers that the self he chooses has a boundless multiplicity within itself inasmuch as it has a history, a history in which he acknowledges identity with himself. This history is of a different kind, for in this history he stands in relation to other individuals in the race and to the whole race, and this history contains painful things, and yet he is the person he is only through this history. That is why it takes courage to choose oneself, for at the same time as he seems to be isolating himself most radically he is most radically sinking himself into the root by which he is bound up with the whole (Kierkegaard, 1843/1987, p. 216).

Thus, a human self is, as embodied being-there, radically embedded in a history. To be an embodied self means to live a history through. History as the history of embodied selves is full of discontinuities, broken life stories, unfulfilled hopes and new beginnings. Consequently, part of an existential approach to consciousness and history is the sense of the *contingency of history* (cf. in particular Kierkegaard, 1846/1992, e.g. pp. 134 ff.). One only understands a history, be it one's own or someone else's, or history on a larger scale as a world history, if one understands that it could have been otherwise. Only then one realizes that it is a history of existences caught in processes of becoming and relating to themselves in these processes. We are also subjected to our history in the sense that we are still to live it.

Selfhood: Self in Relation, Self as Relation

In seeking to account for the embodied and embedded nature of human consciousness we have in various ways encountered a remarkable feature of the human being, a double character or a *redoubling*: to exist is to be in a process of becoming *and* to relate to oneself in this process; a human being is finite *in relating* to itself as finite; it is a synthesis in relating to *itself* as corporeal and temporal; a human being is subjected to its own history in relating to its own past and future possibilities. The famous opening of Kierkegaard's *The Sickness unto Death* takes this redoubling as the definition of a human being as a self:

> A human being is spirit. But what is spirit? Spirit is the self. But what is the self? The self is a relation that relates itself to itself or is the relation's relating itself to itself in

the relation; the self is not the relation but is the relation's relating itself to itself (Kierkegaard, 1849/1980, p. 13).

The passage first answers an implicit question: what is a human being? The answer reformulates the question: a human being is a self, but what is a self? The synthesis definition is then revised: a self is a relation that relates to itself. This definition is remarkable in at least two respects. First, a self is not a substance or some thing, it is a relation, or rather, a process — the relation's relating to itself. It is the process of self-relating. Second, a self is a self *before* that to which it relates itself. 'The criterion for the self is always: that directly before which it is a self' (Kierkegaard 1849/1980, p. 79). In short, self is self-relation (the first quote) and self is self in relation to (the second quote). The two points go together: self is to relate to oneself *in* relating to others and to a world in between.

The definition of self as self-relation captures the double character of the human self. A human being is not simply what she is, but relates to what she is, and this relating becomes part of what she is. She is what she is in taking herself in certain ways, in particular in taking herself to be the person she is. The implication is that to be oneself is not simply to coincide with oneself, but to relate to oneself. To relate to myself implies to relate to what I have done and how I have taken what I have done and experienced. When I relate to my past, be it past experiences or acts, I not only relate to these experiences or acts, but to *myself* as the one who has experienced and has done this. I am the one to account for and live with what I have done and thought.

If we tried to describe another person we would also encounter the double character of the self. Imagine that we list all her traits as far as possible. This would include traits which could, in principle, be shared with other persons as well, such as birth date, family relations, sex, nationality, education, job, social status, etc. Her identity can also be checked by various means (such as passport, photo, teeth prints, finger prints, DNA profile). These ways of identifying a person concern the person as both embedded and embodied. Her history cannot be separated from her body. A person's body can tell a story (for example a scar, the attitude of the body, the eyes or the voice). One's history is unique only as the history of this person being born into a history and with its being, as embodied, subjected to this history. Kierkegaard's synthesis definition implies that one only has history as embodied. An angel would have no history, he notes (Kierkegaard, 1849/1980, p. 49).

Consequently, if we have identified a particular person we would learn more about her if she tells something about herself. To tell who she is would include telling her history: the experiences, events, thoughts and acts that have formed her. The critical point, however, is that we still would have to recognize that the other person is more than what we could describe her as. This is not something obscure, a further or hidden fact, but the core feature that a human being *relates to* what she is. But a person not only relates to what she is. What she is also becomes a matter of how she takes herself. We can, for example, be dissatisfied with what we are; we can wish to be something or even someone else, and this will affect what we are. Kierkegaard's analyses of despair in *The Sickness unto*

Death concern this point. To be in despair means not to be oneself, but this is also a way of being oneself: in despair.

This double character of the self affects what it means to be embodied in being embedded in a history. The identity of a person is complicated by the fact that she relates to what she is, and that this also becomes part of her identity. We might, then, try to describe how she relates to herself. We can do this in at least two ways. First, we could, in the history we tell about her, include how she has taken experiences, events and acts of her history. Second, we can seek to describe her character in the sense of more permanent features of how she takes herself, others and the world shared with others. But not only is this difficult, whether we are right depends on a history that is also yet to come: how the person actually takes herself. She can also relate to her character. One can, for example, with regret describe oneself as impatient, and still be impatient.

If the notion of identity is complicated by the fact that a self relates to itself, it might also appear to be questioned by the fact that a self only is self in relation to. If the human self is not an inner centre, but self-in-relation, what are then the bounds of the self? If the human mind is intrinsically embodied and embedded, in what sense is it a self? If mind is leaky, distributed or rather extended into the environment, if it is out there, where are then the boundaries between self and world (cf. Clark, 1997, pp. 53, 213 ff.)? What at first seems to cause our problem, the notion of self as self-relation, can on a closer look also provide an answer. Precisely in relating oneself and binding oneself to one's world, there is a boundary between self and world. Describing the situation of a neurologically impaired person who relies heavily on a constantly carried notebook, Andy Clark observes: 'Wanton destruction of the notebook, in such a case, has an especially worrying moral aspect: it is surely harm to the person, in about as literal a sense as can be imagined' (Clark, 1997, p. 215). The notebook is personal because the impaired person relies on it. She has extended herself in drawing the notebook into the way she orients herself. In other words, it is because she is a person, relating herself to her world, that such a thing as the notebook can become personal in the sense that she can be harmed by its destruction. The boundary is to be seen exactly in the possibility that she can *herself* be harmed by what happens to the notebook she relies upon.

Thus, the bounds of self are to be found in our ways of relating ourselves to the world. This leads back to the way a human being embodies her perspective. As embodied beings, our perspectives are finite, bound by ourselves, but they are also self-bound in a more intrinsic sense. We are related to ourselves also in the sense that we are to account for the way we, in what we think and do, relate to others, to the world and to ourselves. My perspective is in this sense not to be taken over by someone, or anyone, else.

First Person Perspective

An existential approach is often viewed as a straightforward emphasis on the first person perspective. Kierkegaard, however, emphasizes the problem of subjectivity inherent in the first person perspective. This can be reconstructed in the following three steps:

First, a human self is situated also in the sense that its perspective is finite, as we have seen. It is the perspective of an existing being that is caught in a process of becoming. Its consciousness is part of and takes part in its history. The finitude of a situated self, however, not only means that its perspective is limited, but that it is *itself* bound by its own perspective. It is an embodied self also in the sense that it is *itself* embodied in its way of seeing and understanding.

Second, a human self is not bound by itself in a simple manner. The complex character of self-relation comes in particular to the fore in consciousness as conscience. A human being is a subject also in being subjected to itself, but it can nevertheless seek to escape itself. I can forget, and even seek to forget, that I am the one seeing and acting. I can pretend to see the world just as others do, or act just as others act. Such forms of anonymity are possibilities belonging to a self.

Third, this means that the subjective perspective is a matter of *self-appropriation*: to *realize* what it means that I am the one seeing and acting. The implication is that I am the one to live with the consciousness of being the one seeing and acting as I have done. The existential emphasis put on first person perspective has to do with the negative possibility inherent in being a self. To appropriate oneself as the person seeing and acting makes sense because it is possible to avoid seeing oneself in this way. If to be a self is to be self-accountable, it is also possible for a self not to account for itself. To be a self is a matter of self-appropriation.

Being Ourselves Embodied

Let me conclude the discussion of self and embodiment by focusing on the existential difference. I have been arguing that human embodiment not only consists in the fact that human beings are embodied beings, but also involves the question: how humans *take* their own embodied beings. Of course, the two parts belong together. The fact that humans are embodied beings means that they are themselves caught in time and movement, and in action. That is, they are caught in taking themselves as embodied beings. But the issue of how humans take their being embodied opens up a critical difference in being embodied. Thus, it is possible to forget, or not to realize, that we are *ourselves* embodied. Therefore, human embodiment is also a matter of re-appropriation. As we have seen, first person perspective is not only radical (in the sense that it cannot be embodied by someone else), but also problematic (in the sense that it is a matter of taking it upon oneself). It is a question whether we really ourselves embody our own thoughts and actions. Thus, a central issue in Kierkegaard is the question whether we, as selves, in action embody what we ourselves think and profess, or 'reduplicate' what we say. This can be compared to the distinction, made in Varela *et al.*, whether we actually are present to ourselves or not.[11] As indicated,

---

[11] To be present (to oneself) is interpreted by Varela *et al.* as being 'fully present in one's actions' and as being 'fully present in the world' (Varela *et al.*, 1991, p. 122). This is the possibility for 'total personal reembodiment' (*ibid.*, p. 179, cf. pp. 251 f.).

the parallels between the two approaches (the mindful and the existential) are challenging, but so might also their differences be. One point where they seem to part company is the notion of concerned existence and self-concern, and indeed the notion of self implied in self-concern.

In Kierkegaard, the critical difference (between being present or not present, concerned or indifferent, concrete or abstract, etc.) is existential in the sense that it is a matter of our concern: it concerns our existence and concerns how we relate to it. The existential means that we are ourselves concerned in the sense that something matters to us, and that we are to respond to what happens to us. We should, however, be careful to distinguish between the different senses of self in self-concern. What one is concerned about need not be oneself in a narrow sense or in contrast to others. On the contrary, the critical question, in Kierkegaard, is whether self-concern is free or self-encircling. If one is self-concerned in the sense that one seeks one's own, one becomes self-inclosed in relating to others and to the world in between. In contrast, one can be free in self-concern because something else (other) matters to oneself. That is, the self in self-concern is defined in terms of what matters to oneself. However, there is still an exclusive sense of self-concern at work, but this concerns oneself as the agent, as the one who is committed to respond. That is, the individual herself is concerned in a narrow, or rather singular, sense as the subject of concern.

Whereas Varela *et al.* construe the embodied mind as self-less, I will argue for the notion of the embodied *self*. In their critique of the self, Varela *et al.* take self as ground, unity or centre (cf. e.g. Varela *et al.*, 1991, pp. 59, 64, 123), or as a fixed and permanent self (*ibid.*, pp. 80, 110). But as we have seen, the embodied self is not some sort of substance which first is in itself and then related to a world. On the contrary, it is relational in the strong sense of relating itself, as self-relation. If we would understand the self as a ground or a centre, we would have to presuppose a self that could take this self (e.g. the cogito in Descartes) as ground or centre for itself, that is, we would presuppose a self as self-relation.

The further argument is that in order to understand human embodiment and the critical difference in being embodied, we need a notion of the self. We are *ourselves* being embodied. We are placed in a situation in which something matters to us. We are situated as being concerned. If the situation is that we try to understand, in a more theoretical approach, what human embodiment means, we are still engaged in the project of self-understanding. In that case also, we cannot account for our situation without presupposing a notion of self. This also applies if we would take a more critical stance towards our own attitudes[12] and in

---

[12] The critique of the self in Varela *et al.* (1991), seems to involve a critique of 'the everyday conditioned mind' which is 'full of grasping' (p. 125), and a critique of 'everyday, unreflective life', or experience, with its sense of self (p. 116). However, referring to Nagarjuna, it is also said that there is no distinction between the everyday world (samsara) and freedom (nirvana) (p. 234). The everyday world is to be released from 'the clutches of the grasping mind and its desire for an absolute ground' (p. 254). Thereby we might learn, in a scientific culture, to 'embody groundlessness as compassion' for the world (*ibid.*, cf. p. 252).

particular towards our tendency to grasp ourselves.[13] We would still be the ones grasping and the ones to let go of our own grasping.

What we need is a notion of self as it is implied in self-understanding. Self-understanding does not simply amount to understanding oneself in isolation. It can, on the contrary, consist in taking oneself into account in understanding others and the world that one is part of. This also means to take into account that we are ourselves part of the world we seek to understand and to explain.

Furthermore, the possibility of being mindless is a possibility belonging to a self. What it is to be a self we also see in the negative modes. What I have called the critical difference in being embodied pertains to, or rather demands, a self. If being embodied in some sense implies being (the one) concerned, in being-there, the critical difference implies that it is also possible to be indifferent. If we use the terminology of Heidegger, we could see indifference as a negative mode of concern. This is also what human history is about: how humans take their being embodied, what matters to humans being embedded and subjected to a history, what are their concerns and indifference, sufferings and relief. Being embedded in a history affects humans being embodied.

An alternative way, much in vogue, of reformulating what a self is that also seeks to avoid a substantial definition of the self, is a narrative theory. In conclusion it might be helpful to consider this alternative, as it emphasizes that a human self is embedded in a history, or histories, but also turns out to presuppose a notion of self as self-relation.

Situated Self: Narrative Self?

Kierkegaard's authorship seems to lend itself to a narrative theory of self and identity. His works abound with narratives, combined with philosophical reflections. These narratives are often the narratives of figures which could be called figures of consciousness, to use the terminology of Hegel's *Phenomenology of Spirit*. As such, they embody ways of viewing self, others and the world.

Is a human self narrative? Is self-identity narrative? In order to discuss this we need to differentiate in both directions: what it is to narrate a history and what it is to narrate oneself. *First*, we have to distinguish between living a history and telling a story. An existential approach can focus precisely on the *problem* of narrating existence or telling a lived history. This has to do with the character of human *existence*. It is in-between and in-becoming. It is existence between a beginning and an end that cannot be told by the one existing, and it is existence in becoming with the implication that the individual concerned cannot reach a final perspective on her own existence. One could argue that the history that begins in the moment one comes to consciousness is a history that one can tell. If one lives

---

[13] Cf. Varela *et al.* (1991), e.g. p. 61: 'the origin of human suffering is just this tendency to grasp onto and build a sense of self, an ego, where there is none' (cf. also the conclusion of chapter 4, p. 80). Varela *et al.* then ask: 'What is it in experience that we take for a self?' (p. 63). However, self *is* to take ourselves as (e.g. as a self or as no-self). Being a self is already implied in taking the self as one's ground, or in taking ourselves as groundless.

a history *with* this consciousness, one has the point from where to tell one's history. But this leads to the *second* issue that also concerns the character of human existence: the one existing relates to herself in existing. In this sense, one has a history in relating to it. If one relates it in the form of narrative, then the question is *how* one does so. One can tell one's history with a sense of fulfilment or failure, joy or sorrow, relief or repentance, etc. This means that a human self is not simply a narrative self. Self is not just what comes out of narratives about the self. On the contrary, these narratives, as self-narratives, are only to be accounted for when we take into account that they are already ways of self-relating. The question then is: how does a human being, as a self, relate to what she tells about herself? Let me take the issue in three steps:

First, the existential approach can, as noted, focus on the very problem of narrating oneself, or putting oneself into a narrative. It is a problem of perspective. In the attempt to narrate myself I am already situated and related to myself. I look upon the history to be narrated from a perspective which is part of or takes part in this history as a history yet to be lived, a perspective which I nevertheless cannot just make part of the narrative. The redoubling of the self both makes possible and complicates self-description. As already noted, if we could list the features and tell the story of a person, she would still be more than the listed features and the told story in that she also relates to her own features and her history. If not, they would not be her own. But this double character also gives the possibilities of self-disguise and self-deceit. To describe oneself in such a way that one disguises oneself, or even deceives oneself, is a radical possibility of selfhood. This indicates the complex nature of first person perspective. I can ascribe various facts or even traits to myself, I can tell parts of my history, but I am not simply what I tell. In describing or narrating myself I relate to what I am. This means that I am also the one relating to what I am. That is not just an additional reflective option I have. The way I understand myself is part of what I am. I do not simply live my life but live it in certain *ways* that are also ways of self-understanding. How I describe or narrate myself could be taken as ways of making this self-understanding explicit. But here again the double character of self is crucial. I relate to myself in describing and narrating myself. This can, for example, imply that I need to describe myself in a certain way to others in order to see myself in the way I want. If I persist in doing this, my way of describing and narrating myself becomes part of my history.

Second, the implication is that there is no simple identity in self narratives, between self and narrative. When we seek to narrate ourselves in the form of our histories, we do not just tell who we are. The problem of narrating oneself comes to the fore in questions to be asked such as: why do we tell the narratives about ourselves that we do? What are we doing in telling our narratives? We do not simply inform about who we are, but seek, for example, to be confirmed or even to assert ourselves. The picture that comes out of the narrative matters to us. If we would hold that the identity of a self is a narrative identity, the critical point will be that this identity is at stake for us in the narratives we tell about ourselves. Self narratives might be a matter of self-understanding or self-appropriation. It could be argued, then, that the self actually is what comes out of self narratives, but a self relating to itself is already implied in the narrative *situation*. It relates to itself in narrating and through the narratives it tells about itself. Thus, in order to account for the complexity involved in narrating oneself we need a notion of self as self-relating. The critical question is: do we actually understand ourselves through our narratives?

Third, that narratives are important to us in order to understand ourselves reflects that we are, as selves, situated; but a situated self is not simply a narrative self. The question is how we relate to ourselves in seeking to tell who we are. We are not just what we tell ourselves to be. That we relate to ourselves through our narratives can be seen in our *ways* of telling them. As Kierkegaard's synthesis definition indicates, human subjectivity is bodily and historically determined, but it is so in relating to itself *as* corporeal and *as* temporal. This self-relating in being embodied and embedded is reflected in our narratives. As we carry our history with us in our bodies, so we tell our stories as embodied beings. We tell our stories in expressing ourselves bodily and metaphorically (e.g. using the metaphor of being on life's way); and telling our narratives are ways of dealing with our temporality: oneself as another in time, changing and being oneself in the course of one's history. In sum, narrativity presupposes self-relation. We are already related to ourselves in being temporally and bodily determined, and we are relating to ourselves in telling our narratives. How we tell our stories tells something about us.

Self Situated

Let me add a short note on self as narrative, in order to further set off the notion of self as self-relation. There are various ways of construing human self as a narrative self. One is put forward by Daniel Dennett who holds that the self is a 'center of narrative gravity'. It is 'a theorist's fiction'. The theorist sees some complicated things moving about in the world, human beings and animals, and 'it turns out to be theoretically perspicuous to organize the interpretation around a central abstraction: each person has a *self*'. This self then turns out to be not only the theorist's fiction, but a narrative construction on the part of the self. We treat each other in the same way as we would get a novelist to write more novels on demand to answer our question to his fictional characters: 'that is the way we are', Dennett says. 'That is, it does seem that we are all virtuoso novelists, who find ourselves engaged in all sorts of behavior, more or less unified, but sometimes disunified, and we always put the best "faces" on it we can. We try to make all of our material cohere into a single good story. And that story is our autobiography' (Dennett, 1992; cf. Dennett, 1991, chapter 13: 'The Reality of Selves').

Such a theory of the narrative self, or the self as narrative, cannot account for the self involved: *we* find *ourselves* engaged in all sorts of behaviour, *we* try to make all our material cohere into a single good story, *we* put the best 'faces' on it. That is, the theory of the narrative self cannot account for the narrative *situation* (in much the same way as Hume overlooks the self involved in the situation where he is looking for a self and cannot find it). We are already engaged, we find ourselves more or less disunified, we try to make ourselves cohere into a single good story. Thus, a self is not just what comes out of our narratives, we are already selves in putting the best 'faces' on ourselves.[14] We are already the ones that need to tell stories in order to cohere.[15] That is, we use fictions in order to come to terms with ourselves. That we are not 'the captains of our ships', but 'somewhat disunified', is a problem *for* us,[16] or, if we find the requirement of being unified intolerable, we can find the experience of being disunified relieving, that is, we try to solve the problem by accepting ourselves as more selves. Dennett's theory of the self as narrative presupposes a subject that has itself as material in order to write the good story that it can identify with. In contradistinction to this, the notion of self as self-relation implies that we do not have ourselves at our disposal as material for our narratives (so that we were captains of our narratives). Whether we are how we tell us to be is an open question: it might turn out, in the history we are yet to live, that our narrative was not only a fiction, but an illusion. Also in this sense are we, as selves, embedded in our history.[17]

References

Clark, A. (1997), *Being There: Putting Brain, Body, and World Together Again* (Cambridge, MA: MIT Press).

Dennett, D.C. (1991), *Consciousness Explained* (Boston, MA: Little, Brown and Company).

Dennett, D.C. (1992), 'The Self as a Center of Narrative Gravity', in *Self and Consciousness: Multiple Perspectives*, ed. F. Kessel *et al.* (Hillsdale, NJ: Erlbaum).

Heidegger, M. (1927/1972), *Sein und Zeit* (Tübingen: Niemeyer).

Hegel, G.W.F. (1807/1952), *Phänomenologie des Geistes* (Hamburg: Felix Meiner).

Kierkegaard, S. (1843/1987), *Either/Or II: Kierkegaard's Writings*, Vol. 4, trans. Howard V. Hong and Edna H. Hong (Princeton NJ: Princeton University Press).

Kierkegaard, S. (1844/1980), *The Concept of Anxiety: Kierkegaard's Writings*, Vol. 8, trans. Reidar Thomte (Princeton NJ: Princeton University Press).

Kierkegaard, S. (1846/1992), *Concluding Unscientific Postscript: Kierkegaard's Writings*, Vol. 12.1, trans. Howard V. Hong and Edna H. Hong (Princeton, NJ: Princeton University Press).

Kierkegaard, S. (1849/1980), *The Sickness unto Death: Kierkegaard's Writings*, Vol. 19, trans. Howard V. Hong and Edna H. Hong (Princeton NJ: Princeton University Press).

Taylor, C. (1975), *Hegel* (Cambridge: Cambridge University Press).

Varela, F.J., Thompson, E. and Rosch, E. (1991), *The Embodied Mind: Cognitive Science and Human Experience* (Cambridge, MA: MIT Press).

---

[14] What Dennett calls 'our material' in writing ourselves must in some sense be ourselves — otherwise we would not find ourselves disunified, and not have to make ourselves cohere into a single good story.

[15] In a remarkable passage on Multiple Personality Disorder, Dennett writes about children who have been kept in extraordinarily terrifying and confusing circumstances and preserve themselves by a desperate redrawing of their boundaries: 'What they do, when confronted with overwhelming conflict and pain, is this: They 'leave'. They create a boundary so that the horror doesn't happen *to them*' (Dennett, 1991, p. 420). What this shows is, I think, that they are already selves, relating to themselves in what happens to them.

[16] This is implied in the notion of a human being as a synthesis: we are heterogeneous to ourselves, and our identity as unity is a problem to ourselves.

[17] This study was funded by The Danish National Research Foundation. My thanks to Anthony Freeman for constructive suggestions to a previous version of this paper.

Peter Poellner

Self-Deception, Consciousness and Value

The Nietzschean Contribution

Nietzsche's central criticisms of the evaluative hierarchies he claims to be inscribed in the philosophical tradition and in various everyday practices are based on the idea that the self is opaque to itself. More specifically, he proposes that these hierarchies cannot be adequately explained without reference to a particular form of self-deception he labels **ressentiment**. *What makes this type of self-deception distinctive is that it is alleged to concern the subject's own contemporaneous conscious states. It is shown that none of the three main current models of self-deception can accommodate the type of phenomenon Nietzsche claims to have discovered. Rather than this failure providing grounds for rejecting the concept of* **ressentiment** *as incoherent, it is argued that a reconstruction of some of Nietzsche's own observations, in conjunction with insights from later phenomenology, can explain the possibility envisaged by Nietzsche of a subject's intentionally misinterpreting her own current affective experiences. Nietzsche's analysis continues to be of importance in highlighting central aspects of the kind of theory of (self-) consciousness needed to do justice to the actual complexity of affective experience.*

I: Introduction

Among the most widely influential philosophical and intellectual tendencies of the cultural paradigm of high modernity, sometimes also referred to as 'modernism' (covering roughly the period between the 1880s and the 1960s), are an *anti-metaphysical impetus* and the idea that *the conscious self is opaque to itself.* While the shift of intellectual orientation marked by these clusters of ideas no doubt had many contributing factors, in the philosophical domain one figure was particularly influential in preparing the cultural soil for it: Friedrich Nietzsche.

Indeed, in Nietzsche's work we find versions of both of those tendencies in close connection. According to Nietzsche, what explains the traditional pre-eminence of apparently purely theoretical and, in particular, of metaphysical concerns in the European philosophical tradition, is an evaluative disposition whose actualizations in consciousness are typically misinterpreted by its possessors. The evaluative priority accorded by that tradition to knowledge of the essential properties of reality as it is in itself is to be analysed phenomenologically as involving at some level either a conscious indifference to the world as it ordinarily presents itself to us, or an unacknowledged intention to negate the apparent goods associated with that everyday world.[1] This 'world we are' (WP 583),[2] which Nietzsche often refers to simply as 'life', consists *inter alia* of interacting affective subjects situated in an environment of only relatively enduring spatiotemporal objects; it is a world of 'appearance, change, becoming, death, want, desire' (GM III, 28). Famously, Nietzsche not only accuses the evaluative hierarchies inscribed in the philosophical tradition, but also many of the ordinary practical evaluative commitments of modern European humanity, of often expressing an *unacknowledged*, yet *conscious*, detractive intent or *ressentiment*. Indeed, perhaps his most notorious claim is that the origin and persistence of many of those commitments cannot be fully understood without reference to such an intent among some of their adherents. Irrespective of whether this radical claim is plausible — as I shall argue, in Section VI, it is not — the general pattern of psychological analysis adverted to by Nietzsche seems to have a powerful critical potential, and it no doubt for this reason was widely imitated among the critics of traditional or otherwise established normative frameworks in the first half of the twentieth century. If a subject can be brought to acknowledge that her explicit evaluative commitments in reality serve a hidden or disguised purpose incompatible with their avowed point, she cannot, if she is rational, unproblematically retain them. The acceptance by a subject of Nietzsche's analysis of her commitments therefore represents not merely a putative increase in theoretical self-knowledge, but rather is bound to have a *transformative effect* on a rational subject. It is this transformative impact that is above all aimed at in Nietzsche's ultimately practical, anti-contemplative conception of philosophy.

Nietzsche not only maintains the existence of unacknowledged conscious contents, but explains their failure to be noticed as, in many cases, the result of an *activity* of the agent, a 'lying to oneself' (AC 55) motivated by a 'desiring *not* to see' (*ibid.*). The agent here, by Nietzsche's lights, quite literally *deceives herself* about the contents of her own consciousness. In what follows, I propose to examine his most detailed case study of self-deception: the phenomenon of

---

[1] For a discussion of these Nietzschean claims, see Poellner (2001).

[2] The following standard acronyms will be used in references to Nietzsche's writings: AC = *The Anti-Christ*; BGE = *Beyond Good and Evil*; GM = *On the Genealogy of Morals*; WP = *The Will to Power*; Z = *Thus Spoke Zarathustra*; KGW = *Werke. Kritische Gesamtausgabe*. Translations from AC, BGE and Z are by R. J. Hollingdale, translations from GM and WP are by W. Kaufmann and R. J. Hollingdale, with some modifications. KGW translations are my own. The last numeral in each reference denotes the numbered section or fragment of the work in question.

ressentiment. The purpose of this investigation does not lie, however, primarily in moral psychology or the theory of value. Rather, the aim is to get clearer about the requirements imposed by the actual complexity of affective experience on the theory of consciousness. To put it differently: granted that the characterizations offered by Nietzsche of certain affective states capture actual psychological phenomena, what sort of theory of (self-) consciousness is needed to accommodate and account for them?

II: *Ressentiment* as Self-Deception

The psychological condition of *ressentiment* is at the heart of the later Nietzsche's most central philosophical preoccupation: the critique of 'moral values' (GM, Preface, 6). It is a far from straightforward task to give a satisfactory general description of what Nietzsche means by 'moral values' and 'morality'. Briefly, these expressions seem to refer on the one hand to certain meta-ethical beliefs, including the idea that there are norms or goods which impose obligations universally on every human or even any rational being, irrespective of what their contingent desires happen to be, and which are in this sense *external* to their actual motivational systems (cf. BGE 272).[3] Secondly, at the level of first-order evaluative commitments, 'morality' in Nietzsche's sense includes a diverse catalogue of putative goods, including a conception of justice as involving claims to equal consideration by every agent merely *qua* free and rational agent, and individual virtues such as compassion and humility. Nietzsche's thesis is that these values, if held sincerely, originate in the psychological condition he calls *ressentiment*.

In the first essay of *On the Genealogy of Morals, ressentiment* is presented as a particular evaluative attitude of a subject S (henceforth: the *ressentiment* subject) motivated by the painful confrontation with another subject (a 'not-self'; GM I, 10) experienced by S as the cause of her suffering or discomfort. In Nietzsche's famous example, the suffering is the servitude inflicted upon the members of a subjected populace (the 'slaves') by their masters in the historical setting of a Homeric or Roman feudal society ruled over by a warrior 'nobility' (GM I, 10). (It is perhaps just as well to stress at this point the importance of not confusing the contingent peculiarities of Nietzsche's deliberately provocative examples with what is essential to the phenomenon he is analysing.) S's discomfort or suffering produces in her a resentment of the Other who is taken to be its cause and motivates her to adopt a set of general evaluative norms which permit a negative appraisal of whatever values or desires are manifested in the behaviour and beliefs of the agents responsible for her suffering (I shall refer to the latter as the *objects* of *ressentiment*). If the latter, like the 'nobles' in Nietzsche's example, esteem and behaviourally express putative values like pride, agonistic prowess, carefree unreflectiveness, respect for hierarchies of birth, then the values adopted by S might include ostensible virtues opposed to those, like modesty or humility, peaceableness, prudence and an egalitarian conception of justice. The

---

[3]   For the distinction between external and internal practical reasons, see Williams (1981).

implicit, unacknowledged purpose of the adoption of these values by the subject of *ressentiment* is to make it possible to blame, disparage, reduce in thought, the Others who are the objects of *ressentiment*. It is thus characteristic of the condition of *ressentiment* as conceived by Nietzsche that a negative affective response to another subject — a 'not-self' experienced as 'hostile', 'different' and possibly overpowering (GM I, 10) — precedes and conditions the subject's explicit awareness and conception of value, the latter being a reactive construction, drawn in opposition to whatever values happen to be represented by the Other who is resented for prior and independent reasons:

> Every ideal presupposes *love* and *hatred*, *admiration* and *contempt*. Either the positive emotion is the *primum mobile* or the negative motion. For example, in all *ressentiment* ideals *hatred* and *contempt* are the *primum mobile*. (KGW VIII.2.10.9)

The *ressentiment* subject's self-interpretation in terms of those reactively acquired avowed values enables her to overcome her original, hedonically negative, state through a favourable comparative appraisal of her own 'virtue' *vis-à-vis* the moral deficiency of the Other who is the object of *ressentiment*. Nietzsche stresses that this overcoming of suffering through a 'self-affirmation' made possible by the consciousness of a moral superiority over the resented Other is the fundamental purpose served by the dynamic of *ressentiment*. The process described above would not occur if it did not enable the subject to deal with her suffering through acquiring a sense of self-worth involving essentially a consciousness of superiority over the object of *ressentiment*. But Nietzsche maintains not merely that the dynamic of *ressentiment* serves a need and is in this minimal sense purposeful, but that it is intentionally initiated by the subject for the reason of attaining a consciousness of pre-eminence in virtue:

> And what mendaciousness is employed to disguise that this hatred is hatred! . . . What do they really want? At least to *represent* justice, love, wisdom, superiority — that is the ambition . . . And how skilful such an ambition makes them! Admire above all the forger's skill with which the stamp of virtue . . . is here counterfeited. They monopolize virtue, . . . there is no doubt of it: 'we alone are the good and just,' they say . . . The will of the weak to represent some form of superiority, their instinct for devious paths to tyranny over the healthy — where can it not be discovered, this will to power of the weakest! (GM III, 14)

It transpires from this passage that the subject of *ressentiment* does not simply find herself, by the operation of some to her inscrutable mental mechanism, with 'moral values' which happen to be resources answering to her desires. Rather, the re-interpretation of her hatred of the object of *ressentiment* as a righteous disapproval of wickedness is the result of intentional action: hatred is 'masked' and 'counterfeited' (GM III, 14) as virtue. Given Nietzsche's further claim that *all* moral values (in the sense sketched earlier) ultimately originate in *ressentiment*, his talk of *ressentiment* 'creating' values (GM I, 10) should therefore be taken literally rather than as rhetorical hyperbole.

It is very important to bear in mind that the process Nietzsche is describing is not a *transformation* of an emotion of one type into a different emotion. It is not the case, for instance, that the hatred of an oppressive class is, because it cannot be expressed, actually transformed into a different emotion, say, a love of egalitarian justice. If Nietzsche was describing a 'sublimation' of this kind, the charge frequently made against him of committing the genetic fallacy — confusing the nature of the origin of some phenomenon with the legitimacy of its content — would be appropriate. But it is quite clear that no transformation of this kind is supposed to occur in *ressentiment*. Rather, the original negative emotion towards a 'not-self' *continues* to motivate the subject, but it is 'masked', 'counterfeited', 'lied into' (*umgelogen*, GM I, 14) something it is not, namely, love of some putative good — humility, prudence, justice — for its own sake, and a consequent disapproval of moral 'evil'. Yet, this 'lie' is not merely a pretence for the consumption of others, but is sincerely believed by the subject. There is copious textual evidence that Nietzsche regards the subject of *ressentiment* as genuinely *self*-deceived:

> The man of *ressentiment* is neither upright nor naïve nor honest and straightforward with himself. His soul *squints*; (GM I, 10).

> The subject . . . makes possible to the majority of mortals . . . the sublime self-deception (*Selbstbetrügerei*) that interprets weakness as freedom and their being thus-and-so as a *merit*. (GM I, 13)

> I call lie: wanting not to see something one does see, wanting not to see something *as* one sees it . . . The most common lie is the lie one tells to oneself. (AC 55)

These passages, as well as the extract from GM III, 14 cited previously, suggest strongly that the original negative affective state the subject 'sees' but 'want[s] not to see' continues to be 'visible', i.e. phenomenally conscious, to the self-deceiver. Indeed, what explains Nietzsche's confidence — so perplexing to many readers — that a 'genealogy' of moral values should be the method to be employed for an effective critique of those values, is precisely the conviction that their negative, detractive origin is, if they are held sincerely, still present in their adherents' consciousness. That 'origin' is therefore not so much a cause in the remote historical past, but continues to be a constitutive feature of consciousness in thrall to morality.[4] Since such a consciousness cannot, however, survive a reflective acknowledgement of that constitutive 'origin', a proof of the latter is equivalent to a critique of morality itself.

Ressentiment as described by Nietzsche may then schematically be characterized as a mental episode with the following essential constituents (derivatively, one may speak of a *ressentiment* disposition as a propensity towards occurrent mental states of this type):

---

[4] This is why Nietzsche often qualifies the apparently 'historical' character of his analyses: 'Still retaining the criteria of pre-history (this pre-history is in any case present in all ages or may always reappear) . . .' (GM II, 9). This qualification is most explicit in a notebook entry: 'The history of origins [*die Geschichte der Entstehung*] does not explain the qualities. These must already be known. *Historical* explanation is reduction to a conjunction *familiar* to us: by means of analogy'. (KGW VII.3.34.69).

(1) A discomfort or pain experienced as caused by another subject (the object of *ressentiment*).

(2) A negative affective response ('hatred') towards the object, motivated by (1).

(3) A desire for mastery or superiority over the object, motivated by (1) and (2).

(4) A commitment to general standards of appraisal (henceforth referred to as *ressentiment* values) permitting an ostensibly impartial negative judgment of the object as violating those norms ('blame').

(5) An instrumental intention in adopting the *ressentiment* values, motivated by (3). They are not being adopted for their own sake but because the blame they make possible satisfies the subject's desire for (a kind of) superiority or power over the object. The *ressentiment* values are adopted *for this reason*.

(6) An act of 'masking' (*Maskerade*; GM III, 14) or 'mendacious' disavowal (*Verlogenheit, Uneingeständlichkeit; ibid*.) of the original motivating emotion ('hatred') and of the actual instrumental intention in adopting the *ressentiment* values, i.e. of (2), (3) and (5).[5]

Ressentiment is thus fundamentally a state of self-deception about what the subject values. It is *self*-deceptive in a two-fold sense. The subject is alleged not only to deceive *herself*, but also to deceive herself *about her own current mental state*. The self is simultaneously agent (as deceiver), victim (as deceived) and object (as topic) of the deception.

Nietzsche's formulations strongly suggest that all of the components (1)–(6) of *ressentiment* are typically phenomenally conscious. But if this is his view, it might be objected that it falls victim to the two central paradoxes critics have traditionally identified in a literal interpretation of the expression 'self-deception'. First, Nietzsche's account seems to require that the individual is both aware and not aware of some aspects of a state of herself (in particular, of (2), (3) and (5) above). If she was *not* aware of (2) and (3), there would appear to be no motive initiating the dynamic of *ressentiment*. If she had no awareness at all of (5), there prima facie seems to be no reason to speak of her as in *error* about her own condition. Yet, if she *was* aware of all of these components of her mental state, how

---

[5] This characterization differs in a number of respects from others in recent literature on Nietzsche. There has been a tendency to include among the essential features some which are only peculiar to Nietzsche's example. For instance, Leiter (2002, pp. 202–3) and Reginster (1997, pp. 286–7) suggest in their otherwise sensitive discussions that the experienced impotence or *inability* of the subject really to remove or to overcome the source of painful stimulation is essential to *ressentiment*. It is what motivates its attempted removal through re-interpretation. While this may sometimes be the case, we can also easily think of the dynamic of *ressentiment* being triggered where there is no such experienced inability. A subject may simply be drawn to *ressentiment* through habit or education, as the most convenient way to deal with environments experienced as problematic. Indeed, it is possible to think of a culture of *ressentiment* in which subjects are socialized into responding to Others who are in relevant respects 'different', or simply unfamiliar, in this manner. Scheler seems to envisage this possibility when he speaks of certain deep-seated, habitual *ressentiment* dispositions as directing 'even instinctive attention — which is independent of the sphere of the voluntary — to such phenomena in the environment as may provide material for the typical forms of these affective processes. Even the forming of perceptions, expectations, and memories is co-determined by these [*ressentiment*] attitudes. They select from the phenomena they encounter automatically those elements and aspects which might justify … these emotions and affects, and they suppress others' (Scheler, 1978, p. 31).

could this awareness fail to thwart the purpose of adopting the *ressentiment* values, since she would then realize that she was not really committed to those values for their own sake at all and thus would not be justified in her moral judgment. This apparent requirement that the subject be both aware and not aware of the facts is a version of the so-called static paradox of self-deception. What magnifies the problem in this instance is that, unlike in the standard cases usually discussed in the self-deception literature (see below), the facts concern the subject's own current state of consciousness: she is said to be both aware and not aware of some of her own experiences *as* what they, *qua* conscious experiences, in fact are.

Secondly, Nietzsche's theory might be thought to be threatened by a further, the so-called dynamic, paradox. Since the subject's lack of awareness of (2), (3) and (5) is explained as the result of an intentional action (a project) to 'mask' the actual character of those experiences, the subject must both pursue this intentional strategy 'skilfully' (GM III, 14) — which seems to necessitate at least a precise knowledge of the target features — and be ignorant of pursuing it, for if she was aware that she was pursuing it, this awareness would undermine its success: I cannot believe that the facts are as the 'evidence' suggests if I also know that I have tampered with the evidence in order to make them appear that way. One may be tempted to reply that the project of 'masking' may after all remain *unconscious*, in the sense of: lacking any distinctive phenomenology or what-it-is-likeness for the subject. However, leaving aside for now other difficulties raised by this response, the textual evidence suggests that this route is closed to Nietzsche. His talk of 'lie' and 'mendaciousness' indicates that he thinks of the project of self-deception as carried out by the subject *herself* and this position cannot be maintained once we think of that project as strictly unconscious (see below). But what if the deceptive intention was 'unconscious' in a looser sense: if it was not *noticed* by the subject, while in principle being noticeable, say, through a shift of attention? Alternatively, one might argue that the problematic components of *ressentiment*, such as the self-deceptive intent, are in fact not essential, and perhaps not even possible, and should simply be dropped in an analysis of the phenomenon. All the solutions just sketched have in fact been proposed in different contexts by representatives of the three main approaches that have dominated recent discussions of the so-called paradoxes of self-deception. In order to be in a position to judge whether any of these approaches can account for the phenomenon which concerns Nietzsche, we need to examine them in more detail. This will be the burden of the following three sections. Having found none of these theories fully satisfactory for present purposes, I shall in the final section reconstruct a possible solution pointed to by some of Nietzsche's own remarks.

III: *Ressentiment* and Split Mind Theories

For the reasons outlined above not all the constituent features of *ressentiment* as described by Nietzsche can be known to the subject while she is in that state.

Instead of concluding that *ressentiment* is therefore impossible, one might seek to save the phenomenon by denying that all its components are cognitively accessible to the subject at the time. In particular, this might be argued for the problematic items (2), (3) and (5). To say that they are 'masked' would, on this interpretation, mean that they are 'repressed' beyond the subject's cognitive access. Furthermore, this action of repression — corresponding to (6) in our list — itself takes place without the subject's cognizance, in a mental subsystem inaccessible to the mind's main system. It is tempting to identify the main system with the subject or *self* that experiences the individual's phenomenally conscious thoughts and perceptions, makes her conscious decisions and controls her voluntary bodily movements. It would then be plausible to say that what inferentially insulates the problematic contents, making them inaccessible to the main system at the time, is in part that they are not phenomenally conscious to it — they have no introspectible phenomenology or qualitative what-it-is-likeness from the point of view of the main system.[6] The *locus classicus* for an account of this kind, splitting the mind into several subagencies, is of course Freud's theory of repression.[7] More recently, David Pears has developed a downsized version of this type of approach to explain certain cases of motivated irrationality.[8] The general idea behind his theory is this. Under certain conditions, typically when some belief that p might obtrude itself to a subject but would, if it did so, cause anxiety for her, a mental subagency is set up or activated which manipulates the main system's cognitive processes with the intention of protecting the main system from the anxiety-generating belief. The subsystem is to be thought of as itself a rational agent; it has belief-like representations (about the main system), aims (for the main system to be protected from painful beliefs), and the capacity to act on them (by interfering with the main system's epistemic economy). In order for it to be able to carry out its protective strategy successfully, its beliefs about the main system need to be quite complex and precise: it needs to know about the evidence available to the main system, its epistemic practices, its susceptibility to error, and so forth. Yet, the relation of cognitive transparency is asymmetrical: while the main system must be transparent in all relevant respects to the subsystem, the latter's machinations must be hidden from the main system (at least at the time).

---

[6] Phenomenal consciousness is contrasted with access consciousness by Block (1995). According to Block, a content is access-conscious if it is poised for use in the rational control of the subject's behaviour. It is phenomenally-conscious if there is something it is like to entertain that content (p. 230). Block's thesis that phenomenal consciousness is not conceptually necessary for access consciousness (p. 233) is implausible in this general form because it is, at the fundamental level, through their *phenomenal* properties that items are presented to *me*, the subject, as being thus-and-so. If nothing displays any phenomenal properties at all to me, how can anything in my mental life constitute a cognitive content that actually contributes to *my* reasons to act or to judge in one way rather than another?

[7] See e.g. Freud (1991). Some interpreters would dispute that the subsystem in Freud's split mind theory should be construed as an agent. See Gardner (1993).

[8] Pears (1985). Pears (1991) qualifies some of the stronger claims made in that work. For a more modest version of the subsystemic approach, denying the need for treating the intentional subsystem as an agent, see Davidson (1982, 1985a, 1985b). With respect to the issues relevant in the present context, the differences between the two versions are not crucial and I shall focus on the more full-blown variant.

While this kind of homuncularism may strike the reader as extravagant or far-fetched, one may perhaps think of it less sceptically as a survival-conducive outcome of evolutionary processes, potentially enhancing the overall homoeostatic condition of the individual by reducing proneness to anxiety. In any event, if we are prepared to countenance for the moment the existence of a rational subagency along these lines, the hypothesis would seem to open up an elegant solution to the particular versions of the paradoxes of self-deception threatening Nietzsche's theory of *ressentiment*. For we are then permitted to think of the individual's intentional act of re-interpreting her own affective state (her 'lying') as attributable to the subsystem hidden from the conscious main system, and its activity of 'counterfeiting' as a removing of the offending items from the main system. In order to accommodate Nietzsche's claim that these unacknowledged emotions and desires are in fact components of the subject's *real* state of mind, one further needs to assume that they continue to be efficacious — presumably in the subsystem — in shaping the individual's behaviour (cf. Fox, 1973/4, p. 170). Thus the 'slaves' in Nietzsche's example are neither phenomenally aware that they hate their masters (for *being* their masters), nor are they aware of their real aim to disparage their masters, and of their actual indifference towards the *ressentiment* values outside this particular instrumental context. Yet, if these mental states can correctly be said to persist, they must determine those individuals' actions from their unconscious subsystems. By contrast, the main system really does believe — possibly (but not necessarily) also due to the manipulative interference of the subsystem — that it is committed to the values of humility, justice and so forth, in *general*, irrespective of their applicability in the self-deceiver's own situation.

Split mind theories render self-deception analogous to interpersonal deception, i.e. lying to someone else, and thereby allow a seemingly elegant and logically unproblematic solution to the alleged paradoxes. The subject has a motivated false belief about herself. She is genuinely mistaken about her own condition in virtue of an intentional act of deception. But neither this deceptive act nor her real motives are contemporaneously phenomenally conscious (and therefore in principle accessible) to her, and hence they cannot interfere with the success of the deceptive strategy. Yet her hidden motives can be said to be her *real* motives because they continue to determine her behaviour.

If we suppress for the moment misgivings we may have about the speculative character of the stronger, homuncularist forms of split mind theories, are there any good reasons for resisting this sort of interpretation of *ressentiment*? In fact, most of the standard complaints against intentionalist construals of self-deception in general, and split mind theories in particular, carry little force in the Nietzschean context. First, the individual's state of mind and comportment are not in any obvious sense irrational,[9] because in the *ressentiment* case the theme of self-deception is not an actual or potential state of affairs in the external world, but the subject's own current mental state, her *affective relation* to a part

---

[9] For versions of this objection, see Johnston (1988), p. 83, and Lazar (1999), pp. 272–4.

of that world. Secondly, there can be no question here of the subject's having to ignore countervailing evidence or to violate her normal epistemic standards (Johnston, 1988, pp. 84–5). For we do not primarily ascribe mental states to ourselves in the present tense on the basis of evidence made available through inference or observation (see Section IV for a development of this point and its further implications). If I avow that I detest someone's current actions because I consider them brutal or unjust, I do not have to engage in observations or other investigations to ascertain my avowed state of mind. The fact that a certain psychological self-description just seems to me 'the right thing to say', with no observational or inferential evidence to underwrite it, does not distinguish the self-deceptive case from ordinary present-tense psychological self-ascription.

Nevertheless, there is a related but more serious difficulty for a split mind construal of *ressentiment*. Conscious mental states, including affective states, are not isolated from a person's dispositions and behaviour. If an individual, on the occasion of his house being looted and its inhabitants tortured by a gang of violent thugs,[10] becomes aware of his commitment to *general* values such as non-violence, mutual respect and justice, this awareness has consequences for his subsequent comportment. Unless he suffers from dissociative pathologies or memory failure or the like, he will for example be distressed when hearing of similar horrors having happened to others, or he will participate in educational projects seeking to propagate his irenic values. Yet, according to the split mind account of *ressentiment*, while the subject's *consciousness* is genuinely given over to the *ressentiment* values, his *behaviour* is, unbeknownst to himself, determined by his quite different unconscious intention to take revenge on his torturers. If there were no such discrepancy, there would after all be no justification for Nietzsche's talk of counterfeit or mendaciousness. How are we to envisage such counter-indicative behaviour? It would presumably have to be behaviour manifesting a general indifference towards the avowed values in relevantly similar cases *other than* that which directly involves the objects of *ressentiment* (the particular individuals against whom *ressentiment* is directed). Only if there is such differential behaviour in otherwise similar cases is there any warrant for saying that the subject's real objectives are other than they appear to be (to others *and* to himself). But if my earlier point about the normal behavioural consequences of conscious states is correct, this would mean that the subject would therefore have to be prone to systematically *conflicting* behaviour. Nietzsche stresses that the *ressentiment* subject is not mentally divided at the conscious level (e.g. WP 377), and one must therefore assume that he does not *notice* the inconsistency of his behaviour. But since this failure to notice is topic-specific, we would need some explanation accounting specifically for the subject's failure in self-monitoring in respect of this particular aspect of his life. At this point we can see that the split mind theory offers no adequate solution to our original difficulty, but simply reproduces it at another level: how can the subject fail to notice, in a topic-specific manner, that some of his behaviour systematically conflicts with

---

[10] Cf. Nietzsche's infamous description of the pastimes of the barbarian 'nobles' in GM I, 11.

other action-dispositions of his and with his conscious convictions? On pain of an infinite regress, a different type of explanation is required at this point. We can therefore conclude that, at the least, split mind theories cannot provide *sufficient* explanations, in principle, of the sort of phenomena which concern Nietzsche.

We should also not leave this theory without noting that it fits rather awkwardly with Nietzsche's persistent attacks on the 'mendaciousness' of the adherents of 'slave morality'. These are only intelligible on the assumption that the deceptive project can be ascribed to them at the personal level and, moreover, that human beings are in principle capable of abstaining from such 'lying'.[11] But on the split mind approach, none of these assumptions would be true. At the personal level, the 'slaves' would be innocently deceived victims, and the originator of the lie would be a subpersonal agency that a human subject in principle can have no voluntary control over. Nietzsche's rhetoric strongly suggests that he would accept neither of these implications.

IV: *Ressentiment* and Nonintentional Motivated Error

The currently most popular theories of self-deception construe it as a motivated, purposeful, but nonintentional process involving a biased treatment of available evidence which causes the subject to arrive at a false belief.[12] Typically, the motivational states which are said to result in the defective handling of evidence are the subject's desires or emotions. The presence of strong desires or emotions will often tend to produce false beliefs, among other things by causing us to gather evidence selectively and to focus selectively on the evidence available to us.[13] Yet the biased treatment of evidence in these circumstances is itself normally not noticed by us and we do not intentionally violate our best epistemic standards *in order* to end up with a desired belief. Thus, in the standard example, the husband's anxiety about his wife's possibly having an affair, and his desire for a harmonious marriage, results in his misinterpreting or overlooking evidence which would confirm his wife's infidelity and to over-interpret apparent countervailing evidence. His falling short of his normal epistemic standards is in this case motivated and topic-specific, but it is not *intended* by him under any description. He is in error by virtue of his desires or emotions interfering in his assessment of the facts, but he is not intentionally being deceived, either by himself or by some homuncular subagency. The element of a literal interpretation of 'self-deception' that is abandoned here is the act of deceiving or lying, and the strategy is therefore appropriately referred to as 'deflationary' (Mele, 1997,

---

[11] Nietzsche's fatalism of course commits him to the view that for those who *are* subject to *ressentiment*, things contingently could not have turned out differently (cf. GM I, 13). But even among them, some may be susceptible to a liberation from it, and to bring this about is part of the point of Nietzsche's analysis.

[12] Versions of this account have been proposed by Johnston (1988), Mele (1987, 1997), Barnes (1997) and Scott-Kakures (2002).

[13] For discussions of various biasing mechanisms, see Nisbett and Ross (1980), and Trope *et al.* (1997).

p. 91). In the best-known version of this theory, the following conditions are held to be jointly sufficient for entering a state of self-deception:

(1) The belief that p which S acquires is false.
(2) S treats data relevant, or at least seemingly relevant, to the truth value of p in a motivationally biased way.
(3) This biased treatment is a nondeviant cause of S's acquiring the belief that p.
(4) The body of data possessed by S at the time provides greater warrant for ~p than for p. (Mele, 1997, p. 95).

Some advocates of the deflationary approach balk at this close assimilation of self-deception to wishful thinking (or to fantasy; cf. Lazar, 1999, pp. 284–7) and therefore add as a further condition a *failure of reflective self-knowledge* (Scott-Kakures, 2002).

Can deflationary theories of self-deception explain *ressentiment*? I do not think so. The crucial element distinguishing Nietzschean *ressentiment* from the sorts of case usually discussed in the deflationist literature is that the motivated error is supposed to concern the subject's own current mental state: the subject is supposed falsely to ascribe an occurrent regard for the intrinsic worth of humility, justice or peacableness to herself, while failing to acknowledge her actual vengeful, detractive, superiority-craving intent in avowing these putative values. On the deflationary interpretation this self-ascription would have to occur on the basis of a biased treatment of evidence, but without any intention to disguise the truth. Hence, by the deflationist's lights, items (5) and (6) in my statement of Nietzsche's analysis should be deleted. But there is a difficulty here. It is a familiar point in the philosophy of mind that our logically primary self-ascriptions of mental states in the present tense have a kind of immediacy that preclude their being made on the basis of evidence at all. We normally neither need to observe ourselves or some 'inner object', nor make any conscious inferences from other facts known to us (e.g. from our behaviour) when we ascribe conscious mental states to ourselves in the present tense. Moreover, there are powerful reasons to think that any such inferential or spectatorial self-knowledge not only is not in fact, but *could not* be our primary kind of awareness of our own experiences.[14] Hence there can be no question of the *ressentiment* subject being unwittingly misled to make false present-tense ascriptions of mental states to herself on the basis of a non-intentionally biased treatment of evidence. In fact, the only way desire or interest could lead to a false psychological self-interpretation of the relevant sort is to cause it to be the case that this self-description simply, immediately, and without appeal to evidence, strikes the subject as correct. But can we even make sense of the idea that a self-interpretation which *in principle* does not utilize evidence, might be literally false (or indeed true)? There seem to be two ways of holding on to the truth-assessability of such self-interpretations in the light of the considerations just broached. We either say that present-tense

---

[14] For an argument to this effect based on Husserl's analysis of pre-objective self-awareness, see Poellner (2003), pp. 45–56. Zahavi (1999, 2004), and Moran (2001), pp. 124–48, offer other reasons for the same conclusion.

psychological self-interpretations, while not strictly describing an independent object about which evidence could in principle be gathered, nevertheless articulate or *explicate* the character or content of previously conscious, but more inchoate, less articulated mental states, and that in the case of *ressentiment*, the distorting influence of the subject's desires results in an inadequate articulation.[15] In order to judge this proposal we would need a better grasp of the relation between pre-articulated and interpreted conscious episodes and the deflationary theory has nothing to say on this. But this relation has been a central concern of the phenomenological approaches to be considered in the next section, to which I therefore defer discussion of this issue. Alternatively, one might reject the idea of pre-articulated, conscious, intentional states and hold instead that in *ressentiment* the subject's desire brings about a self-interpretation that is false, not because it is inadequate to anything allegedly pre-propositionally 'given', but because it conflicts with the subject's behavioural patterns. I considered a similar refinement when discussing split mind theories, but its prospects seem better in the present context. For the deflationist has an answer to why the subject fails to notice the discrepancy between her self-interpretation and her actions: she may not notice it due to a failure of attention and other cognitive shortcomings which are themselves non-intentionally caused by the subject's desires. As a result, the subject may simply not realize that (say) she never gets particularly upset about instances of injustice except where it is perpetrated by individuals who have independently caused her displeasure.

However, such a state of affairs may appear more plausible than it actually is only as long as we neglect that the self-interpretations at issue are the subject's primary mode of awareness of her own mental states on the present construal. As such they must be what Moran calls 'avowals', that is, they must be in part constituted by the subject's being struck by aspects of the world in a certain way (Moran, 2001, esp. ch. 4). 'Interpreting myself', in this sense, as a lover of justice on the occasion of a particular encounter with injustice is not just to come up with a description of myself which I happen to like, but to experience the event in a certain way, for example as *painful because* someone's rightful possessions are taken away from him, or because his freedom is arbitrarily infringed upon. Being genuinely struck by aspects of the world in this way normally implies, as we saw earlier, dispositions to respond alike to similar situations as well as various other action-dispositions. Once this is recognized, it becomes very difficult to see how a subject who, like the person of *ressentiment*, does not suffer from a severe form of self-division or dissociation, might simply *systematically not notice* the discrepancy between her self-interpretation and her patterns of behaviour. But granting it for now as at least a theoretical possibility, since the cognitive defect — the failure to notice systematic practical inconsistency — is not intended by the subject, she should be perfectly amenable to correction once it is pointed out to her by others. Such openness to correction through a guided

---

[15] This sort of account of explicit psychological self-interpretation has in recent years been associated especially with Charles Taylor. See e.g. his (1982, 1985).

re-direction of attention is, to say the least, not common in cases of self-deception of the kind Nietzsche is interested in.

V: *Ressentiment* as 'Bad Faith'

The accounts of self-deception considered in the two preceding sections each abandoned some part of Nietzsche's characterization of *ressentiment*; either the claim that all the main components of *ressentiment* are conscious, or the idea of an intentional strategy of deception. By contrast, Sartre's analysis of bad faith stresses precisely these problematic aspects and thus seems closely analogous to Nietzsche's own story. While Sartrean *mauvaise foi* is a very specific form of bad faith that concerns the fundamental structure of what it is to be a human being, the essentials of his account are transferable to other types of self-deception. In bad faith, according to Sartre,

> it is from myself that I am hiding the truth. Thus the duality of the deceiver and the deceived does not exist here [*pace* split mind theories]. Bad faith on the contrary implies in essence the unity of a *single* consciousness . . . One does not undergo one's bad faith; one is not infected with it; it is not a state [*contra* deflationism]. But consciousness affects itself with bad faith. There must be an original intention and a project of bad faith; this project implies a comprehension of bad faith as such and a pre-reflective apprehension (of) consciousness as affecting itself with bad faith. It follows first that the one to whom the lie is told and the one who lies are one and the same person, which means that I must know in my capacity as deceiver the truth which is hidden from me in my capacity as the one deceived. Better yet I must know the truth very exactly in order to conceal it more carefully — and this not at two different temporal moments, which at a pinch would allow us to re-establish a semblance of duality — but in the unitary structure of a single project. (Sartre, 1969, p. 49).

Sartre later concedes that this passage overstates his position. The self-deceiver does not *know* he is self-deceived: 'non-thetic consciousness is not to *know*' (Sartre, 1969, p. 69). The notion of non-thetic or pre-reflective consciousness alluded to here plays a crucial role in Sartre's solution to the apparent paradox of self-deception re-iterated in this passage. He takes this idea from Husserl who had already outlined and made use of it, albeit less expansively and systematically than Sartre. Pre-reflective consciousness is the most basic mode of awareness of our own conscious mental states. Its characteristics are grasped best by contrasting it with *reflective* consciousness which has provided the model for many of the inadequate 'inner theatre' theories of self-consciousness, from Locke onward, that have dominated the modern philosophical tradition. In reflective self-consciousness we *attend* to our own mental state; this attending or thematizing an experience is a necessary condition of the possibility of the experience being presented to us as an *object*. But for many reasons reflection (or 'introspection') cannot be our primary mode of awareness of our experiences.[16] We

---

[16] Cf. Husserl (1991), pp. 122–4. For a detailed discussion of this and the claims in the following sentences, and of the relevant concept of object, see Poellner (2003), pp. 45–56. See also note 14.

are, and must be, able to be aware of them prior to reflection (or *pre-reflectively*), which is to say that they are then phenomenally conscious, but *not* as intentional objects. Any *conceptual* mental content is, necessarily, a representation of an intentional object in Husserl's sense. This entails that in pre-reflective consciousness experiences are presented nonconceptually and thus cannot be objects of propositional attitudes such as belief, and thus *a fortiori* cannot be known (hence Sartre's self-correction on this point). Husserl in one place uses the potentially misleading analogy with visual background objects to characterize the non-thematic mode of givenness of pre-reflective experiences:

> [Intentional experiences] do not only exist when they are themselves objects of a reflecting consciousness, but they are already present when not reflected upon, as 'background' and thus as in principle *available for perception*, like unattended things in our external field of vision. (Husserl, 1983, pp. 98–9).

At least since Heidegger's analysis of *Besorgen*, it has been a common theme in the philosophy of intentionality that much of our everyday practical dealing with things involves such non-thematic background awareness; we skilfully 'cope' with, or take account of things as implements without paying attention to them, when we intentionally and purposefully use the keys on the keyboard, or the pen in writing, or the steering wheel or gear handle of the car. We have a similarly non-thematic awareness of our own body and its movements in our normal voluntary bodily comportment. This suggests the following solution to the alleged paradox. Those contents of consciousness we cannot acknowledge without realizing our practical inconsistency are indeed conscious, but pre-reflectively: they are unattended yet nevertheless skilfully negotiated 'background'. Avoiding explicit awareness of them is no more unproblematic than avoiding bumping into a piece of furniture without paying attention to it while perambulating engaged in intense conversation in a familiar environment.[17]

Sartre's own solution makes essential use of the idea of non-thematic consciousness, but is based on the more general thesis that what makes self-deception possible is that its object is 'not given or is given indistinctly' (Sartre, 1969, p. 67): 'Bad faith apprehends evidence but it is resigned in advance to not being fulfilled by this evidence' (*ibid.*, p. 68). In Sartre's own example, the young woman can continue to engage in the desired flirtatious conversation with her admirer, which her 'virtuous' self-image would otherwise prohibit, because her interlocutor's behaviour is ambiguous and allows her to entertain an unthreatening interpretation of it as the expression of a purely intellectual interest. She is self-deceived, not because the evidence available to her necessarily favours the threatening interpretation of the situation, but because she intentionally rests content with the *ambiguity* of the evidence *in order* to be able to hold on to the desired interpretation and be permitted to continue the game. This intention, Sartre insists, is itself phenomenally conscious: 'I shall not be able to hide from myself that I believe [in the face of inconclusive evidence] in order not to believe [the undesirable hypothesis]' (Sartre, 1969, pp. 69–70). Yet the intention

---

[17] For a recent exposition of this approach, see Fingarette (1998).

is itself pre-reflective and hence 'non-thetic'. Not being thematized, it is not the object of a reflective judgment and is therefore not available to the subject for relevant inferences. But only if it was thus available could her awareness of it undermine her project.

If we apply this Sartrean model to Nietzsche's *ressentiment*, the idea of pre-reflective self-consciousness makes it possible to see how (6) — the intentional concealing of the motivational nexus (2)/(3)/(5) — could be conscious, while yet being unnoticed by the subject of *ressentiment*. It may, in phenomenological parlance, be unthematically 'lived through' (*erlebt*), just as many of our experiences and their intentional contents are, both in simple behavioural routines and in relatively complex, skilled, absorbed action. But the difference here is that, unlike in the normal, non-self-deceived case, there is a resistance to reflection. This is why Sartre speaks of the 'original project' of the self-deceiver as involving an *iterated* or second-order bad faith: 'We must note in fact that the project of bad faith must itself be in bad faith. I am not only in bad faith at the end of my effort' (Sartre, 1969, pp. 67–8). What is characteristic of bad faith is thus that the self-deceiver intentionally adopts a non-reflective stance *vis-à-vis* her own intentional behaviour in certain contexts; and this stance includes *itself* among the items it pre-reflectively resists being made the objects of critical reflection and detection. This is why phenomenologists of self-deception sometimes use the metaphor of 'fleeing' to characterize the self-deceiver's consciousness: the types of self-deception which are of interest to them involve essentially a *fugitive* consciousness — a consciousness which has pre-reflectively determined itself not to reflect on certain aspects of itself.[18]

However, while the Sartrean approach has a good answer to the question how *ressentiment* can consistently involve a project of concealment (6), it is not clear how it can plausibly account for *what* is concealed. In *ressentiment* the facts to be concealed are not external to the individual but consist in the motivational nexus (2)/(3)/(5), leading from hatred of a not-self to a desire for superiority or power over that Other, and thence to an instrumental use of 'moral values' as a tool for reducing the Other in thought. What would it mean for this experiential complex to be presently given to the subject 'indistinctly'? Not all of it can be given as pre-reflective 'background', for Nietzsche states emphatically, and very plausibly, that the states of consciousness initiating the dynamic of *ressentiment* are states with a high affective intensity:

> Here a *ressentiment* without equal rules, that of an unsatisfied instinct and will to power which desires to become master . . . over life itself . . .; here the gaze is directed venomously and maliciously against physiological flourishing itself, in particular against its expressions: beauty, joy' (GM III, 11).

Indeed, if the negative affects at the core of *ressentiment* were merely unnoticed background, like my intention of shifting gear when driving round a corner in my car, or like a mild headache I pay no attention to while engaged in a fascinating conversation, it is entirely incomprehensible why the subject's hedonic balance

---

[18] For the metaphor of fleeing, see especially Heidegger (1962), §§ 29, 40.

should even *require* the extensive efforts of re-interpretation described by Nietzsche. Sartre's account of bad faith, therefore, while illuminating the possibility of a *ressentiment project*, seems to offer us little help in understanding the nature and mode of givenness of the *items to be concealed* or the manner in which their concealment is effected. What could the method of concealment or 'masking' (GM III, 14) of a present conscious state with high affective intensity possibly consist in, given that such states are necessarily in the foreground of consciousness, conspicuously manifesting their presence?

VI: *Ressentiment* and Value

None of the three main contemporary models of self-deception can satisfactorily accommodate the kind of phenomenon Nietzsche claims to be the condition of possibility of 'moral values' — a subject's intentional misinterpretation of her own current conscious state. The failure, in particular, of Sartre's literal and apparently congenial interpretation of self-deception to make intelligible *ressentiment* as Nietzsche describes it may suggest that it is simply not a coherently conceivable state of mind at all. Nevertheless, it is worth investigating whether Nietzsche's own remarks might provide the materials for a revised concept of *ressentiment* which preserves some of the critical potential of the original while avoiding its defects. One notable feature of Nietzsche's analysis is his emphasis on the comparative or relational character of the *ressentiment* subject's orientation towards the positive values or virtues she 'counterfeits' or 'imitates' (*nachmacht*; GM III, 14). Her attitude towards those values or virtues typically manifests itself in a thematizing, not of their intrinsic character, but of their *relation* to the vices or disvalues associated with the Others who are the objects of *ressentiment*:

> Slave morality from the outset says No to what is 'outside', what is 'different, what is 'not itself'; and this No is its creative deed. This inversion of the value-positing eye — this need to direct one's view outward . . . — is of the essence of *ressentiment* . . .

> The 'well-born' felt themselves to be 'happy'; they did not have to establish their happiness artificially by looking at their enemies, or to persuade themselves, *deceive* themselves, that they were happy (as all men of *ressentiment* are in the habit of doing) . . . (GM I, 10).

The difference Nietzsche is concerned with in these passages is not some ostensible statistical fact of empirical psychology, but is explicitly identified by him as deriving from the 'essence of *ressentiment*' and its opposite. In fact, Nietzsche's 'nobles', whether they do embody the ethos of a historical Homeric warrior nobility or not, also represent (like his 'slaves') an *idealization* in at least one respect which is central to the present discussion. For most actual human beings, instances of the values most important to them are often not directly self-given to them, but are absent objects of desire: whether it is love, prestige, beauty, wordly success, knowledge, or whatever else that may matter most to us, we are regrettably often bereft of it. By contrast, Nietzsche's nobles are portrayed as subjects who are always in the direct presence of the goods that matter most to them. The reason why this portrait seems to be not obviously an idealization is that the goods most important to them happen to be their own virtues of excellence: 'every noble morality develops from a triumphant affirmation of itself' (*ibid*.).[19] This does not imply that these goods are primarily given to them in self-observation or reflection. Nietzsche on the contrary repeatedly stresses the nobles' lack of reflection, their 'naïve' comportment (GM I, 10). Unlike the *ressentiment* subjects, the nobles only reluctantly thematize the disvalues represented by their antipodes, the 'slaves': their 'negative concept "low", "common", "bad" is only a subsequently invented, pale, contrasting image', from which they 'look away' with 'impatience' (*ibid*.).

Now, I want to suggest that both of these features of Nietzsche's nobles, *non-reflectiveness* and the *reluctance to thematize disvalue*, derive from the circumstance that they are idealized subjects who are stipulated to be invariably in the presence of what they value most. Implicit in Nietzsche's account is the idea that the self-givenness[20] of what is valued greatly essentially captures a subject's awareness, such that the subject 'lives in' the orientation of her consciousness towards the value-features self-given to it. That is to say, her awareness will necessarily be *directed onto* any significant good insofar as its significance-constituting properties are indeed themselves genuinely present to her. The more the subject values the good thus self-given to her, the greater will be this fixation upon it, and the more will she mentally resist its being removed or withdrawing from the direct grasp her consciousness has upon it.[21] If the value in question is exemplified by an item in the external world, or by an aspect of the subject's own activity of a kind incompatible with reflection (like most complex skill-involving actions), this focus *precludes* the subject's simultaneously focusing on her own mental state. Thus the non-reflective, naive and non-comparative 'living in' what is given as of intrinsically great value — this orientation being partly constitutive of the 'noble' disposition — is explicable by the fact that on one level Nietzsche's account simply is a description of an ideal evaluatively 'fulfilled' consciousness. Being fixated or captivated by the phenomenal character of its

---

[19] Cf. Migotti (1998), p. 749.

[20] 'Self-givenness' is here used in Husserl's sense, referring to the direct presentation (not necessarily complete) of an item in intentional consciousness. For example, an object's secondary qualities, considered as particular instances, are self-given in sensory perception. Self-givenness is to be distinguished from symbolic (e.g. linguistic), imagistic (*bildlich*), and imaginative (*phantasiemässig*) forms of presentation. For Husserl, self-givenness as well as imagistic and imaginary presentifications (but not 'empty' symbolic representations) count as *intuitively fulfilled* forms of presentation sustaining various levels of *acquaintance* with the items presented.

[21] This is why in the classical accounts of the 'highest good' (*summum bonum*), the possession of it was represented as a condition in which there is no endogenous tendency or desire for change, including for a change of attention away from the 'contemplation' of it (see Aquinas, 1981, IaIIae, qu. 1, art. 5, pp. 586–7). Such conceptions of what it is to be in 'possession' of the highest good were arguably motivated less by a contingent or even arbitrary preference for stability over change than by the consideration that the highest conceivable good would necessarily have to be that whose presence satisfies desire completely, and for as long as desire is satisfied completely there can be no desire for change.

object itself, and therefore being in the relevant sense non-comparative, is what an ideally fulfilled evaluative consciousness *essentially is*.

Returning now to the contrasting state of *ressentiment*, we have seen that Nietzsche describes it as involving an *essential* preoccupation with the locus of (ostensible) disvalue. In *ressentiment*, there is a '*need* to direct one's view outward' to what is an object of 'hatred and contempt' (KGW VIII.2.10.9) for the subject who thereby 'constructs [his] happiness artificially by looking at [his] enemies' (GM I, 10). The *ressentiment* subject acquires his evaluative standards by avowedly embracing values that negate whatever values happen to be represented by the Other who is resented. His adoption of these standards, and the 'happiness' ensuing from thinking of himself as living under their authority, are therefore essentially dependent upon a comparative and favourable assessment of his own virtue in relation to the representation as vicious or 'evil' of the object of *ressentiment*. This questionable 'happiness' — a certain sort of consciousness of superiority — is of course what the adoption of the *ressentiment* values *aims* at. One way in which one may expect this essential relationality or comparative character of the subject's consciousness of value to express itself is a tendency, when directly confronted with instances of the *ressentiment* values, to describe these not with monadic evaluative predicates (as 'just', 'generous', 'compassionate', etc.), but comparatively: as 'more just than x', 'more virtuous than x', and so forth.

These considerations invite the following proposal towards a coherent and empirically adequate construal of *ressentiment* as a form of self-deception. The *essentially* comparative character of the *ressentiment* subject's evaluative orientation implies that he has no appropriately 'fulfilled' consciousness of, i.e. acquaintance with, the values he avows. This is, I suggest, how we should interpret Nietzsche's talk of *ressentiment* as merely 'counterfeiting' or 'imitating' virtue. By contrast, the subject *is* conscious of the motivational nexus from discomfort or suffering caused by another subject (1), to hatred of that Other (2), and thence to a desire for superiority over the Other (3), which desire supplies the reason for the intentional adoption of the values of *ressentiment* (5).

Items (3) and (5) are plausibly interpretable in terms of a broadly Husserlian or Sartrean account of pre-reflective consciousness: they are conscious, but as 'background', i.e. without being thematized by the subject. The resolve not to engage in reflection in certain experiential contexts is itself an unthematic intention essential to the form of self-deception which *ressentiment* exemplifies. This aspect, emphasized by Sartre, is at least in part what entitles us to speak of a *project* of self-deception.[22]

However, as I argued earlier, the notion of pre-reflective (self-) consciousness cannot account for (1) and (2), since these are conscious states with high

---

[22] An alternative, deflationary reading would dispense with (5) altogether and hold instead that desire (3) directly, non-intentionally, causes the adoption of the *ressentiment* values (4). But this is implausible: surely the fact that these values justify a condemnation of the objects of *ressentiment* is consciously registered by the subject and this awareness plays a reason-giving motivational role in their adoption.

affective intensity and thus not convincingly construed as unobtrusive background. They are therefore undoubtedly focally conscious, yet re-interpreted (*umgedeutet*) as, respectively, pain at, and hatred of, not the object of *ressentiment*, but the general moral disvalues ('evil') which happen to be instantiated by that object:

> We good men — *we are the just* — what they desire they call, not retaliation, but 'the triumph of justice'; what they hate is not their enemy, no! they hate 'injustice', they hate 'godlessness' (GM I, 14).

This re-interpretation of negative affect as disapproval of 'immorality' makes possible its acknowledgement as well as its modification (into an experience of moral superiority). The problem of how current, conscious, emotional episodes like hatred could possibly be actively concealed from the subject therefore vanishes — they could not and do not need to be intentionally concealed. Yet, does this solution not merely replace one problem with another? For we have seen that Nietzsche's description entails that the *ressentiment* subject has no fulfilled awareness, i.e. no genuine acquaintance with, the values making possible the re-interpretation of negative affect. But if she has no acquaintance with, say, humility *as a value* at all (as opposed to an acquaintance with certain behavioural routines described non-evaluatively and typically recognized as expressing it in her cultural environment), she has no adequate grasp of the *concept* of humility. For an acquaintance with what the concept applies to is here no less essential for grasping the concept than in the case of other concepts of experience-involving properties, like *red*.

How, then, can a concept like *humility* be used in *ressentiment* to legitimate and modify negative affect by re-interpreting its intentional object? There appear to be several possible responses to this problem, but all of them are incompatible with Nietzsche's claim that *ressentiment* 'creates' values, and that 'moral values' in particular owe their origin to *ressentiment*. Rather, it turns out that *ressentiment* is only possible as a derivative or parasitic phenomenon, presupposing a prior givenness to *someone* of the values it instrumentalizes. It is conceivable, for instance, that in *ressentiment* a subject utilizes values which she has no acquaintance with, if she is aware that these values are recognized by *others* in her culture. But it is also possible — although Nietzsche himself does not seem to consider this possibility — that the subject does have, in other contexts, a genuine (non-self-deceived), albeit relatively weak, grasp of the values instrumentalized in *ressentiment*, while being motivated in the *ressentiment* situation itself, not by this commitment (due to its relative weakness), but by other aspects of the situation — in Nietzsche's example, by the Other being in a position of *power* over her. In such a case, the subject misinterprets her 'hatred' of the Other as being directed at certain morally relevant properties ('immorality') whose contraries she is in some limited measure acquainted with, while in fact its intentional object is simply the superior power of the Other. What makes possible the false construal of the intentional object of negative affect in either of these cases is, crucially, the subject's *expectation*, which may or may not be thematic, to be able to intuitively fulfil her avowed commitment (and the strength of that commitment) to the *ressentiment* values, if she so wishes. What makes this a case of self-deception is (a) that this expectation is mistaken and (b) that the subject pre-reflectively, but intentionally, desists from seeking to verify it *in order* to avoid the possible falsification of her expectation. This supplies a further sense, in addition to what was said above in relation to items (3) and (5) of Nietzsche's own analysis, in which *ressentiment* can be said to involve a *project* of self-deception, although of course not under this description. It is also what, in my judgment, supplies the only philosophically defensible interpretation of Nietzsche's talk of the subject's 'masking' her actual sentiments (item (6)).

VII: Conclusion

I have argued that Nietzsche's notion of *ressentiment* should be interpreted as the concept of a form of self-deception about some of the subject's own present conscious mental states, more specifically about the subject's evaluative commitments apparently manifested in some of them. We have found that none of the prevalent contemporary theories of self-deception can satisfactorily explain the possibility of *ressentiment*. Nevertheless, rather than abandoning the concept as incoherent, a reconstruction has been proposed which draws both on Nietzsche's own formulations and on elements of Sartre's theory of pre-reflective consciousness, itself influenced by Husserl's analysis of pre-objective self-awareness. While this reconstruction has not been able to vindicate Nietzsche's account in its entirety, it does arguably remain faithful to much of its spirit. However, Nietzsche's more radical critical project — the attempt to show that 'moral values' in some sense are 'created' by *ressentiment* — has not been found defensible. If *ressentiment* is to be possible, it is dependent upon a prior recognition by someone of the values it instrumentalizes.

References

Aquinas, T. (1981), *Summa Theologica* (London: Sheed and Ward), Vol. 2.
Barnes, A. (1997), *Seeing through Self-Deception* (Cambridge: Cambridge University Press).
Block, N. (1995), 'On a confusion about a function of consciousness', *Behavioral and Brain Sciences*, **18**, pp. 227–47.
Davidson, D. (1982), 'The paradoxes of irrationality', in *Philosophical Essays on Freud*, ed. R. Wollheim and J. Hopkins (Cambridge: Cambridge University Press), pp. 289–305.
Davidson, D. (1985a), 'Incoherence and irrationality', *Dialectica*, **64**, pp. 345–54.
Davidson, D. (1985b), 'Deception and division', in *Actions and Events: Perspectives on the Philosophy of Donald Davidson*, ed. E. LePore and B. McLaughlin (Oxford: Blackwell), pp. 138–48.
Fingarette, H. (1969), *Self-Deception* (London: Routledge).
Fingarette, H. (1998), 'Self-deception needs no explaining', *Philosophical Quarterly*, **48**, pp. 283–301.
Fox, M. (1973/4), 'On unconscious emotions', *Philosophy and Phenomenological Research*, **34**, pp. 151–70.
Freud, S. (1991), 'The unconscious', in *On Metapsychology: The Theory of Psychoanalysis*, The Penguin Freud Library, Vol. 11 (Harmondsworth: Penguin), pp. 159–222.

Gardner, S. (1993), *Irrationality and the Philosophy of Psychoanalysis* (Cambridge: Cambridge University Press).

Heidegger, M. (1962), *Being and Time* (Oxford: Blackwell).

Husserl, E. (1983), *Ideas Pertaining to a Pure Phenomenology and to a Phenomenological Philosophy*, First Book (Dordrecht: Kluwer).

Husserl, E. (1991), *On the Phenomenology of the Consciousness of Internal Time (1893–1917)* (Dordrecht: Kluwer).

Johnston, M. (1988), 'Self-deception and the nature of mind', in *Perspectives on Self-Deception*, ed. B. McLaughlin and A. Oksenberg Rorty (Berkeley: University of California Press), pp. 63–91.

Lazar, A. (1999), 'Deceiving oneself or self-deceived? On the formation of beliefs "under the influence" ', *Mind*, **108**, pp. 265–90.

Leiter, B. (2002), *Nietzsche on Morality* (London: Routledge).

Mele, A. (1987), *Irrationality: An Essay on Akrasia, Self-Deception and Self-Control* (Oxford: Oxford University Press).

Mele, A. (1997), 'Real self-deception', *Behavioral and Brain Sciences*, **20**, pp. 91–102.

Migotti, M. (1998), 'Slave morality, Socrates, and the Bushmen: A reading of the first essay of *On the Genealogy of Morals*', *Philosophy and Phenomenological Research*, **58**, pp. 745–79.

Moran, R. (2001), *Authority and Estrangement: An Essay on Self-Knowledge* (Princeton: Princeton University Press).

Nietzsche, F. (1967–), *Werke. Kritische Gesamtausgabe*, ed. G. Colli, M. Montinari *et al.* (Berlin: De Gruyter).

Nietzsche, F. (1968), *The Will to Power*, ed. W. Kaufmann (New York: Vintage).

Nietzsche, F. (1969), *Thus Spoke Zarathustra* (Harmondsworth: Penguin).

Nietzsche, F. (1973), *Beyond Good and Evil* (Harmondsworth: Penguin).

Nietzsche, F. (1989), *On the Genealogy of Morals / Ecce Homo* (New York: Vintage).

Nietzsche, F. (1990), *Twilight of the Idols / The Anti-Christ* (Harmondsworth: Penguin).

Nisbett, R. and Ross, L. (1980), *Human Inference: Strategies and Shortcomings of Social Judgment* (New Jersey: Prentice Hall).

Pears, D. (1985), *Motivated Irrationality* (Oxford: Oxford University Press).

Pears, D. (1991), 'Self-deceptive belief-formation', *Synthese*, **89**, pp. 393–405.

Poellner, P. (2001), 'Perspectival truth', in *Nietzsche*, ed. B. Leiter and J. Richardson (Oxford: Oxford University Press), pp. 85–117.

Poellner, P. (2003), 'Non-conceptual content, experience and the self', *Journal of Consciousness Studies*, **10** (2), pp. 32–57.

Reginster, B. (1997), 'Nietzsche on *Ressentiment* and valuation', *Philosophy and Phenomenological Research*, **57**, pp. 281–305.

Sartre, J.P. (1969), *Being and Nothingness* (London: Methuen).

Scheler, M. (1978), *Das Ressentiment im Aufbau der Moralen* (Frankfurt: Vittorio Klostermann).

Scott-Kakures, D. (2002), 'At "permanent risk": Reasoning and self-knowledge in self-deception', *Philosophy and Phenomenological Research*, **65**, pp. 576–603.

Taylor, C. (1982), 'Responsibility for self', in *Free Will*, ed. G. Watson (Oxford: Oxford University Press).

Taylor, C. (1985), 'Self-interpreting animals', in *Human Agency and Language: Philosophical Papers 1* (Cambridge: Cambridge University Press).

Trope, Y., Gervey, B. and Liberman, N. (1997), 'Wishful Thinking from a Pragmatic Hypothesis Testing Perspective', in *The Mythomanias: The Nature of Deception and Self-Deception*, ed. M.S. Myslobodsky (Hillsdale, NJ: Erlbaum).

Williams, B. (1981), 'Internal and external reasons', in *Moral Luck* (Cambridge: Cambridge University Press).

Zahavi, D. (1999), *Self-Awareness and Alterity* (Evanston: Northwestern University Press).

Zahavi, D. (2004), 'Back to Brentano?', *Journal of Consciousness Studies*, **11** (10–11), pp. 66–87 [this volume].

Dan Zahavi

Back to Brentano?

For a couple of decades, higher-order theories of consciousness have enjoyed great popularity, but they have recently been met with growing dissatisfaction. Many have started to look elsewhere for viable alternatives, and within the last few years, quite a few have rediscovered Brentano. In this paper such a (neo-)Brentanian one-level account of consciousness will be outlined and discussed. It will be argued that it can contribute important insights to our understanding of the relation between consciousness and self-awareness, but it will also be argued that the account remains beset with some problems, and that it will ultimately make more sense to take a closer look at Sartre, Husserl, and Heidegger, if one is on the lookout for promising alternatives to the higher-order theories, than to return all the way to Brentano.

I: The Rise and Fall of Higher-Order Theory

It is customary to distinguish between two uses of the term 'conscious', a transitive and an intransitive use. On the one hand, we can speak of our being conscious of something, be it x, y, or z. On the other we can speak of our being conscious *simpliciter* (rather than non-conscious). For the past two or three decades, a dominant way to account for intransitive consciousness in cognitive science and analytical philosophy of mind has been by means of some kind of higher-order theory (cf. Armstrong, 1968; Rosenthal, 1986; Lycan, 1987; Carruthers, 1996; etc.). The distinction between conscious and non-conscious mental states has been taken to rest upon the presence or absence of a relevant meta-mental state. One way to illustrate the guiding idea is by comparing consciousness to a spotlight. Some mental states are illuminated; others do their work in the dark. Those that are illuminated are intransitively conscious, those that are not, are non-conscious. What makes a mental state conscious (illuminated) is the fact that it is taken as an object by a relevant higher-order state. It is the occurrence of the higher-order representation that makes us conscious of the first-order mental state. In short, a conscious state is a state we are conscious of, or as Rosenthal puts it, 'the mental state's being intransitively conscious simply consists in one's being transitively conscious of it' (Rosenthal, 1997, p. 739). Thus, intransitive consciousness is taken to be a non-intrinsic, relational property (Rosenthal, 1997, pp. 736–7), that is, a property that a mental state only has in so far as it stands in the relevant relation to something else.

There have generally been two ways of interpreting this. Either we become aware of being in the first-order mental state by means of some higher-order perception or monitoring (Armstrong, 1968; Lycan, 1997), or we become aware of it by means of some higher-order thought, that is, the state is conscious just in case we have a roughly contemporaneous thought to the effect *that* we are in that very state (Rosenthal, 1993a, p.199). Thus, the basic divide between the higher-order perception (HOP) and the higher-order thought (HOT) model has precisely been on the issue of whether the conscious-making meta-mental states are perception-like or thought-like in nature.[1] In both cases, however, consciousness has been taken to be a question of the mind directing its intentional aim upon its own states and operations. Self-directedness has been taken to be constitutive of (intransitive) consciousness, or to put it differently, higher-order theories have typically explained (intransitive) consciousness in terms of self-awareness.[2] As Van Gulick puts it, it is 'the addition of the relevant meta-intentional self-awareness that transforms a nonconscious mental state into a conscious one' (Van Gulick, 2000, p. 276).

For a period, the higher-order theories enjoyed great popularity, but in recent years they have been met with growing dissatisfaction (cf. Byrne, 1997; Siewert, 1998; Zahavi, 1999; Van Gulick, 2000; Thomasson, 2000; Baker, 2000; Lurz, 2003a; Kriegel, 2003a). The criticism has been multifaceted, but let me mention a few of the counter-arguments.

All higher-order models, be they of the HOT or the HOP variant, share common assumptions. One of the most frequently criticized is the idea that the relation between two otherwise non-conscious processes can make one of them conscious. Conscious states are not something that one simply has, like coins in one's pocket. On the contrary, conscious states are characterized by having a subjective 'feel' to them, i.e., a certain phenomenal quality of 'what it is like' or what it 'feels' like to have them. According to the higher-order theories a certain mental state must stand in the right relation to a second-order thought or perception in order for it to manifest itself phenomenally. But it is quite unclear how a state without subjective or phenomenal qualities can be transformed into one with such qualities by the mere relational addition of a meta-state having the first-order state as its intentional object (cf. Van Gulick, 2000, p. 294).

One of the questions that a higher-order theory has to answer is the following: What is it that makes one mental state conscious of another mental state? For Rosenthal a 'higher-order thought, B, is an awareness of the mental-state token, A, simply because A is the intentional object of B' (Rosenthal, 1993b, p. 160).

---

[1] For an informative comparison of the HOT and HOP models, see Van Gulick (2000).

[2] In the following, I will not distinguish 'self-consciousness' and 'self-awareness', but rather use the two terms interchangeably.

Rosenthal readily admits, however, that the relation between the higher-order state and the first-order state is of a rather special kind. On the one hand, we only regard mental states as being conscious if we are conscious of them in some suitably unmediated way, namely non-inferentially. Otherwise, a non-conscious mental process would qualify as conscious, simply because we could infer that we would have to be in it (Rosenthal, 1997, p. 737). On the other hand, Rosenthal argues that for a mental state to be conscious, it is not sufficient that we are non-inferentially conscious of the state, we also have to be conscious of being *ourselves* in that very mental state. 'Only if one's thought is about oneself as such, and not just about someone that happens to be oneself, will the mental state be a conscious state' (Rosenthal, 1997, p. 750, cf. p. 741).[3] To put it differently, it is not enough to explain how a certain state becomes conscious, the theory also has to explain how the state comes to be given as *my* state, as a state that *I* am in. Why? Because this first-personal givenness is an ineliminable part of what it means for a state to be conscious — it concerns the fact that a conscious mental state feels like something *for somebody* — and for a theory of consciousness to leave this aspect out is to leave something absolutely crucial out.

The decisive question, however, is whether the higher-order theories are capable of accounting for this feature in a satisfactory manner.

Rosenthal has argued that if one wishes to come up with a non-trivial and informative account of consciousness one must at any price avoid the claim that consciousness is an intrinsic property of our mental states. To call something intrinsic is, for Rosenthal, to imply that it is something unanalysable and mysterious, and consequently beyond the reach of scientific and theoretical study: 'We would insist that being conscious is an intrinsic property of mental states only if we were convinced that it lacked articulated structure, and thus defied explanation' (Rosenthal, 1993b, p.157). Although Rosenthal acknowledges that there is something intuitively appealing about taking consciousness to be an intrinsic property, he still thinks that this approach must be avoided since it will impede a naturalistic (and reductionistic) account, which seeks to explain consciousness by appeal to non-conscious mental states, and non-conscious mental states in non-mental terms (Rosenthal 1993b, p. 165; 1997, p. 735). But as Baker has recently pointed out, although Rosenthal's account of consciousness requires a first-person perspective — a first-order mental state is to be conscious by being accompanied by a non-conscious higher-order state that only a being with a first-person perspective could have — his theory simply presupposes this first-person perspective, or to put it differently, 'the first-person perspective that is required for the explanation of conscious states is itself left unexplained'(Baker, 2000, p. 84).

This objection can be elaborated and amplified by means of some of the classical analyses of first-personal self-reference found in the writings of Castañeda, Perry, Shoemaker, and others. These analyses have purported to show that the types of self-reference available from a first-person perspective and from a

---

[3]   In making this claim, Rosenthal explicitly refers to the work of Castañeda, Chisholm, Lewis, and Perry (Rosenthal, 1997, p. 750).

third-person perspective are utterly different. I can refer to a publicly available object by way of a proper name, a demonstrative, or a definite description, and occasionally this object happens to be myself. When I refer to myself in this way, that is, when I refer to myself from the third-person perspective, I am referring to myself in exactly the same way that I can refer to others, and others can refer to me (the only difference being that I am the one doing it, thus making the reference into a self-reference). But this type of objectifying self-reference is neither necessary nor sufficient if one is to be aware of oneself in the proper first-personal manner. In order for a perception of a sunset to be given as *my* perception, as a perception *I* am in or living through, it is not sufficient for me to know that Dan Zahavi or a 36-year old Dane is currently perceiving a sunset etc., since I can be in possession of knowledge that identifies me from a third-person perspective, and still fail to realize that I am the person in question. Since there is always a gap between grasping that a certain third-person description applies to a person, and grasping that I am that person, i.e., since there is no third-person description such that grasping that it fits a certain person guarantees that I realize that I am that person, first-personal self-reference cannot be regarded as involving the identification of an object by any third-person description (Castañeda, 1967). Nor is such third-person identificatory knowledge necessary, since I can be in a state of complete amnesia and be ignorant of all those properties that would identify me from a third-person perspective, and still remain in possession of first-personal self-reference, still remain aware that this unpleasant experience is *mine*, and that it is *me* who is undergoing it.

Why is first-personal self-reference different from third-personal self-reference? A natural reply is that first-personal self-reference owes its uniqueness to the fact that we are acquainted with our own subjectivity in a way that differs radically from the way in which we are acquainted with objects. In first-personal self-reference one is not aware of oneself as an object that happens to be oneself, nor is one aware of oneself as one specific object rather than another. Rather, first-personal self-reference involves a non-objectifying self-acquaintance. It involves what has alternately been called 'self-reference without identification' (Shoemaker, 1968) and 'non-ascriptive reference to self' (Brook, 1994).

But why is it impossible to account for first-personal self-reference in terms of a successful object-identification. Why is self-awareness not a type of object-consciousness? Shoemaker has provided a classical argument. In order to identify something as oneself one obviously has to hold something true of it that one already knows to be true of oneself. This self-knowledge might in some cases be grounded on some further identification, but the supposition that *every* item of self-knowledge rests on identification leads to an infinite regress (Shoemaker, 1968, p. 561). This even holds true for self-identification obtained through introspection. That is, it will not do to claim that introspection is distinguished by the fact that its object has a property which immediately identifies it as being me, since no other self could possibly have it, namely the property of being the private and exclusive object of exactly my introspection. This explanation will not do, since I will be unable to identify an introspected self as myself by the fact that it is introspectively observed by me unless I know it is the object of *my* introspection, i.e., unless I know that it is in fact *me* that undertakes this introspection, and this knowledge cannot itself be based on identification if one is to avoid an infinite regress (Shoemaker, 1968, pp. 562–3). More generally, one cannot account for the unique features of self-awareness by sticking to a traditional model of object-consciousness and then simply replacing the external object with an internal one. When one is aware of one's thoughts, feelings, beliefs, and desires, one does not seem to be given to oneself as an *object* at all (cf. Shoemaker, 1984, pp.102–5).

Any convincing theory of consciousness has to account for the first-personal givenness of our conscious states, and has to respect the difference between our consciousness of a foreign object and our consciousness of ourselves. Any convincing theory of consciousness has to be able to explain the distinction between *intentionality*, which is characterized by an epistemic *difference* between the subject and the object of experience, and *self-consciousness*, which implies some form of *identity*. But this is precisely what the higher-order theory, which seeks to provide an extrinsic and relational account of consciousness, persistently fails to do (cf. Zahavi, 1999; 2002; 2003a).[4] Every higher-order theory operates with a duality. One mental state is taking another mental state as its object, and consequently we have to *distinguish* the two. Given that their relation is supposed to account for the *mineness* of the first-order state, i.e., for the fact that the conscious mental state is given as *my* state, as a state *I* am in, the process must somehow circumvent the division or difference between the two states and posit some kind of identity, namely that of belonging to the same mind or stream of consciousness. But how is that supposed to work? Just as I cannot recognize something as mine unless I am already aware of myself, a non-conscious second-order mental state (that per definition lacks consciousness of itself) cannot recognize or identify a first-order mental state as belonging to the same mind as *itself*. To suggest that the second-order state might be furnished with the required self-intimacy by being taken as intentional object by a third-order mental state — and what other option does a higher-order theory have — would obviously generate an infinite regress.

---

[4] On some occasions, Rosenthal has explicitly argued that a higher-order thought might occur in the absence of the mental state it is purportedly about. He even writes that 'a case in which one has a higher-order thought along with the mental state it is about might well be subjectively indistinguishable from the case in which the higher-order thought occurs but not the mental state' (Rosenthal, 1997, p. 744). This might make Rosenthal's HOT position safe from the objection just outlined, but it also turns his theory into a rather strange type of higher-order theory. If one can have a higher-order thought about a first-order state even when the first-order state doesn't exist, consciousness is not really explained in terms of a relation between two different states, nor does it really make sense to say that intransitive consciousness is a relational property, a property that the first-order state acquires if one is transitively conscious of it. In fact, since there can be phenomenal consciousness even in the absence of a first-order mental state, it looks as if the higher-order thought itself is sufficient for phenomenal consciousness (cf. Byrne, 1997, p. 123). But — to repeat — in that case, it seems rather doubtful that we are still dealing with a higher-order account of consciousness that takes consciousness to be a relational and non-intrinsic property.

II: The Return of Brentano

The growing disenchantment with higher-order theories has made people look elsewhere for a viable alternative, and within the last couple of years quite a few have taken a closer look at Brentano (cf. Zahavi 1998; Thomasson, 2000; Hossack, 2002; Kriegel, 2003b,c).

Brentano's main contribution to the topic under discussion can be found in his *Psychologie vom empirischen Standpunkt* (1874). According to Brentano, all mental states — or psychical phenomena, as he calls them — are characterized by their intentional directedness, they are all conscious of objects. But are they themselves also necessarily conscious, or should one rather admit the existence of non-conscious (or unconscious) psychical phenomena (Brentano, 1874, pp. 142–3)?

One of the traditional arguments in defence of the existence of *non-conscious* mental states insists that only the non-conscious can save us from a vicious infinite regress. *If* all occurrent mental states were conscious, in the sense of being taken as objects by an inner consciousness, and if this inner consciousness were itself conceived of as a new occurrent mental state, it itself would also have to be taken as an object by a further inner consciousness, and so forth *ad infinitum*. Furthermore, as Brentano points out, this would not be the only problem. If, say, the perception of a sunset were really the object of a higher-order awareness, the sunset would be given as an object twice (first as an object for the perception, and second as an object for the higher-order state). And in the third-order awareness of the second-order awareness of the perception of the sunset, we would have the sunset as object thrice, whereas the original perception would be given twice as object, and so forth. Thus, the regress would be of an exceedingly vicious kind, implying in addition to the simple infinite iteration a simultaneous complication of its single members. Since this consequence is absurd, that is, since it is absurd that even as simple an experience as the perception of a sunset should involve an infinite complex series of conscious states, one has to end the regress by accepting the existence of non-conscious intentional states (Brentano, 1874, p. 171).

Needless to say, this is precisely the position adopted by the defenders of the higher-order theory. For them the second-order perception or thought does not have to be conscious. This will only be the case, if it is accompanied by a (non-conscious) third-order thought or perception (cf. Rosenthal, 1997, p. 745).

In *Psychologie vom empirischen Standpunkt*, however, Brentano rejects this 'solution'. He claims that it has an implication that is just as absurd as the position it seeks to avoid, the implication namely that consciousness can be accounted for in terms of the non-conscious. (It is worth emphasizing that the vicious infinite regress outlined at the end of section I cannot be avoided by means of the non-conscious; quite on the contrary). Obviously, Brentano also wants to avoid the infinite regress, however. How does he manage to pull off that trick? Brentano denies one of the crucial premises, and argues that the inner consciousness in question, rather than being a new mental state, is simply an internal feature of the primary experience. Thus, a mental state is conscious not by being taken as an object by a further mental state, but by taking itself as object, and according to Brentano, this prevents any infinite regress from getting off the ground.

While seeing a sunset, I am aware of seeing it. What is the structure of my consciousness in this case, according to Brentano? I have a perception of the sunset, and an awareness of the perception, and consequently two objects: The sunset and the perception. Contrary to appearance, however, I do not have two different mental states. As Brentano points out, the perception of the sunset is united so intrinsically and intimately with the awareness of the perception of the sunset, that they only constitute one single psychical phenomenon. Their apparent separation is merely due to a conceptual differentiation:

> In the same mental phenomenon in which the sound is present to our minds we simultaneously apprehend the mental phenomenon itself. What is more, we apprehend it in accordance with its dual nature insofar as it has the sound as content within it, and insofar as it has itself as content at the same time. We can say that the sound is the *primary object* of the *act* of hearing, and that the act of hearing itself is the *secondary object* (Brentano, 1874, pp. 179–80 [1973, pp. 127–8]).

Brentano consequently claims that every intentional experience has a double object, a primary and a secondary. In the case of the seeing of a sunset, the primary and thematic object is the sunset; the secondary and unthematic object is the seeing. Thus, it is important to emphasize that the focus of attention is on the primary object, and that our awareness of the mental state itself is normally secondary and incidental. In fact, according to Brentano, the experience is in principle incapable of observing itself thematically, it cannot take itself as its own primary object. Only in recollection, where one psychical act can take a preceding act as its primary object, can we pay attention to our own mental life (Brentano, 1874, pp. 41, 181).

How does Brentano's theory differ from the higher-order theories? At first sight the difference seems obvious. In contrast to the higher-order model that claims that consciousness is an extrinsic property of those mental states that have it, a property bestowed upon them from without by some further states, Brentano argues that the feature that makes a mental state conscious is located within the state itself; it is an intrinsic property of those mental states that have it.[5] But on closer inspection, this difference might conceal some striking similarities (cf. Kriegel, 2003c, pp. 486–9). Both the higher-order theories and Brentano's one-level theory construe consciousness in terms of self-awareness. In both cases, consciousness is taken to be a question of the mind directing its intentional aim upon its own states and operations. Moreover, both types of theory argue that conscious states involve two representational contents. In the case of a conscious perception of a sunset, there is an outward directed first-order content (that takes the sunset as its object), and an inward directed second-order content (that takes the perception as its object), and their only disagreement is over the question of

---

[5]   And of course, one should distinguish the view that consciousness is intrinsic to those states that possess it from the more radical view that consciousness is intrinsic to all mental states (cf. Thomasson, 2000, p. 197).

whether there are two distinct mental states, each with its own representational content, or only one mental state with a twofold representational content. Thus, both types of theory argue that for a state to be conscious means for it to be represented, and they only differ in whether it is represented by itself or by another state. To use Kriegel's notation:

A mental state M of a subject x at a time t is conscious only if x is aware of M at t.

Since awareness of an object involves a mental representation of that object, a mental state M is conscious if the subject has a mental state M*, such that M* represents the occurrence of M. The question is merely whether M = M* or whether they are two different mental states (Kriegel, 2003b, pp. 107–8).

For Kriegel this structural similarity between the higher-order model and Brentano's one-level theory counts as an argument in favour of a (neo-) Brentanian account. If two theories are almost identical, but if one has the added advantage of being phenomenologically adequate (since it conceives of consciousness as an intrinsic property), it is the latter that wins the day (Kriegel, 2003c, p. 488). Not all neo-Brentanians agree with this appraisal, however. The close proximity between the two accounts could also be taken as an indication that both are problematic. Thomasson, for instance, concedes that although Brentano has been seen by some as an early defender of a higher-order take on consciousness (cf. Güzeldere, 1997, p. 789; Siewert, 1998, p. 358), he was in fact seeking to develop an alternative to the higher-order theories, an alternative that conceived of consciousness in terms of a one-level model. But as she then continues, the question is whether Brentano really succeeded in staying clear of the pitfalls of the higher-order view. Is it really consistent to defend a one-level account while at the same time claiming that each conscious state involves not only a primary awareness of its object but also a secondary awareness of itself, or does the latter claim turn Brentano's supposedly one-level theory into a higher-order theory in disguise (Thomasson, 2000, pp. 190–2, 199)?

According to Thomasson, it is misleading to speak as if consciousness involves an awareness *of* our mental states. To speak in such a manner suggests that in order to have conscious mental states we must be aware of them as objects (Thomasson, 2000, p. 200). Thus, it could be argued that Brentano's claim that every conscious intentional state takes two objects, a primary (external) object, and a secondary (internal) object, remains committed to a higher-order account of consciousness; it simply postulates it as being implicitly contained in every conscious state. 'It wants', as Thomas puts it, 'the benefits of a first order account of consciousness while illegitimately smuggling in a second order (higher order) view as well' (Thomas, 2003, p. 169).[6]

This danger is rather apparent in Kriegel's reconstruction of Brentano's theory. Although Kriegel admits that self-awareness has special features that

---

[6] Van Gulick has argued that it might be worthwhile trying to develop a higher-order theory that stresses the identity between the lower and the higher-order state (Van Gulick, 2000, p. 296). This proposal, which is considerably more attractive than the standard higher-order theory, might in fact remind one of Brentano's position. But it is also vulnerable to the same kind of objections.

distinguish it from other mental phenomena, he nevertheless speaks of it in terms of an intentional self-representation (Kriegel, 2003c, p. 497). But one thought that comes to mind is whether 'self-representation' is the right term, or whether it would not have been better to speak of self-presentation, self-presence, or self-manifestation.[7] Our acquaintance with our own experiences seems to have a presentational immediacy that is not easily captured by the term '*re*presentation'. In fact, in most cases my experiences are present to me, rather than represented to me. There is no representational mediation. Moreover, to argue, as Kriegel does, that consciousness of an object involves a mental representation and that our mental states must therefore also be represented if we are to be conscious of them, strongly suggests that self-awareness is taken to be a species of object-consciousness. Kriegel is, as already mentioned, prepared to admit that there might be something special about self-awareness, and he therefore proposes that the self is represented as a subject and not as an object in self-awareness. But given the representational structure involved, what this means is supposedly that we in self-awareness is intentionally confronted with a rather peculiar kind of object, namely a subject. This reading is supported by the fact that Kriegel suggests that the special character of self-awareness might also be captured by saying that the gap between subject and object collapses, so that the self is represented both as subject and as object (Kriegel, 2003a, p. 19).[8] Thus, object-consciousness apparently remains the paradigm.

Is there a better way to capture Brentano's core insight? Thomasson's simple but ingenious suggestion is that we should adopt an adverbalist interpretation of the secondary awareness. We should construe the secondary awareness as a property of the primary act, and the best way to do so is by thinking of consciousness in adverbial terms. Rather than saying that our conscious mental states are in possession of a secondary awareness of themselves, rather than saying that there is a perception of an object, and in addition an awareness of the perception, it is better to say that we simply see, hear or feel consciously (Thomasson, 2000, p. 203). The decisive advantage of this phrasing is that it avoids interpreting the secondary awareness as a form of object-consciousness. This temptation will remain as long as we keep talking about conscious states as states we are conscious of. But what is gained by adding the adverb 'consciously'? As Thomasson points out, the difference between those mental states that remain non-conscious and those that make us consciously aware of (external) objects is that in the latter case objects seem a certain way to us. The difference between a non-conscious perception of a sunset, and a conscious perception of the sunset, is that there is something it is like to consciously perceive a sunset. So although my attention is on the object, the experience itself remains conscious. Not in the sense that I am

---

[7] At one point, Kriegel actually does use both of the latter terms (Kriegel, 2003a, p. 13). But he doesn't do so consistently, and he doesn't seem to realize that they both have quite different connotations from the term 'self-representation'.

[8] A rather similar idea has been defended by Fichte in 1797 (cf. Fichte, 1920, pp. 527–9) and criticized by Henrich (1966).

aware *of* it, but in the sense that there is something it is like to be in that state, it has phenomenal qualities (Thomasson, 2000, pp. 203–4).

In my view, Thomasson's adverbalist account has some decisive advantages over Brentano's own view. In fact, the question is whether we are still moving within a broadly conceived Brentanian framework, or whether we are rather faced with a new theory. Thomasson herself admits that the view she is proposing might look as if it is rather far removed from Brentano, since she is precisely discarding his idea of an 'inner consciousness'. But in her view, the idea of an inner consciousness, the idea that consciousness is based on an awareness of our own mental states as objects, was never central to Brentano to start with. Rather what is crucial to the Brentanian model is the idea that consciousness is an aspect of the mental state that possesses it, rather than something that is conferred upon it by a higher-order state, and this is precisely the idea that she is trying to develop (Thomasson, 2000, p. 204).

I disagree with this appraisal. First I take the distinction between the primary and the secondary object of consciousness as well as the idea that mental states are either non-conscious or given as objects to be integral features of Brentano's theory. And I think that if one jettisons these ideas, as one rightly should, one will also take leave of the Brentanian framework. And second, even more importantly, there is as little reason to designate every one-level account of consciousness as Brentanian or neo-Brentanian as there is to call every non-reductionistic theory of intentionality, Brentanian or neo-Brentanian.[9] This might perhaps have been defensible if Brentano's theory had been the only one-level game in town. But that is not the case, since a number of twentieth-century phenomenologists have defended a one-level account of consciousness much more unequivocally than Brentano.

In section IV, I will have more to say about the phenomenological alternatives, but let us first take another look at some of the recent attempts to develop a one-level account of consciousness.

III: Consciousness and Self-consciousness

As we have just seen, Thomasson argues that there is something it is like to consciously perceive an object. This link between phenomenality and conscious intentionality has also recently been explored by Lurz in his criticism of the higher-order theories (Lurz, 2003a,b). Lurz's specific target is the higher-order thought theory. The HOT theory argues that the only way to be conscious of one's mental states is to be conscious of the fact *that* one has them. But as Lurz points out, this view confronts the HOT position with a rather uncomfortable dilemma when it comes to ascribing consciousness to animals and infants. It can claim that both groups lack the cognitive resources to entertain higher-order beliefs. And in that case, they must obviously also lack conscious mental states. This position has been explicitly defended by Carruthers. In his view, the

---

[9] Thus, I would personally take exception to being described myself as a recent defender of a neo-Brentanian account (Kriegel, 2003, p. 481).

subjective feel of experience presupposes a capacity for higher-order awareness, and as he continues, 'such self-awareness is a conceptually necessary condition for an organism to be a subject of phenomenal feelings, or for there to be anything that its experiences are like' (Carruthers, 1996, p. 152, cf. p. 154). To be more precise, Carruthers argues that in order to be able to think about your own thoughts and experiences you must be in possession of the concepts of thought and experience. Since such concepts get their significance from being embedded in a folk-psychological theory concerning the structure and functioning of the mind, what this ultimately means is that only creatures in possession of a theory of mind are capable of enjoying conscious experiences (Carruthers, 1996, p. 158; 2000, p.194). In other words, creatures that lack a theory of mind — such as most animals, young infants, and supposedly autists — will also lack conscious experiences. There is nothing it is like for them to feel pain or pleasure (Carruthers, 1998, p. 216; 2000, p. 203). Carruthers concedes that most of us believe that it must be like something to be a bat, a cat or a newborn baby, and that the experiences of these creatures have subjective feels to them, but he considers this common-sense belief to be quite groundless (Carruthers, 1996, p. 223).[10] But apart from being counterintuitive — and it is extremely counterintuitive to claim that there is nothing it is like for infants or animals to feel pain or pleasure — and apart from being vulnerable to the previously mentioned objections against the higher-order theories, Carruthers' conclusion is also confronted with the problem that quite a lot of animal and infant behaviour can be predicted and explained rather well by ascribing conscious mental states to the creatures in question (Lurz, 2003a). The other possibility, of course, is for the higher-order thought theory to concede that even animals and infants are in possession of higher-order beliefs about their own mental states and that this makes them in possession of conscious mental states. But although it certainly seems plausible to ascribe conscious mental states, such as emotions or perceptual experiences, to infants and (some) animals, it seems quite implausible to claim that, say, cats and newborn babies are in possession of something as cognitively sophisticated as higher-order thoughts about their first-order mental states, i.e., it seems implausible to claim that they are aware of the fact *that* they are having mental states. Thus, we should not forget that the HOT theory — in contrast to the HOP theory — denies that we are *observationally* acquainted with our first-order mental states. And to claim that a cat in order to have conscious experiences must have thoughts about unobservable states occurring inside its own body is surely not a very attractive option (cf. Lurz, 2003a).

Lurz's own proposal is that a creature can be conscious of its thoughts and experiences by being conscious of *what* it thinks or experiences and that this does not entail that it has to be conscious of the fact *that* it thinks or has experiences (Lurz,

---

[10] Although Carruthers is in general quite unequivocal about denying conscious experiences to young infants (cf. Carruthers 1996, p. 221; 2000, pp. 202–3), he occasionally leaves a door open for a different conclusion. As he writes at one point, it might be that infants are capable of discriminating between their experiences (and hence capable of enjoying conscious experiences) even while still being incapable of conceptualizing them (Carruthers 1996, p. 222).

2003b, p. 24). When, say, an infant points at a doll and says 'that is my doll' she appears to say what she believes, and how should she be able to say that unless she was conscious of what she believes? But although the infant is conscious of *what* she believes, i.e., of what a particular belief of hers is about — and how could she be that if she were not conscious of the belief — it is not obvious that the infant is conscious of the fact *that* she believes something. The case is similar with (some) animals. A cat can be paying attention to movements in the bushes. But if it were completely unaware of what it was seeing, it would not be able to attend to what it was seeing. Insofar as it makes sense to say that the cat is paying attention to what it is seeing, it makes sense to say that it is conscious of what it is seeing. But that does not mean that the cat is conscious of the fact *that* it sees movements in the bushes. In being conscious of what it sees, the cat is simply conscious of what its visual state is about, and it is hard to understand how the cat could be conscious of this if it were not in some way conscious of the mental state itself (Lurz, 2003a; 2003b, p. 31–2).

In recent writings, Dretske has argued that we should call states conscious if they make us conscious of other things, and that we should not conclude that because the states are conscious, then we must also be conscious of them. In short, conscious mental states are states we are conscious with, not states we are conscious of (Dretske, 1995, pp. 100–1). But one problem with this view is that it gives us no means to distinguish between conscious and non-conscious intentional states, all of which make us directed at objects in environment. For Dretske they would all be conscious. Is Lurz committed to the same view? Is every state that is about something also a conscious state? No, rather Lurz's account permits him to distinguish between the case where a subject is perceiving an object, the case where the subject is conscious of *what* she is perceiving, and the case where she is conscious of the fact *that* she is perceiving. A blindsight subject, for example, might (non-consciously) be perceiving something in the blind region of her visual field, as evinced from her performance on a forced-choice test, but she would not be conscious of what she was perceiving (Lurz, 2003b, pp. 232–5).

In short, Lurz's proposal is that we can distinguish between two different ways of being acquainted with our own thoughts and experiences. We can be acquainted with them by being conscious that we have them, and we can be acquainted with them by being conscious of what our thoughts and experiences are about. Whereas the first type of self-acquaintance is a form of higher-order consciousness, the latter type is not. One advantage of this proposal is that it can avoid the dilemma confronting the HOT theory. It does not have to deny conscious states to animals, but neither does it have to argue that animals have higher-order thoughts about their own mental states. One problem with the proposal, however, is that Lurz apparently thinks that in order to be conscious of what our thoughts and experiences are about we also need to be conscious *of* the mental states themselves. But it is easy to amend his proposal by means of an adverbalist reformulation. We could stay clear of the idea that in order to have conscious mental states we must be aware of them as objects by saying that we are conscious of what our thoughts and experiences are about when we consciously perceive or believe something.

How does this analysis relate to the idea that consciousness should be accounted for in terms of self-awareness? Does it support the idea that a conscious state differs from a non-conscious state precisely by entailing self-awareness? Yes, and rather neatly, in fact, although Lurz doesn't address the issue himself. The whole thrust of the argument is that for a state to be conscious is for the subject to be aware of what the state is about, and that this presupposes that the subject has direct experiential access to the mental state itself. But this is precisely what self-awareness — according to one classical definition — amounts to: Experiential access to one's own consciousness. Thus, to undergo a conscious experience (to taste coffee, to feel pain, to remember a past journey on the Rhine) necessarily means that there is something 'it is like' for the subject to have that experience. But insofar as there is something it is like for the subject to have the experience, the subject must in some way have access to the experience, must in some way be acquainted with the experience. Moreover, although conscious experiences differ from one another — what it is like to taste ice-cream, is different from what it is like to smell a bunch of roses or to admire a statue of Michelangelo — they also share certain features. One commonality is the quality of *mineness*, the fact that the experiences are characterized by a first-personal givenness. When I am aware of an occurrent pain, perception, or thought from the first-person perspective, the experience in question is given immediately, non-inferentially and non-criterially as *mine*. That is, the experience is given (at least tacitly) as an experience I am undergoing or living through. First-personal experience presents me with an immediate and non-observational access to myself. All of this suggests that we are dealing with a (minimal) form of self-awareness. This self-awareness is not something that only emerges the moment one scrutinizes one's experiences attentively, rather it is there the moment I consciously experience something. It does not exist apart from the experience, as an additional mental state. Rather, it is an intrinsic feature of the experience, and is not brought about by some kind of reflection or introspection or higher-order monitoring. Given this outlook, it is obvious that a discussion of self-awareness is of pertinence for an understanding of phenomenal consciousness. In fact, phenomenal consciousness must precisely be interpreted as entailing a primitive form for self-awareness (cf. Zahavi, 1998, 1999, 2002, 2003b).[11]

A rather similar view has recently been defended by Kriegel, who has introduced a distinction between *transitive* and *intransitive* self-consciousness.

---

[11] Let me forestall a possible objection, namely that this definition of self-awareness is too broad and that it simply includes too much. That is, since it doesn't match our everyday notion of self-awareness (that tends to link the notion with our ability to recognize or identify ourselves in a thematic way) the present use of the term is inappropriate. I don't think this objection carries a lot of weight. From a conceptual point of view, there are no intrinsic problems whatsoever in using the term 'self-awareness' to designate a situation where consciousness has access to or is being acquainted with itself. Moreover, it is a simple fact that many of the classical philosophical theories of self-awareness as well as the more recent contributions by such thinkers as Brentano, Husserl, Sartre, Henry, Henrich, Frank, etc. have exactly been discussions of this broad notion (cf. Zahavi, 1999).

Whereas transitive self-consciousness designates the situation where a subject is self-conscious of her thought that p (or of her perception of x), intransitive self-consciousness can be captured by saying that the subject is self-consciously thinking that p (or perceiving x).[12]

What is the difference between the two types of self-consciousness? Kriegel lists four differences, and claims that whereas the first type is introspective, rare, voluntary, and effortful, the second is none of these (Kriegel, 2003b, p. 104). But Kriegel also points to another relevant distinction. As he points out, in transitive self-consciousness the state of self-consciousness is numerically distinct from the thought that p, since the latter is the object of the former. Thus the state is self-conscious in virtue of the object it takes. In intransitive self-consciousness by contrast, the self-consciousness simply modifies the thought, it does not take it as an object, and one might therefore say that the state is self-conscious in virtue of the way it is had by the subject (Kriegel, 2004).

According to Kriegel, the latter type of self-consciousness, intransitive self-consciousness, captures one of the important senses of consciousness. We use the adjective 'conscious' to indicate the presence of intransitive self-consciousness. This is why Kriegel can claim that intransitive self-consciousness is a necessary condition for phenomenal consciousness. In fact, intransitive self-consciousness should be understood as an implicit type of self-consciousness that is shared by all our conscious mental states (Kriegel, 2003a, p. 20; 2003c, p. 478). Unless the mental state is intransitively self-conscious there is nothing it is like to be in the state, and therefore the state cannot be a phenomenally conscious state. Or to put it differently, a mental state that lacks intransitive self-consciousness is a non-conscious state (Kriegel, 2003b, pp. 103–6). As Kriegel writes, 'It is impossible to think or experience something consciously without thinking or experiencing it self-consciously, i.e., without being peripherally aware of thinking or experiencing it' (Kriegel, 2004).

Kriegel's distinction between transitive and intransitive self-consciousness bears a striking resemblance to the classical phenomenological distinction between reflective and pre-reflective self-awareness; a distinction I will return to in a moment. This similarity is also readily acknowledged by Kriegel (2004). But there is also a noticeable difference, which has to do with the fact that Kriegel — as we have already seen — ultimately persists in taking self-awareness as a species of object-consciousness.

To say that a subject has a mental state self-consciously is to say that the subject is implicitly or peripherally aware of her having the state, or of the state being her own. Thus, for Kriegel the distinction between intransitive and transitive self-consciousness can also be cashed out by means of the distinction between focal and peripheral awareness. We are confronted with transitive self-

---

[12] I find the locutions 'self-conscious of her thought that p' and 'self-consciously thinking that p' problematic, since they can easily be misunderstood. I think it would have been better if Kriegel had simply said that a subject is in possession of transitive self-consciousness when 'she is conscious of her thought that p' and in possession of intransitive self-consciousness when 'she is consciously thinking that p'.

consciousness when the subject is focally aware of being in a specific mental state, whereas we are dealing with intransitive self-consciousness when the subject is only peripherally aware of being in the mental state (Kriegel, 2004).

It is certainly quite appropriate to distinguish focal and peripheral modes of consciousness.[13] There is an obvious distinction to be made between my focal awareness of my computer, and my peripheral awareness of the myriad of objects surrounding it. We also need to dismiss any narrow conception of consciousness that equates consciousness with attention and claims that we are only conscious of that which we pay attention to. But the question is whether this distinction between focal and peripheral consciousness — a distinction between two types of object-consciousness — is pertinent when it comes to an understanding of the relation between the two types of self-consciousness. In a regular intentional experience, I am directed at and preoccupied with my intentional object. When I consciously perceive the computer, I do not ordinarily attend to myself and my perceptual experience. But although I lack a focal awareness of myself, and although I do not take my experience as a thematic object, I am still in possession of intransitive self-consciousness. I agree with this analysis, but I do not agree with the claim that intransitive self-consciousness entails that my experiences remain in the background as potential themes in precisely the same way as, say, the hum of the refrigerator. This would suggest that intransitive self-consciousness is a kind of peripheral, inattentive, *transitive* object-consciousness, but that cannot be right. As Husserl pointed out in 1906:

> One should not mistake the consciousness of the objective background [*gegenständlichen Hintergrund*] and consciousness understood in the sense of experiential being [*Erlebtseins*]. Lived-experiences as such do have their own being, but they are not objects of apperception (in this case we would end in an infinite regress). The background, however, is given to us objectively, it is constituted through a complex of apperceptive lived-experiences. We do not pay attention to these objects [...], but they are still given to us in a quite different manner than the mere lived-experiences themselves [...]. The attentional consciousness of the background and consciousness in the sense of mere experiential givenness must be completely distinguished (Husserl, 1984a, p. 252).

The attempt to model intransitive self-consciousness on peripheral object-consciousness is misleading since it remains stuck in the subject–object model and is vulnerable to the arguments presented against the higher-order theories. A common line of thought is that our experiential life must either be given as an object or not be given at all, and that the only remaining question (and allowed variable) is whether it is given as an object focally or merely peripherally. But this line of thought is flawed, since it erroneously assumes that there is only one type of givenness or manifestation, namely object-givenness. But had that in fact been the case, real self-awareness would have been impossible. Object-consciousness necessarily entails an epistemic divide, a distinction between that which appears and that to whom it appears, between the object and the subject of experience. For something to be given as an object of experience is for it to differ

---

[13] For a classical account cf. Gurwitsch (1974).

from the subjective experience, that takes it as an object. This is one reason why object-consciousness is singularly unsuited as a model for understanding self-awareness. Another reason, which was already spelled out in section I, is that the attempt to construe self-awareness as a type of object-consciousness generates an infinite regress.

IV: Back to Phenomenology

In the following, I wish to call attention to some of the philosophical resources to be found in the phenomenological tradition. In particularly, I wish to show that it contains a clear and sustained defence of a one-level account of consciousness that is free from the equivocations still to be found in Brentano.

Let us start by taking a look at a very early phenomenological appraisal of Brentano's theory of inner consciousness; an appraisal that can be found in the first edition of Husserl's *Logische Untersuchungen* (1901).

How does Husserl assess Brentano's theory? Rather negatively, in fact. Husserl denies that there is any phenomenological evidence in support of the claim concerning the existence of a constant and continuous inner perception, and he consequently rejects Brentano's theory as a piece of construction (Husserl, 1984b, pp. 367, 759). There are two ways to interpret Husserl's criticism. In the one, Husserl is taking Brentano to be claiming that we are constantly thematically aware of our occurrent experiences. If this reading is correct, Husserl would be right in rejecting the thesis, but wrong in ascribing it to Brentano. As we have already seen, Brentano explicitly warns against taking inner consciousness as a kind of thematic observation (cf. Brentano, 1874, p. 181). The other possibility is that Husserl is criticizing Brentano for having held the view that we are constantly objectifying our own experiences. This criticism would be right on target, and there is no question that this is a view that Husserl rejects. In the First Investigation, Husserl writes that the sensations are originally simply lived through as moments of the experience; they are not objectified and taken as objects. This only happens in a subsequent psychological reflection (Husserl, 1984b, p.80). This assertion is then followed up in the Second Investigation, where we find the following significant observation:

> That an appropriate train of sensations or images is *experienced*, and is in this sense conscious, does not and cannot mean that this is the *object* of an act of consciousness, in the sense that a perception, a presentation or a judgment is directed upon it (Husserl, 1984b, p. 165 [2001, I, p. 273]).

Obviously the central word is the term 'conscious'. Husserl is denying that our sensations are a phenomenological nought. On the contrary, they are conscious, that is, experientially given, when they are lived through, and as he points out this givenness does not come about as the result of an objectification, does not come about because the sensations are taken as objects by an (internal) perception. The sensations are given, not as objects, but precisely as subjective experiences. The very same line of thought can be found in the Fifth Investigation. There Husserl writes that the intentional experiences themselves are lived through and experienced (*erlebt*), but that they do not appear in an objectified manner, they are neither seen nor heard. They are conscious without being intentional objects (Husserl, 1984b, p. 399). This is not to deny that we can in fact direct our attention towards our experiences, and thereby take them as objects of an inner perception, but this only occurs the moment we reflect (p. 424).

In the light of these statements, the conclusion is rather easy to draw. In contrast to Brentano, Husserl does not seek to identify the givenness of our experiences with the givenness of objects. Husserl does not believe that our experiences are conscious by being taken as secondary *objects*. As he explicitly states in the Sixth Investigation: 'To be experienced is not to be made objective [Erlebtsein ist nicht Gegenständlichsein]' (Husserl, 1984b, p. 669 [2001, II, p. 279]). Thus, Husserl operates with a distinction between perceiving (*Wahrnehmen*) and experiencing (*Erleben*): prior to reflection one perceives the perceptual object, but one experiences (*erlebt*) the perception. Although I am not intentionally directed towards the perception (this only happens in the subsequent reflection, where the perception is thematized), the perception is not nonconscious but conscious, that is, pre-reflectively given.

In general, one should not overestimate the homogeneity of the phenomenological tradition. It is a tradition spanning many differences. But when it comes to the question concerning the relation between consciousness and self-consciousness, literally all of the major figures (Husserl, Scheler, Heidegger, Sartre, Merleau-Ponty, Henry, Ricoeur, etc.) reject the higher-order model and advocate some kind of one-level account.

The phenomenologist best known for advocating this view is Sartre, and since it would be impossible to cover all the different figures in detail, let me focus on him.

Sartre's account of the relationship between consciousness and self-awareness can primarily be found in three different texts: In his first philosophical publication *La transcendance de l'ego* from 1936, in his principal work *L'être et le néant* from 1943, and in an article from 1948 entitled 'Conscience de soi et connaissance de soi'.

According to Sartre consciousness is essentially characterized by intentionality. It is as such a consciousness *of* something. He also claims, however, that each and every intentional experience is characterized by self-awareness. Thus, Sartre takes self-awareness to constitute a necessary condition for being conscious of something. To consciously perceive a signpost, an ice-cream, or a comfortable chair without being aware of it, i.e., without having access to the experience in question, is for Sartre a manifest absurdity (Sartre, 1943, pp. 18, 20, 28; 1948, p. 62).

This line of thought is elaborated in the important introduction to *L'être et le néant*, where Sartre claims that an ontological analysis of intentionality leads to self-awareness since the *mode of being* of intentional consciousness is to be *for-itself* (*pour-soi*), that is, self-aware. An experience does not simply exist, it exists for itself, i.e., it is given to itself, and this self-givenness is not simply a quality added to the experience, a mere varnish, but on the contrary constitutes the very mode of being of the experience:

> This self-consciousness we ought to consider not as a new consciousness, but as *the only mode of existence which is possible for a consciousness of something* (Sartre, 1943, p. 20 [1956, p. liv]).

Originally, my intentional experiences are not (possible) objects for consciousness, but (actual) modes of consciousness, and as such they are self-aware.

As we can see, Sartre emphasizes quite explicitly that the self-awareness in question is *not* a new consciousness. It is not something added to the experience, it is not an additional mental state, but rather an intrinsic feature of the experience. Thus, when he speaks of self-awareness as a permanent feature of consciousness, Sartre is not referring to what he calls reflective self-awareness. Reflection (or to use the more current name 'higher-order representation') is the process whereby consciousness directs its intentional aim at itself, thereby taking itself as its own object. But according to Sartre, this type of self-awareness is derived. It involves a subject-object split, and the attempt to account for *self*-awareness in such terms is for Sartre bound to fail. It either generates an infinite regress or accepts a non-conscious starting point, but Sartre considers both of these options to be unacceptable (Sartre, 1943, p. 19).

Sartre readily admits the existence of reflective self-consciousness. We can for instance reflect upon — and thereby be thematically conscious of — an occurrent perception of a Swiss Army knife. In reflection we can distinguish the reflecting experience and the experience reflected-on. The first takes the latter as its object. But for Sartre both of these experiences are already self-conscious prior to reflection, and in both cases the self-awareness in question is of a non-reflective and non-positional kind, i.e., it does not have a reflective structure, and it does not posit that which it is aware of as an object (Sartre, 1936, pp. 28–9).[14] As Sartre writes: '[T]here is no infinite regress here, since a consciousness has no need at all of a reflecting consciousness in order to be conscious of itself. It simply does not posit itself as an object' (Sartre, 1936, p. 29 [1957, p. 45]). Thus, Sartre speaks of pre-reflective self-awareness as an immediate and non-cognitive 'relation' of the self to itself (Sartre, 1943, p. 19).

> In other words, every positional consciousness of an object is at the same time a non-positional consciousness of itself. If I count the cigarettes which are in that case, I have the impression of disclosing an objective property of this collection of cigarettes: *they are a dozen*. This property appears to my consciousness as a property existing in the world. It is very possible that I have no positional consciousness of counting them. Then I do not know myself as counting. [...] Yet at the moment when these cigarettes are revealed to me as a dozen, I have a non-thetic consciousness of my adding activity. If anyone questioned me, indeed, if anyone should ask, 'What are you doing there?' I should reply at once, 'I am counting.' This reply aims not only at the instantaneous consciousness which I can achieve by reflection but at those fleeting consciousnesses which have passed without being reflected-on, those which are forever non-reflected-on in my immediate past. Thus reflection has no kind of primacy over the consciousness reflected-on. It is not reflection which reveals the consciousness reflected-on to itself. Quite the contrary, it is the

---

[14] Whereas the early Sartre speaks of an irreflective or non-reflective self-awareness, he later increasingly opts for the term 'pre-reflective self-awareness'.

non-reflective consciousness which renders the reflection possible; there is a pre-reflective cogito which is the condition of the Cartesian cogito (Sartre, 1943, pp. 19–20 [1956, p. liii]).

If I am engaged in some conscious activity, such as the reading of a story, my attention is neither on myself nor on my activity of reading, but on the story. But if my reading is interrupted by someone asking me what I am doing, I reply immediately that I am (and have for some time been) reading; and the self-consciousness on the basis of which I answer the question is not something acquired at just that moment but a consciousness of myself which has been present to me all along.

When Sartre says that every positional consciousness of an object is simultaneously a non-positional consciousness of itself, it is essential to emphasize that this pre-reflective self-awareness is not to be understood as an intentional, objectifying, or epistemic act, and consequently neither to be interpreted as some kind of inner perception, nor more generally as a type of knowledge (Sartre, 1936, pp. 23–4, 66; 1943, p. 19). This implies that the self-awareness in question might very well be accompanied by a fundamental *lack of knowledge*. Although I cannot be unconscious of my present experience, I might very well ignore it in favour of its object, and this is of course the natural attitude. In my daily life I am absorbed by and preoccupied with projects and objects in the world. Thus, pervasive pre-reflective self-awareness is definitely not identical with total self-comprehension, but can rather be likened to a pre-comprehension, that allows for a subsequent reflection and thematization.

To put it differently, consciousness has two different modes of existence, a pre-reflective and a reflective. The first has priority since it can prevail independently of the latter, whereas reflective self-consciousness always presupposes pre-reflective self-consciousness. So to repeat, for Sartre pre-reflective self-awareness is not an addendum to, but a constitutive moment of the original intentional experience. The experience is aware of itself at the time of its occurrence. If I consciously see, remember, know, think, hope, feel or will something I am *eo ipso* aware of it.[15]

What about Thomasson's objection? Is it not inconsistent to claim on the one hand that we are aware *of* our thoughts and experiences when they are conscious and on the other that consciousness is not given to itself as an object

---

[15] As already indicated this view is shared by most of the other phenomenologists. To provide just one further example: In the early lecture course *Grundprobleme der Phänomenologie* from 1919/1920, Heidegger argues that one of the tasks of phenomenology is to disclose the non-objectifying and non-theoretical self-understanding that belongs to experience as such (Heidegger, 1993, pp. 155–7). Thus, Heidegger clearly acknowledges the existence of a pre-reflective self-acquaintance that is part and parcel of experience. Any worldly experiencing involves a certain component of self-acquaintance and -familiarity, any experiencing is characterized by the fact that 'I am always somehow acquainted with myself' (p. 251). And as Heidegger repeatedly emphasizes, this basic familiarity with oneself does not take the form of a reflective self-perception or a thematic self-observation, nor does it involve any kind of self-objectification. On the contrary, we are confronted with a process of lived self-acquaintance whose distinctive feature is its non-reflective character, and which must be understood as an immediate expression of life itself (pp. 159, 165, 257–8). For a more extensive account of Heidegger's position, cf. Zahavi 2003c.

pre-reflectively? In other words, doesn't Sartre commit the same mistake as Brentano? But Sartre has anticipated this objection. As he points out, it is only the necessity of syntax which has compelled him to write that we are pre-reflectively aware *of* our experiences and that there is a pre-reflective consciousness *of* self. (In French the term for self-consciousness — *conscience de soi* — literally means consciousness of self). Thus Sartre readily admits that the use of the 'of' (or 'de') is unfortunate since it suggests that self-consciousness is simply a sub-type of object-consciousness, as if the manner in which we are aware *of* ourselves is structurally comparable to the manner in which we are aware *of* apples and clouds. We cannot avoid the 'of', but in order to show that it is merely there in order to satisfy a grammatical requirement, Sartre places it inside parentheses, and frequently speaks of a 'conscience (de) soi' and of a 'conscience (de) plaisir' etc. (Sartre, 1943, p. 22; 1948, p. 62). Thus, although Sartre ultimately opts for another typographical solution than Thomasson's adverbalist proposal, his motivation for avoiding a phrasing that might misleadingly suggest that we in order to have conscious mental states must be aware of them as objects is precisely the same as hers.

Sartre's phenomenological account of self-awareness is far more complex and wide-ranging than suggested by this brief presentation. But hopefully it should already have become evident that Sartre's defence of a one-level account of consciousness is preferable to Brentano's. Whereas Brentano flirts with the higher-order account, Sartre's rejection is unequivocal.[16] Both share the view that self-awareness (or inner consciousness) differs from ordinary object-consciousness. The issue of controversy is over whether self-awareness is merely an extraordinary object-consciousness or not an object-consciousness at all. In contrast to Brentano, Sartre (and the other phenomenologists) thinks the latter, more radical, move is required. The fact that Sartre's analysis is furthermore integrated into and to be found in the context of an examination of a number of related issues, such as the nature of intentionality, embodiment, selfhood, temporality, attention, sociality, etc. should only count in its favour. Thus, as part of his analysis of the structure of consciousness Sartre also discusses — to mention just a few of the topics — (1) whether one should opt for an egological or non-egological account of consciousness, i.e., whether or not every episode of experiencing always involves a distinct subject of experience; (2) how to understand the temporality of the stream of consciousness; (3) whether pre-reflective

---

[16] This has unfortunately been overlooked by some of the few analytical philosophers who actually refer to Sartre. In *The Significance of Consciousness*, for instance, Siewert writes that Sartre argues that all consciousness is consciousness of itself, and he then claims that the argument presupposes Sartre's flawed identification of (a) an unconscious state, (b) a state that ignores itself, and (c) a state of which there is no consciousness (Siewert, 1998, p. 357). But as we have just seen, Sartre does not make such an identification. Siewert then continues his criticism by arguing that since Sartre is on the one hand claiming that all consciousness is consciousness of itself and on the other hand denying that this ubiquitous self-consciousness is reflective, thetic, positional, epistemic, and objectifying, his account is inconsistent, confused, extremely misleading, and totally unclear (Siewert, 1998, p. 360). Is this rather harsh judgement justified? I think not. When Sartre claims that all consciousness is consciousness of itself he means something quite specific, and it is only if one overlooks his quite explicit remarks concerning the problematic use of the proposition 'of' that one would be led to the idea that he was contradicting himself.

self-awareness is characterized by any internal differentiation or infrastructure; (4) to what extent self-awareness is always embodied and embedded; (5) how social interaction might change the structure of self-awareness; (6) whether reflection is able to disclose the structure of pre-reflective consciousness or whether it necessarily distorts its subject matter; (7) and to what extent self-awareness although not being itself a form of object-consciousness nevertheless presupposes the intentional encounter with the world.[17] Although some of Sartre's further findings and conclusions might be problematic, he is pointing to issues that should be taken into account by a theory of (self-)consciousness; issues that Brentano to a large extent remained silent about.

V: Conclusion

Let me by way of conclusion briefly recapitulate the main line of thought. Intransitive consciousness should be accounted for in terms of self-awareness, i.e., a conscious mental state differs from a non-conscious mental state by entailing self-awareness. Given that the attempt to provide a relational, higher-order, account of this self-awareness has been unsuccessful, it makes better sense to opt for a one-level account. Some have suggested that Brentano's account in *Psychologie vom empirischen Standpunkt* might serve as a good starting point, and have then gone on to defend neo-Brentanian positions. In contrast, I have argued that a number of twentieth-century phenomenologists have defended a one-level account of consciousness more unequivocally than Brentano. And I would suggest that it would make considerably more sense to take a closer look at Sartre, Husserl, and Heidegger, if one is on the lookout for promising and worked out alternatives to the higher-order theories, than to return all the way to Brentano.[18]

References

Armstrong, D.M. (1968), *A Materialist Theory of the Mind* (London: Routledge and Kegan Paul).

Baker, L.R. (2000), *Persons and Bodies* (Cambridge: Cambridge University Press).

Block, N., Flanagan, O. & Güzeldere, G. (ed. 1997), *The Nature of Consciousness* (Cambridge, MA: MIT Press).

Brentano, F. (1874/1924), *Psychologie vom empirischen Standpunkt* I (Hamburg: Felix Meiner).

Brentano, F. (1973), *Psychology from an Empirical Standpoint*, tr. A. C. Rancurello, D. B. Terrell & L.L. McAlister (London: Routledge & Kegan Paul).

Brook, A. (1994), *Kant and the Mind* (Cambridge: Cambridge University Press).

Byrne, A. (1997), 'Some like it HOT: Consciousness and higher-order thoughts', *Philosophical Studies*, **86**, pp. 103–29.

Carruthers, P. (1996), *Language, Thoughts and Consciousness. An Essay In Philosophical Psychology* (Cambridge: Cambridge University Press).

Carruthers, P. (1998), 'Natural theories of consciousness', *European Journal of Philosophy*, **6** (2), pp. 203–22.

Carruthers, P. (2000), *Phenomenal Consciousness. A Naturalistic Theory* (Cambridge: Cambridge University Press).

Castañeda, H.-N. (1967), 'The logic of self-knowledge,' *Nous,* **1**, pp. 9–22.

Dretske, F. (1995), *Naturalizing the Mind* (Cambridge, MA: MIT Press).

Fichte, J.G. (1797/1920), *Erste und Zweite Einleitung in die Wissenschaftslehre* (Leipzig: Felix Meiner).

---

[17] For a more extensive account of Sartre's theory, cf. Zahavi (1999).

[18] Thanks to Galen Strawson and Uriah Kriegel for comments to an earlier version of the article. This study has been funded by the Danish National Research Foundation.

Gurwitsch, A. (1974), *Das Bewußtseinsfeld* (Berlin: de Gruyter).

Güzeldere, G. (1997), 'Is consciousness the perception of what passes in one's own mind?' in Block *et al.* (1997).

Heidegger, M. (1993), *Grundprobleme der Phänomenologie* (1919/1920). Gesamtausgabe Band 58. (Frankfurt am Main: Vittorio Klostermann).

Henrich, D. (1966), 'Fichtes ursprüngliche Einsicht', in *Subjektivität und Metaphysik. Festschrift für Wolfgang Cramer*, eds. D. Henrich & H. Wagner (Frankfurt am Main: Klostermann), pp.188-232.

Hossack, K. (2002), 'Self-knowledge and consciousness,' *Proceedings of the Aristotelian Society*, **102** (2), pp. 163–81.

Husserl, E. (1984a), *Einleitung in die Logik und Erkenntnistheorie*, Husserliana XXIV (Den Haag: Martinus Nijhoff).

Husserl, E. (1984b), *Logische Untersuchungen II*, Husserliana XIX/1-2 (Den Haag: Martinus Nijhoff).

Husserl, E. (2001), *Logical Investigations* I-II (London: Routledge).

Kriegel, U. (2003a), 'Consciousness as sensory quality and as implicit self-awareness', *Phenomenology and the Cognitive Sciences*, **2**, pp.1–26.

Kriegel, U. (2003b), 'Consciousness as intransitive self-consciousness: Two views and an argument', *Canadian Journal of Philosophy,* **33** (1), pp. 103–32.

Kriegel, U. (2003c), 'Consciousness, higher-order content, and the individuation of vehicles', *Synthese,* **134**, pp. 477–504.

Kriegel, U. (2004), 'Consciousness and self-consciousness,' *Monist,* **87** (2), pp. 185–209.

Lurz, R.W. (2003a), 'Neither *HOT* nor *COLD*: An alternative account of consciousness', *Psyche*, **9** (2), http://psyche.cs.monash.edu.au/v9/psyche-9-01-lurz.html.

Lurz, R.W. (2003b), 'Advancing the debate between HOT and FO accounts of consciousness', *Journal of Philosophical Research*, **28**, pp. 23–44.

Lycan, W.G. (1987), *Consciousness* (Cambridge, MA: MIT Press).

Lycan, W.G. (1997), 'Consciousness as internal monitoring', in Block *et al.* (1997).

Rosenthal, D.M. (1986), 'Two concepts of consciousness', *Philosophical Studies,* **94** (3), pp. 329–59.

Rosenthal, D.M. (1993a), 'Thinking that one thinks', in *Consciousness: Psychological and Philosophical Essays*, ed. M. Davies & G.W. Humphreys (Oxford: Blackwell).

Rosenthal, D.M. (1993b), 'Higher-order thoughts and the appendage theory of consciousness', *Philosophical Psychology*, **6**, pp.155–66.

Rosenthal, D.M. (1997), 'A theory of consciousness', in Block *et al.* (1997).

Sartre, J.-P. (1936), *La transcendance de lego* (Paris: Vrin).

Sartre, J.-P. (1957), *The Transcendence of the Ego*, tr. F. Williams & R. Kirkpatrick (New York: The Noonday Press).

Sartre, J.-P. (1943/1976), *L'être et le néant* (Paris: Tel Gallimard).

Sartre, J.-P. (1956), *Being and Nothingness*, tr. H.E. Barnes (New York: Philosophical Library).

Sartre, J.-P. (1948), 'Conscience de soi et connaissance de soi', *Bulletin de la Société Française de Philosophie*, **XLII**, 49–91.

Shoemaker, S. (1968), 'Self-reference and Self-awareness', *The Journal of Philosophy*, **LXV**, pp. 556–79.

Siewert, C.P. (1998), *The Significance of Consciousness* (Princeton: Princeton University Press).

Thomas, A. (2003), 'An adverbial theory of consciousness', *Phenomenology and the Cognitive Sciences*, **2**, pp. 161–85.

Thomasson, A.L. (2000), 'After Brentano: A one-level theory of consciousness,' *European Journal of Philosophy*, **8** (2), pp. 190–209.

Van Gulick, R. (2000), 'Inward and upward: Reflection, introspection, and self-awareness', *Philosophical Topics*, **28** (2), pp. 275–305.

Zahavi, D. (1998), 'Brentano and Husserl on self-awareness', *Etudés Phénoménologiques*, **27–28**, pp. 127–68.

Zahavi, D. (1999), *Self-awareness and Alterity. A Phenomenological Investigation* (Evanston, IL: Northwestern University Press).

Zahavi, D. (2002), 'First-person thoughts and embodied self-awareness. Some reflections on the relation between recent analytical philosophy and phenomenology', *Phenomenology and the Cognitive Sciences*, **1**, pp. 7–26.

Zahavi, D. (2003a), 'Phenomenology of Self,' in *The Self in Neuroscience and Psychiatry*, ed. T. Kircher & A. David (Cambridge: Cambridge University Press).

Zahavi, D. (2003b), 'Inner time-consciousness and pre-reflective self-awareness', in *The New Husserl: A Critical Reader*, ed. D. Welton (Bloomington, IN: Indiana University Press).

Zahavi, D. (2003c), 'How to investigate subjectivity: Heidegger and Natorp on reflection,' *Continental Philosophy Review*, **36** (2), pp. 155–76.

Sonja Rinofner-Kreidl

Representationalism and Beyond

A Phenomenological Critique
of Thomas Metzinger's Self-Model Theory

Thomas Metzinger's self-model theory offers a framework for naturalizing sub-jective experiences, e.g. first-person perspective. These phenomena are explained by referring to representational contents which are said to be interrelated at diverse levels of consciousness and correlated with brain activi-ties. The paper begins with a consideration on naturalism and anti-naturalism in order to roughly sketch the background of Metzinger's claim that his theory renders philosophical speculations on the mind unnecessary. In particular, Husserl's phenomenological conception of consciousness is refuted as uncriti-cal and inadequate. It is demonstrated that this critique is misguided. The main deficiencies of Metzinger's theory are elucidated by referring to the conception of phenomenal transparency which is compared to a phenomenological idea of transparency. The critical horizon is then enlarged by focusing on some implications of representationalism, including reification of consciousness, brain-Cartesianism and exclusion of the social dimension. Finally meta-theoret-ical reflections on the naturalism debate are taken up.

I: Cognitive Science versus Phenomenology: Points of Departure

Cognitive scientists usually take for granted that it is, on principle, possible to naturalize subjective experiences. There is much debate on the conditions and possibility of this enterprise. However, there is hardly any fundamental doubt concerning the feasibility and adequacy of naturalization projects. The idea of subjectivity involved in these theories mainly refers to qualia and diverse modes of self-reference. Accordingly, a considerable part of the debate on the prospects of naturalization programmes in the field of cognitive science focuses on the relation between presentational and representational contents of mind, both being grasped in terms of multi-realizable functional states.

Phenomenologists insist on the practical dimension of subjectivity and make a point of questioning the methodical and conceptual presuppositions of cognitive scientific models of the mind.[1] From this point of view it is obvious that an effective refusal of *strong naturalization projects which ignore or distort our life-worldly experience* requires more than exploring the consistency and empirical plausibility of the theories in question. A phenomenological critique of such theories transcends the limits of an immanent critique, however elaborately this may be done. Therefore, the onus rests with the phenomenologists to show that their objections cannot be passed over lightly or ridiculed as dogmatically ignoring the efficiency of modern natural science.

The core of what phenomenologists have to say with regard to strong projects of naturalizing the human mind is this: Refuting naturalism is tantamount to appreciating the work of natural science whose impressive success is exactly enabled by the fact that natural science, due to its methodical idealizations and specific theoretical interest, is always an undertaking of limited scope (cf. Husserl, 1962). Naturalism arises whenever this fact is obscured, displaced or explicitly denied. Neglecting the limited scope of scientific theories goes hand in hand with neglecting the function and status of the subject whose experiences are the starting-point of all scientific theorizing. It may therefore be said that self-forgetfulness is a significant mark of the natural scientific attitude (Husserl, 1952a, pp. 183–4). It manifests itself in a strong affinity to a purely mechanical or technical approach to scientific methods. Heidegger's fundamental ontology, which claims to go beyond traditional distinctions such as subject/object or theory/practice via an existential analysis of being-human (*Dasein*), represents an alternative, phenomenological critique of naturalism. According to this project the limited scope of scientific investigations is explained by referring to the *ontological difference*, i.e. the difference between Being (*Sein*) and particular spheres of entities (*Seiendes*), by querying the presuppositions implied in the theoretical attitudes of science and philosophy and, more specifically, by maintaining a foundational relation between a logical idea of science and an existential idea of science (Heidegger, 2001, § 69b). If phenomenologists are right in arguing that the abilities and achievements of the subject (Husserl) or of being-human (Heidegger) underlie all scientific investigations, then it goes without saying that what is at stake in the naturalism debate is nothing less than our idea of science. If the exclusion of the subject or of being-human is the most fundamental objection to strong and dogmatic types of naturalism, then it seems plausible that cognitive scientists aim at strengthening their position by demonstrating that subjective experiences can be naturalized. In reply to this phenomenologists argue that constructions of a naturalized subjectivity, again, can be understood only by referring to a subjectivity both embedded in a life world and not naturalized. In the following we will confine ourselves to a

---

[1] It has been argued that Husserl's project fails due to its lack of a pragmatic dimension. See Varela *et al.* (1993), p. 19. However, there are still pragmatic aspects to be discovered in transcendental phenomenology, given that we do not commit ourselves to narrow concepts of pragmatic dimension. Cf. Rinofner-Kreidl (2003b), pp. 168–205.

Husserlian-style, anti-naturalistic reasoning, for the naturalization project at issue explicitly refers to Husserl's idea of intentionality. The latter is given prominence as the most influential old-fashioned and unscientific model of the human mind which cognitive science is expected to overcome.

II: The Naturalism Debate: Some Issues of General Interest

Cognitive scientists and phenomenological anti-naturalists often talk through one another. They usually begin with different ideas of naturalism and, consequently, pursue different ideas of why we should or should not support naturalization projects. Equally, the opponents take divergent views on what can be expected from these projects, given that they can be fully realized. Until now all persistent efforts to settle the quarrel on naturalism have failed. This indicates serious meta-theoretical problems involved in this debate. For instance, it is not at all clear how strong a naturalistic theory has to be in order to be relevant or, vice versa, how weak it should be in order to be tenable. Insofar as a phenomenologist's task, among other things, is to question seemingly complete alternatives such as subjectivism vs. objectivism, realism vs. idealism, or platonism vs. psychologism, from a more comprehensive point of view which cannot be reduced to either of the positions at issue, it is misleading to talk straightforwardly about 'phenomenological anti-naturalism' as I did before. Phenomenology is non-naturalistic insofar as it forces us to understand what it *means* to take a naturalistic or anti-naturalistic standpoint. This, in turn, cannot be done from a strong naturalistic position.

Another meta-theoretical problem refers to the fact that we do not know how the disagreement between naturalists and anti-naturalists could be removed in a manner agreeable to both opponents. Given that the naturalism-debate concerns the presuppositions and philosophical interpretations of natural scientific research (note: arguing like this already involves a specific non-naturalistic point of view), we cannot hope to solve the problem within the framework of any natural scientific theory whatsoever, which is exactly what a naturalist will demand by referring to successful scientific explanations. This being the case, our attempts to settle the dispute cannot dispense with considerations which bring to light the above-mentioned asymmetry. Whereas a transcendental philosopher, on his own theoretical ground, is able to discuss the opposition of naturalism and anti-naturalism, this does not hold for a strong naturalist (Rinofner-Kreidl, 2003b, pp. XI–XIII, 7–9, 13–18). Because every interesting, i.e. non-trivial, version of naturalism touches on our idea of objectivity and how this should be related to the idea of subjectivity, the difficult question is how one can judge the legitimacy of naturalism or anti-naturalism without begging the question.

III: Husserl and Metzinger:
Two Incompatible Models of the Human Mind

Phenomenology is, basically, interested in phenomenality. It claims to grasp phenomena, i.e. things and processes, solely with respect to their appearance. For conceptual reasons, there is no phenomenon *in itself*. Phenomena are intrinsically related to some consciousness for whom they are presently given. According to our natural attitude we do not encounter phenomena but those things we are directed at for multifarious reasons, for instance, in order to gain some knowledge about them, technically modify them or consume them. To become aware of phenomena means to become aware of the fact that there is an intentional structure lying beneath our ordinary way of handling things and looking at the world. This awareness requires a change of attitude which involves a reflective stance. Husserl's transcendental phenomenology establishes an attitude towards attitudes (Husserl, 1952a, pp. 174, 179). This higher order reflexivity can, among other things, be directed at scientific attitudes. In this case it must be shown that every theory is based on a specific correlation between a method and its object of investigation. For example, natural science always operates on the basis of a tacit agreement concerning what qualifies as *nature* or *natural object* (Husserl, 1952a, p. 2; Husserl, 2001, p. 10). Moreover, every theoretical attitude (including a philosophical one, cf. Husserl, 1952a, p. 146) refers to a specific theorizing subject, the latter being a methodical fiction which must not be confused with a full-blooded human person. It goes beyond the specific theoretical interest of natural science to dig into these correlations of method, object and subject (cf. Husserl, 1952a, pp. 287–8, 355).[2] Phenomenology, on the other hand, is the endeavour to disclose the hidden structure of intentionality in a methodically disciplined manner. It makes explicit the correlation between consciousness and world with regard to a variety of intentional relations.

Reading the works of Husserl we constantly stumble on the term 'consciousness'. This might be misleading. Phenomenology is not interested in investigating consciousness as an *object* of scientific, e.g. psychological, concern cutting off its relations to other regions of being. Consciousness is of *philosophical* interest only insofar as it functions as the medium of experiences embedded in a pre-given world. If we take consciousness in its pure intentional function, leaving aside the existential assumptions we normally attach to it with regard to both the experience and its object, we discover that 'pure' consciousness incorporates all other regions of being: everything can be considered a phenomenon. Every physical

---

[2] This holds true with regard to our modern, methodologically biased idea of science. Compared to a philosophically informed science this, however, represents a degenerate concept of science. Heidegger insists that science is restricted insofar as it does not even realize its own blindness to restrictions which occurs whenever scientific investigation takes place (Heidegger, 1996, pp. 212–13, 219, 221–2). With a view to this methodically induced self-concealment, science engenders the need to go beyond science. 'Science is only possible as philosophy' (Heidegger, 1996, p. 401). Cf. Husserl (1952b), pp. 12–13, 139, 160–1; (2001), pp. 7, 13–19. All translations from German texts cited in the bibliography are mine,

or higher-order object or process can be considered as intentionally related to consciousness.[3] According to Husserl's transcendental-phenomenological ideal-ism, pure consciousness, which renders possible the appearance of any object whatsoever, cannot, on its turn, be conceived of as appearing in the mode of an object.[4] The result would otherwise be an infinite regress of consciousness, since we would have to ask *for whom* this appearing consciousness-*phenomenon* were given and so forth ad infinitum.

Phenomenologically viewed, consciousness is the place where the world is brought to appearance. Consciousness, due to its physical foundation, always occupies a certain place within the world. On the other hand, the world is brought to appearance by consciousness *in terms of meaning constitution.* (A pure ego not embodied could not have any appearances.) Husserl's *paradox of subjectivity* refers to this double role of constituting world and being part of an already constituted world. This is far from being an artificial or purely theoretical philo-sophical problem. It accurately describes the fact that we experience ourselves both as self-conscious agents and as physically pre-structured entities situated both temporally and spatially (cf. Rinofner-Kreidl, 2003b, pp. 125–205). A phenomenological critique of naturalism is based on vigorously acknowledging *the legitimate naturalization of consciousness.*[5] This naturalization turns into a kind of natural*ism* which has to be refuted if one falsely ignores its 'natural' lim-its (cf. Husserl, 1952a, pp. 297, 346). The latter are brought to light by analysing the human mind as a complex phenomenon which comprises different ontologi-cal layers. The term 'naturalization' rightly indicates the inseparability of nature and mind in every human consciousness. Strong naturalistic theories, on the con-trary, annul the multi-layered structure of consciousness in favour of describing its physiological organization as if the achievements of consciousness could be exhaustively grasped by confining oneself to its physiological foundation.

Thomas Metzinger's self-model theory takes notice of the physiological con-ditions which give rise to those occurrences we are accustomed to name 'con-sciousness'. His *neurophenomenology* (Metzinger, 1999b, p. 392) is meant to

---

[3] Following Husserl the term 'transcendental' refers to pure consciousness (in the above-mentioned sense) which 'is' nothing but a manifold relatedness to transcendent objects. 'Transcendental' and 'transcendent' are correlative terms. Here, 'transcendent' refers to everything which is not enclosed in our intentional experiences, i.e. which is not a real part of consciousness.

[4] Accordingly, the self-constitution of my (and everybody else's) transcendental subject by means of original time consciousness cannot be understood in terms of object constitution. It requires a differ-ent concept of constitution. The same holds true for the world as it is given in natural experience, i.e. the world as the indeterminate horizon of all appearing objects and processes (cf. Husserl, 1985, pp. 23–37; Husserl, 2001, p. 15). When considered in their pure experiential structure, the correlating poles of phenomenality, i.e. subjectivity and world, cannot be constituted in terms of object constitu-tion and cannot be subject to any scientific investigation.

[5] 'The fact that body and soul constitute a genuine unity of experience and that the psychic life, in local and temporal respect, takes a particular place due to this unity, makes up the legitimate "naturaliza-tion" of consciousness' (Husserl, 1952a, p. 168). Here, naturalizing the psychic includes naturalizing the intentional (what Husserl refers to as 'Geistiges'). Cf. Husserl (1952a), pp. 202–5, 239, 243–7, 276, 281–5, 297; (1952b), p. 117.

replace traditional phenomenology.[6] It claims to give a naturalistic reformulation of subjectivity centring round phenomenal consciousness and cognitive
self-reference. Metzinger's intention is not to eliminate subjectivity. Instead, he
wants to take our first-person perspective seriously (cf. Metzinger, 1999a, p. 9).
Describing phenomena such as experiencing sensational contents, remembering,
focusing one's attention on something or behaving like a self-conscious agent,
Metzinger assumes that the representational contents of the mind are correlated
with brain activities. Because this correlation is interpreted in terms of
supervenience, the author believes his theory offers a non-reductive naturalization of the human mind. In particular, its naturalistic character is said to consist
in treating consciousness in all its manifestations as a natural phenomenon which
can be explained by natural means in reference to natural history (Metzinger,
1994, pp. 42–3; Metzinger, 1999a, pp. 18, 23–4, 117, 229). If we follow
Metzinger in equating naturalistic theories with empirically founded theories we
are dealing with a weak and trivial conception of naturalism. Looking for more
substantial statements, we learn that there are two which, according to
Metzinger, are essential to naturalistic theories. Theories of this kind refuse both
the idea of material a priori knowledge and the subject/object distinction as a
basic category of our theorizing about the human mind. The former moment
manifests itself in a bottom-up analysis that explains structural and procedural
features of consciousness as resulting from self-organizing processes. These
processes may be said to stand without need of any non-inherently functioning
principles of regulation and control.[7] When Metzinger argues in favour of his
naturalistic theory, he proceeds from the alternative *naturalism vs. essentialism
(sc. metaphysics) or metaphysics of subject vs. self-organizing natural systems.*[8]
He ignores the fact that a phenomenological approach cannot be subsumed under
this alternative. Rather, it gets all its impulse and vigour from the attempt to open
up a third way between naturalism and essentialism.[9] This third way rests on the
attempt to faithfully and painstakingly describe our lived experience.

Metzinger is not concerned with philosophically querying phenomenality in
accordance with Husserl's *First Philosophy*. He does not take a phenomeno-

---

[6] Other approaches to a neurophenomenological science, e.g. Francisco Varela's *enactive* neurophenomenology, do not demand to replace phenomenology but, instead, to cooperate on condition of
mutual restrictions (Petitot *et al.*, 1999, pp. 66–8, 266–314, especially pp. 305–6). I take it that it is the
right direction of any promising neurophenomenology to acknowledge 'the validity of trying to control experimentally the subjective context from the outside' while simultaneously favouring 'a complementary "endogenous" strategy based on using first-person methods' (Thompson *et al.*, 2004, p. 54
(section 9)). However, this requires an analysis of how first-person perspective and third-person
perspective are related to each other in epistemological, methodological and phenomenological respects.
'[Employing] first-person methods in tandem with third-person methods' (*ibid.*, p. 52) could turn out to be
much more difficult than we initially expect it to be. Among these difficulties ranks what I shall
describe as a quarrel about phenomena (section VII).

[7] Contrary to this, a top-down-analysis refers to operational hierarchies.

[8] For a further comment on this *naturalistic strategy of minimizing reasonable alternatives* referring to
Quine's naturalized epistemology see Rinofner-Kreidl (2003b), pp. 1–20.

[9] Cf. my arguments for introducing the term 'mediane Phänomenologie' (Rinofner-Kreidl, 2003b, pp.
V–XV).

logical point of view according to which consciousness is considered the general medium of appearance. Consciousness, rather, is subject to a special methodical grip which replaces its intentional structure by internally produced hierarchies of informational data. These data are investigated with a view to their physical realization. Metzinger's project of presenting an empirically corroborated theory of the human mind is composed of a naturalization of qualia and a naturalization of intentionality. In his theory, 'phenomenal consciousness' both refers to qualia and to those operations which engender a *phenomenal ego*. As for the latter, it is particularly the sub-symbolic constitution of the phenomenal attribute of subject-centring which is of theoretical interest. Qualia are sensational contents whose quality seems to exclude any objective description, for the specific mode of being given to someone is constitutive of the quality at issue (cf. Metzinger and Walde, 2000). Qualia are considered simple, indivisible mental states possessing a peculiar phenomenal content, namely 'a subjective quality of experiencing which is accessible only to the person who has the experience in question' (Metzinger, 1996a, p. 323). According to a phenomenological approach 'phenomenal consciousness' refers to two associated aspects of intentional experiences, namely (a) the appearing of x, and (b) the present, living-through of the experience directed at x. Consequently, intentionality and phenomenality cannot be discussed separately. Contrary to this, Metzinger takes intentionality and phenomenality as representing two issues which can be treated independently from one another.

Metzinger holds that the representational character of contents is exclusively grounded in the causal roles which these contents fulfil as parts of an information processing system. Representation, therefore, is not an intrinsic character of contents of a special kind. Rather, representation has a functional role. The fundamental difference between Metzinger's concept of representation and the phenomenological concept of intentionality may be summarized as follows.

1. Information flows into the system from outside. Information processing, therefore, is referred to as 'inverted intentionality' (Metzinger, 1999a, pp. 128–9). The cognitive scientific concept of representation is based on the assumption that there are causal relations holding between an information processing system and its environment. According to a phenomenological concept of intentionality, intentional and real relations are irreducibly different insofar as the former may not be explained by referring to the latter. Of course, causal relations can concomitantly occur with intentional relations, for instance in the case of sensual perception. Nevertheless, intentional relations constitute a meaning content which cannot be reduced to physical or physiological issues, e.g. relations of stimuli and reaction.
2. The phenomenological concept of intentionality combines two aspects, namely the directedness to an object, via some intentional content, and an immediate awareness of my actually living through the intentional experience in question. Metzinger eliminates the latter moment in favour of a conception that integrates phenomenal states into a self-model and a

world-model by means of self-referentially structured meta-representa-tions.[10] Self-models occur whenever a part of the system analogically repre-sents the system as a whole. Self-models do not involve any propositionally structured self-reference. Those parts of self-models which, in principle, can be represented as contents of phenomenal consciousness, via some meta-representation, are called 'mental'. A phenomenal self is that part of the mental self-model which is the actual content of phenomenal conscious-ness (Metzinger, 1999a, pp. 158–9). *Subjectivity* is a quality of complex information processing systems which manifests itself if and only if the sys-tem succeeds in embedding a self-model into its model of reality.[11]

The cognitive scientific conception of representation rests on a dual structure of internal data-processing and outer reality, which is induced by Metzinger's concept of information. It implies a third-person perspective. The basic concepts of Metzinger's theory presuppose what this theory claims to show, namely that it is possible to naturalize our folk-psychological account of first-person perspec-tive. A human first-person perspective precisely manifests itself in the intrinsic relatedness of consciousness and world, the latter being interpreted in terms of meaningful experiences. Due to its conceptual and methodical framework, Metzinger's self-model theory cuts off this intimate relation between conscious-ness and world. Metzinger refutes Husserl's (and every other 'classical') con-ception of intentionality. In doing so he ignores that a phenomenologist's and a cognitive scientist's idea of consciousness radically differ from each other. Thus it is not surprising that he considers Husserl's phenomenological idealism an incomprehensible and obscure position. Among other things, Metzinger's cri-tique is misguided with regard to the following issues.[12]

- According to Metzinger intentional experiences are present whenever an act (noesis) is directed to an intentional content (noema) as its object. In this view the mediating function of intentional contents gets lost. Whereas Husserl emphasizes that intentional contents are not the objects of our con-cern whenever we live through present intentional experiences (although we can turn our attention to them in subsequent acts of reflection), Metzinger implicitly takes this reflective turn to be constitutive of the 'na-ively' realized intentional relation. From the point of view of phenomenol-ogy this amounts to reifying intentional contents and consciousness respectively, since the fundamental reality of accomplishment (*Vollzug*), that is, of performing intentional experiences, is eliminated. Metzinger, however, denies any reifying interpretation. 'Content is not a mysterious type of *thing*, but an abstract property of a highly fluid and complex

[10] See 'Meaning and the conscious experience of meaningfulness have to be separated. Of course, this does not mean that no such thing as intentional contents exists' (Metzinger and Gallese, 2003a, p. 564).

[11] See Metzinger (1999a), p. 204. A more detailed account of subjectivity is presented in Metzinger (2003a), pp, 37 f, 567 f.

[12] For a more comprehensive discussion of this critique as well as IT and HAT (section IV) see Rinofner-Kreidl (2003b), pp. 27–53.

cognitive dynamics . . .' (Metzinger, 2000, p. 302 (fn. 3)). Representational contents must be described as 'an aspect of an ongoing process and not as some kind of abstract object' (Metzinger, 2003b, p. 358). According to Husserl, intentional contents are both aspects of an ongoing process of experiencing *and* abstract objects, depending on whether they are considered as actually functioning or referred to by means of reflective acts (noematic reflection). Holding this view requires, of course, that we note Husserl's purely formal understanding of object ('everything upon which we may predicate') as well as his peculiar idea of abstract objects. Objects of this kind are said not to be timeless entities as Metzinger takes them to be (Metzinger, 2003a, p. 606) but beyond ordinary temporal location. They can be realized at any time whatsoever (Husserl, 1985, pp. 309–14). Holding the above view furthermore requires us to acknowledge that living through actual experiences and reflecting on experiences are fundamentally different act qualities and that reflection presupposes actual experience. If we talk about a '*mediating* function' of intentional contents, this refers to the fact that every reference to an object involves some intentional content which determines the reference at issue. The relatedness of consciousness and world, *if analysed theoretically*, shows itself to be realized *by means of these contents*. This obviously does not involve a noematic *mediator* in accordance with the idea that consciousness and world are separate spheres of reality in need of being brought together by some ontologically mysterious noema entity representing an 'outer reality'. This view certainly does not correspond to our experience of being intentionally related to something. In other words: it is ontologically and epistemologically harmless to refer to a mediating function of intentional contents if this is interpreted in terms of the above-mentioned one-sided ontological dependence of acts of reflection upon preceding accomplishments.[13] *Acknowledging the mediating function of intentional content is equivalent to denying the representational character of our intentional relations (given that the idea of representation involves a rigid distinction of inside and outside).*

- Phenomenology does not replace real objects with intentional objects. Distinguishing intentional objects from real ones neither implies nor requires that we consider the former as fictitious. On the other hand, if intentional experiences are conceived of as functional states which represent aggregates of causal relations, we should say that intentional contents represent presently given objects *because* mental states are determined by something different from them and located outside them (Metzinger, 1999a, p. 17). However, in cases of remembering, imagining future events, fantasies,

---

[13] From a phenomenological point of view it is not the vehicle–content distinction which is of primary interest but the distinction of accomplishment and reflection. It is only due to the latter that we can avoid reifying consciousness whereas the former distinction, according to Metzinger, 'contains subtle residues of Cartesian dualism in that it always tempts us to *reify* the vehicle and the content, by conceiving of them as distinct, independent entities' (Metzinger, 2003a, p. 166).

hallucinations and similar mental phenomena ('mental simulations'), it is obvious that there is no represented object as part of the present environment (cf. Metzinger, 1999a, p. 66). Following Metzinger we, therefore, have to interpret intentional experiences on a large scale as fantasies which are not caused by any external occurrences.

- A phenomenological conception of intentionality does not assume a privileged first-person accessibility in terms of a full self-referential transparency of consciousness. Arguing like this is based on a dogmatic idea of givenness and a misguided conception of inner certainty (cf. Rinofner-Kreidl, 2000, pp. 178–203; 387–412).

IV: A Scientific Model of Phenomenal Transparency: the Illusive Self

Phenomenal transparency (PT) is one of the basic features of the human mind. Transparency is a property of phenomenal representations in a sub-symbolic medium, i.e. of non-linguistic entities (Metzinger, 2003b, p. 363). It is 'a property of active mental representations satisfying the minimally sufficient constraints for conscious experience to occur' (*ibid.*, p. 355), namely being presently activated and being integrated in a global model of the world. '[Phenomenally] transparent representations are precisely those representations the existence of whose content we cannot doubt' (Metzinger and Gallese, 2003a, p. 563). PT is important with respect to explaining the achievement of cognitive self-reference that always is reference to the phenomenal content of a transparent self-model (Metzinger, 2003b, p. 385). Why do transparent states emerge in information processing systems?

> what makes mental representations transparent is the *attentional unavailability of earlier processing stages in the brain* for introspection (Metzinger, 2003b, p. 356).

PT is problematic with regard to its epistemological implications.[14] PT is meant to elucidate a thesis which may be designated the 'illusion thesis' (IT): the subjectivity of the mental results from a kind of self-confusion. A phenomenal ego appears because the system, in a certain respect, is deprived of information. This possibly is the most important insight of cognitive science concerning philosophical anthropology.[15] We may expound this insight as follows:

(IT) The unity of our phenomenal self is a representational fiction (Metzinger, 1996b, p. 152). The fact that we are faced with a fiction cannot be realized

---

[14] Although PT is said to represent a phenomenological notion and not an epistemological one (Metzinger, 2003b, p. 363), it is obvious that this notion has epistemological implications (see the formulation of the illusion thesis below).

[15] See Metzinger (1998), p. 361; (2003a), pp. 32–42, 163–79, 330–40, 386–95. PT plays a pivotal role with regard to Metzinger's central idea 'that metaphysically speaking no such things as selves exist in the world; that the conscious experience of self*hood* is brought about by the phenomenal transparency of the system-model; and that what philosophers call the epistemic irreducibility of conscious experience — the fact that it is tied to a first-person-perspective — can be exhaustively analyzed as a *representational* phenomenon, which in the future will likely be fully explained on functional and neurobiological levels of description' (Metzinger, 2003a, p. 627). See Metzinger (2003a), pp. 563 f, 577, 625–35.

at the phenomenal, personal level of consciousness (Metzinger, 2003b, p. 363; Metzinger, 1994, pp. 50–1). Semantic transparency is responsible for our pre-reflexive self-acquaintance (Metzinger, 1998, p. 360): A *phenomenal first-person perspective* emerges whenever a system is not able to recognize its self-model as a model. Only from the point of view of sub-personal information processing is it possible to recognize the illusion and to explain why it necessarily occurs, given information processing systems of a certain complexity.[16] Cognitive science helps us to understand why phenomenologists inevitably fall victim to the *myth of the given*. What phenomenologists naively grasp as immediately given truly is a construction based on neural processes.

The argument in favour of IT may be expounded in the following manner. What, in everyday experience, is given to us immediately, is interpreted in a naively realistic mode. Under normal conditions we have the strong, albeit subjective, feeling that we are in direct contact with both ourselves as experiencing subjects and with the world. From a scientific point of view it turns out that what presents itself as immediately given actually results from the inability of human consciousness to simultaneously grasp those rapidly running off brain processes that lie behind the experiences in question (cf. Metzinger, 1999b, p. 401). As soon as we come to know this time lag inherent in all our thinking, perceiving, remembering or desiring, we cannot stick to the former naively realistic interpretation of ourselves and the world. As Metzinger argues, with a view to the Cotard syndrome, this implies that 'if a human being's self-model became fully opaque, then this person would experience herself as non-existent' (Metzinger, 2003d, p. 21).[17] Abandoning naive realism, we recognize that what actually happens when we live through theoretical and practical intentions is that some special system operations occur. Strictly speaking, there *is* no intention directed to an object 'out there'. There is rather an informational process taking place. Intentional relations are substituted by an internal determinism of the information processing system. Metzinger's representationalism implies a constructivistic bias which cannot be challenged within the framework of his theory (cf. Metzinger, 1996a, p. 622).

According to Metzinger traditional theories of intentionality hold an incorrect idea of how the mental modelling of representational relations takes place. They erroneously attribute intentional experiences to a phenomenal self-model instead of attributing them to the brain that engenders the self-model in question.

---

[16] Generally, Metzinger does not take seriously the objection that, referring to the sub-personal level of neural processes, it is, from conceptual reasons, inadmissible to talk about 'illusions' since the brain, or the limbic system as a whole, cannot function as the subject of epistemic evaluations like 'illusive' or 'veridical' , 'true' or 'false'. So we are in the dilemma of either not being able to identify the illusion at issue or of having to admit that, strictly speaking, there is no illusion since there is nobody subject to it. Metzinger only *seems* to consider the latter possibility when talking about 'nobody's illusion' (cf. Metzinger, 1996b, p. 153; Metzinger, 1996c, p. 625 (fn. 46); Metzinger, 2000, p. 301). However, he holds that it makes sense to talk about an illusion nobody is subject to.

[17] The Cotard syndrome is a serious mental disorder which occasionally appears in cases of depression. It manifests itself in a feeling of complete disembodiment.

Referring to the latter we do not find individual causal relations. A self-model exclusively grasps the final products of these underlying processes. From this Metzinger draws the conclusion that there is no consciousness which is directed to the world. There are, rather, complex physical occurrences determining mental models (Metzinger, 1999a, pp. 128–9 (fn. 212)). This amounts to a naturalization of the cogito. Whereas Descartes took our thinking to be inseparable from our ego, we realize nowadays that, according to Metzinger, the ego is nothing but a thought which depends on a physical system *thinking this thought*. This system, for instance the brain of a biological organism, is the thinking thing (Metzinger, 1999a, pp. 154–5).

From the above it is clear that IT requires a highly problematic supplementary thesis which I call the 'hidden agent thesis (HAT)':

> The true cognitive agent of our intentional experiences is not the phenomenal ego represented by a relatively stable and coherent self-model. The true agent is our brain.[18]

PT means that introspective access to a phenomenal mental model is limited to its content properties, as opposed to its vehicle properties (Metzinger, 2003a, p. 394). Mental states do not represent their internal constructional genesis (cf. Metzinger, 1996b, p. 143). The temporality of the underlying processes does not enter the representational content. Accordingly, IT may be reformulated as follows.

> The illusive character of (at least some) representations is due to the fact that their neurological constitution is not part of the representational contents in question.

Let us call this T1. T1 involves a *fallacy of latency*. In order to explain why T1 is fallacious we must now take up the problem of transparency as it presents itself in non-scientific contexts.

V: A Phenomenological Model of Phenomenal Transparency: The Double Aspect of a Self's Behaviour (Accomplishment and Reflection)

Everyday experience is acquainted with a basic transparency of values, interests, purposes and so on which is indispensable for our thinking and acting. Whenever these issues are made the objects of concern two things happen. First, they lose their immediate and reliable guiding function because we recognize that there are alternative values, interests and purposes which could or should be equally realized. Secondly, the intentional objects of the experiences in question change as soon as we stop thinking and acting in a 'naive' mode and start reflecting on the rationales of our thinking and acting. Given that our hierarchies of values, interests and purposes cannot be absolutely justified, the above reasoning leads to this: in order to think and act something, i.e. some problematic ideas, must be kept in latency.

On the other hand, asking whether our thoughts and actions are *reasonable* involves a reflective turn. For the present purposes we may leave untouched

---

[18] Cf. 'Compared with the scientist who wants to understand these abstract qualities [sc. qualia] the brain which produces these qualities is in a privileged position' (Metzinger, 1999a, p. 270).

what it means to give sufficient reasons for our acting and how we could hope to practically implement our principles of acting. With a view to the issue of transparency it may suffice to note that in order to act smoothly these principles have to be made our own in a manner that allows for an 'invisible' or unnoticed functioning. The fact that x functions latently does not indicate that x lacks any rational foundation. It might just as well turn out that it is perfectly rational to act x-like. In the absence of any reflection, practical (as well as theoretical) transparency leaves entirely open whether we are faced with an irrational behaviour or with a rational one *dropped into a special mode of passivity*, where passivity normally includes, as Husserl says, some hidden rationality. Acknowledging latent functions is neutral to epistemological concerns. The latter cannot be formulated as long as the intentional contents in question have not been made explicit. The occurrence of intentional experiences, as far as we know, depends on various latent functions of, for instance, biological organisms. However, describing latent functions does not mean giving a sufficient or even relevant description of the intentional experiences, e.g. thinking about something, whose occurrence is owing to the latent functions at issue.[19] For instance, it is a reasonable hypothesis worthy of being empirically tested that '[identity] disorders, while being diagnosed on the *personal* level of description, result from subpersonal disintegration' (Metzinger, 2003d, p. 24). Nevertheless, trying to explain the occurrence of pathological types of experience by referring to neurophysiological states or functional relations taken to be realized in these states does not and cannot help us to gain a better therapeutic understanding of what it means to have experiences of these kinds.

As we have seen above, relating to the mediating function of intentional content, there is also a transparency thesis implicit in a phenomenological conception of intentionality. When Husserl analyses the mode of givenness of other minds he introduces the following analogy. The apperception of intentional contents that I attribute to other persons' mind is achieved via some bodily appearance in a way similar to the apperception of meaning which is achieved via some linguistic sign, 'meaning' understood here in a narrow logical sense (Husserl, 1952a, p. 240). My body as well as the body of other persons functions transparently with regard to the apperception and communication of intentional contents. The phenomenological transparency thesis illustrates how phenomenologists steer clear of the alternative of metaphysical essentialism and naturalism. Analysing the mind/body relation we have to recognize that, engaged in our life-world practice, we normally do not experience any separation of mind and body. According to Husserl, gaining sympathetic understanding (*einfühlendes Verstehen*) of other persons means to grasp their bodies with a view to inherent

[19] See from a wider perspective Nagel (1997). Metzinger, ultimately, does not clearly distinguish these different levels or aspects. For instance, he explains that the brain makes ' "ontological commitments" [. . .] when representing actions and goals' and that these commitments could be traced at the microfunctional level implemented in the brain's neural networks. '*The same subpersonal ontology* then guides organisms when they are epistemic agents in a social world: Interpersonal relations *become meaningful* in virtue of a shared action ontology' (Metzinger and Gallese, 2003a, p. 550, emphasis mine) — which is of neurophenomenological character!

meaning structures manifesting a unity of sense. Every perception of a person is founded on an apperception of objective intentional content (*objektiver Geist*). On the other hand, there is no apperception of the body as bearer of the psychical in terms of a physical object which had to be supplemented by something different, as if it were taken

> as something related or connected to something else. It, rather, is a higher-level objectification superimposing on a lower-level one to the effect that there results a unified object. Without referring to any kind of connection *which would imply separation,* this synthetic object comprises a lower- and a higher-level-constitution *being distinguished only subsequently.* The unity which is given in course of apperceiving some spiritual being can be distinguished into body and sense *by changing the apperceiving attitude.* (Husserl, 1952a, p. 244, emphasis mine)

The so-called mind/body-problem arises if we theoretically reflect on the possibility of apperceiving other minds. However sophisticated this reflection may be, it always refers back and remains embedded in our experiential practice. *Acknowledging the transparency involved in this original practice amounts to overcoming the Cartesian starting-point of our theorizing both with regard to the original mind/body-unity and the original community of self and others.* Phenomenologically viewed, there is no need to naturalize the mind as long as our theoretical representations of the human mind do not go beyond its true nature, as it presents itself in primordial experience, by introducing some dubious spiritual entity.

The phenomenological transparency thesis differs in an essential way from Metzinger's transparency thesis. First, it is not connected with any illusion thesis. If we explicitly refer to the functioning of bodily appearance and behaviour or linguistic signs, an act which we may accomplish at any time by turning our attention, this does not alter the epistemic appraisal of the intentional content at issue. Acknowledging the indispensability of latent functions does not alter the phenomenal character of those previous experiences that have been effected because of the latent functions in question. Second, and in connection with the epistemic neutrality of reflecting on transparent moments, the phenomenological transparency thesis does not annihilate the distinction between living through experiences and reflecting on experiences. On the contrary, phenomenological transparency implies that this distinction essentially belongs to human consciousness. Third, whether something is explicitly grasped or given transparently, whether it is, to use Husserl's terms, given in a manifest (*patent*) or latent manner, depends on the thematic attitude of the experiencing subject. In order to understand transparency we must inquire into the attitude/object correlations that belong to the intentional life of persons, instead of analysing special attitudes, e.g. attention, *in terms of information processing.*[20] In order to distinguish latent and manifest functions we must make reference to changing attitudes or perspectives, modes of querying. Nothing is *in itself* latent or manifest. The

---

[20] 'attention is a constructive form of representing another representation (or a set thereof) with the help of non-conceptual mental means, a subsymbolic kind of metarepresentation' (Metzinger, 2003b, p. 356). See Metzinger (2003a), pp. 32–8.

appearance of whatever thing and moment depends on particular circumstances and conditions on the side of the subject as well as on the side of the object which must be specified. Every single attitude brings to light particular objects and processes and, simultaneously, makes disappear other objects and processes. For instance, if we decide to neurologically inquire into the genesis of phenomenal transparency, we unavoidably lose sight of the intentional life of persons. IT forfeits its prima facie plausibility if we realize that every scientific finding rests on some particular attitude which fulfils a visualizing and de-visualizing function in the above sense. This function is vital for our scientific division of labour. Nevertheless, we are led astray if we forget its operational implications.

VI: Scientifically Shaped Experience versus Primordial Experience: The Representationalist Predicament

The latency of neural processes implied in Metzinger's PT cannot be conceived of as a structure of experience. There is no subject for whom the processes in question could be made explicit *as structuring her experience*. The brain (or the limbic system) does not constitute a self in any relevant theoretical or practical sense. It cannot constitute a self because this requires meaningful, i.e. semantically interpreted, experiences that involve reference to (hierarchies of) wants, desires, values, interests, and so on. The mere running off of neural processes does not constitute experience. The processes occurring in my brain are not part of my experience (cf. Husserl, 1952a, pp. 164, 218, 230–1; Ricoeur, 1996, p. 164). IT and HAT call for self-application. Every cognitive scientist who investigates the human mind and thereby performs particular intentional experiences too, must be subject to IT and HAT. She has to consider herself as a brain that interprets informational data realized in some mind whose 'true agent' is a brain. From this point of view it may become common in cognitive science to talk about brain-to-brain communications. Arguing like this, however, involves a categorical mistake. Neural processes do not think, communicate, regret their moral imperfection or enjoy some magical erotic moments.

If there are electrodes fixed to my head which transmit the occurrences in my brain to a recorder that simultaneously visualizes them, it does not follow that I am, in any strict or interesting sense, able to experience my own brain. Methodically disciplined modes of experience which are operative in variable experimental designs must not be confused with our ordinary experience (cf. Heidegger, 1996, pp. 188, 196–7). Metzinger naturalizes primordial experience by supposing that *first-person perspective and third-person perspective are equivalent attitudes which can be changed arbitrarily according to different objectives* (Rinofner-Kreidl, 2004). Consequently, we are free to describe our mind from either an external point of view, i.e. as a succession of neurological states, or an internal point of view, i.e. as the experiences we go through (Metzinger, 1996a, p. 256). Here again it is obvious that the naturalization of subjectivity which is expected to be the outcome of Metzinger's theory has been smuggled in from the outset (see section III). It is implied in the basic concepts of his self-model and its mode of questioning empirical data. Contrary to this, a phenomenologist insists that any talk about 'my brain' requires that I have an experience of my own body involving a first-person perspective. Without this original bodily experience I could never conceive of a succession of brain states as belonging to me. Taking first-person perspective and third-person perspective on a par with one another tacitly assumes that brains can be considered self-sufficient entities whose contingent realization in human bodies, including modes of behaviour which cannot be explained 'bottom-up', can be neglected with a view to special theoretical purposes.

A functionalistic view, committed to the thesis of multi-realizability, cannot do justice to our subjective experience of embodied mind. What it means to leave aside the intrinsic 'worldliness' of human consciousness can be explained in relation to a diverse set of issues. Among these is the peculiar weakening of the mind/body unity owing to a functionalistic view, i.e. the displacement of our natural experience of embodiment. In a similar way the loss of world in Metzinger's theorizing manifests itself as a total neglect of intersubjectivity with a view to the constitution of self-reference and, consequently, self-referentially based self-consciousness. Furthermore, Metzinger disregards our ability to grasp immediately the situational horizon of whatever single experience we encounter. It has been rightly argued that scientific models that take consciousness to consist in information processing inevitably fail to consider the 'enworlded' nature of consciousness. This is due to the fact that it is impossible to transform our natural ability of synthetically grasping more or less complex situations into some objective system of data by means of which one could exhaustibly specify the concepts and rules to be applied in concrete cases (Dreyfus, 1985, pp. 214–18). The belief that this can be done, applied to artificial intelligence, could be called 'computer-Cartesianism' (cf. *ibid.*, p. 218). Equally, we may talk about a 'brain-Cartesianism' implicit in those cognitive scientific theories which, due to their representationalism, adhere to a rigid dualism of outer reality and internal system of informational data (see the discussion about our concept of the world in section VII).[21] Both the external and the internal eludes our natural experience.

From another point of view the sterility of Metzinger's theory concerning the demands of intersubjectivity and situational embedding is due to the complete lack of a practical dimension.[22] Metzinger's naturalistic theory of self-modelling exclusively explains the emergence of phenomenal self-consciousness without taking into account the social dimension of subjectivity (Metzinger, 1999a, pp. 175, 225). This dimension is said to be negligible insofar as the physical structures of data are deprived of any semantic content (*ibid.*, p. 251 (fn. 10)). Notwithstanding this severe restriction of his field of investigation, the author does

---

[21] This objection obviously does not hold with regard to *embodied* or *enactive cognitive science*. There is much evidence that following the latter we could avoid the pitfalls of the naturalism/anti-naturalism debate sketched above (Sections I and II) by redefining our idea of what it means to naturalize the human mind.

[22] Perceiving my own as well as other bodies is implied in many higher-order activities of the mind. Intersubjectivity in terms of understanding bodily, e.g. physiognomic, expressions is founded upon a pre-linguistic grasping of situations.

not reckon with any loss of sense with regard to his naturalized subjectivity. Generally, and quite amazingly, it is expected that future research in the field of cognitive science will succeed in incorporating intersubjectivity. Yet how could one expect to adequately describe or explain subjectivity from a solipsistic point of view and, later on, expand one's concern to a social dimension considered as a supplementary field of experience which is not, from the outset, involved in the constitution of subjectivity?[23]

Metzinger's attempt to naturalize subjectivity is based on a reification of consciousness. This reification results from eliminating the distinction of actually living through experiences and being reflectively directed at one's experiences. The representationalism of Metzinger's self-model theory does not leave any room for immediately present experiences. For methodical reasons, Metzinger holds that what cannot be represented as conscious content on the neurophenomenological level of description is not a relevant part of human experience. This assumption occasionally turns up when Metzinger discusses the methodical implications involved in the question of how philosophers and psychiatrists can cooperate in analysing phenomena of identity disorder.

> 'Personal identity' can be either a complex theoretical concept or *a concrete [form] of subjective experience, a conscious content* — but it never is a thing, neither in the brain nor anywhere else. To put the point differently: Psychiatrists must stop being naive realists about personal identity. (Metzinger, 2003d, p. 3, emphasis mine)

Here we have the tacit presupposition of Metzinger's self-model: there are no 'formal' aspects of human experience which cannot be (neurophenomenologically) represented as conscious contents. Depending on whether or not we agree to this general thesis, we achieve completely different ideas of subjectivity. It is characteristic of a phenomenological approach to deny the above thesis (Rinofner-Kreidl, 2003b, pp. 215–21). The peculiar character of subjectivity ultimately lies in the fact that there are 'formal' aspects of our experience which resist representational objectification on whatever level of description. Metzinger holds that this is true with regard to the phenomenal level of description, as it is interpreted in folk psychology, but false with regard to the neurophenomenological level of description. Consequently, a pivotal question of the naturalism debate is how different levels of description are related to each other. However, talking about 'levels' of description is misleading. It wrongly suggests that what neurophenomenologists and phenomenologists do is describe the same phenomena from different points of view.

---

[23] See Metzinger (2003a), p. 590. Concerning persons as moral agents, Metzinger seems to be ready to acknowledge the inadequacy of this methodical approach. Cf. Metzinger (1999a), pp. 152–3, 162, 274–5, 290; (2003a), pp. 601, 606. There are also problems concerning the question of how ontology and ethics are interrelated to each other. It is not at all clear how we could talk about moral agents if we take seriously Metzinger's claim that 'no such things as selves exist in the world. What actually exists is a special kind of self-models and their contents and this content makes us believe that we actually do have, or are identical to, a self' (Metzinger, 2000, p. 289). Agency, here, is understood as 'the representation of subpersonal selection processes on the level of the PSM [the phenomenal self-model]' (Metzinger, 2003a, p. 609). In my view the discussion of an 'ethics of consciousness' does not find any support in Metzinger's theory (*ibid.*, pp. 630–4).

In relation to the superimposing structure of meta-representations which enables the system to re-interpret and overcome phenomenally transparent states we may summarize Metzinger's account as follows. Experiences are part of our cognitive life only if they have been transformed into or acquired in terms of meta-representational contents.[24] Contrary to this, a phenomenological approach emphasizes *the practical moment of accomplishment (living through experiences).* From a phenomenological point of view it is evident that Metzinger de-temporalizes our primordial self-consciousness which is said to consist in a hierarchical structuring of contents by means of meta-representations. It is interesting that Metzinger, vice versa, accuses phenomenologists of eliminating the dynamic character of consciousness ('phenomenological fallacy': Metzinger, 1999a, p. 161; Metzinger, 2003a, pp. 22f) by disregarding the neurological level of description. This objection results from two assumptions which must be dismissed. First, the succession of occurrences in the brain is equated with the original temporality of consciousness based on the subjective experience of before/after relations which are not yet interpreted in terms of objective time units.[25] Second, the mediating function of intentional contents is ignored (see above section III).

VII: Once Again: Meta-Theoretical Issues Involved in the Naturalism Debate

Metzinger's naturalization project revolves around the attempt to conceive of subjectivity in terms of representational relations. Contrary to this, a phenomenologist argues that representation cannot be considered the most fundamental, original mode of consciousness. Given this essential disagreement concerning the idea of consciousness, the most basic question seems to be whether or not cognitive scientists and phenomenologists actually refer to the same phenomena.[26] Do they explain the same phenomena in incompatible ways or do they talk about different things? We obviously cannot soothe this issue by arguing that the opponents talk about different aspects of reality so that, in a certain sense, we might be satisfied with both approaches. This does not do because our idea of reality is part of the issue.[27] If we follow Metzinger in conceiving of intentionality in terms of causal roles, it is unclear how we could ever reach the

---

[24] Cf. 'Conscious experiencing, basically, is a form of remembering' (Metzinger, 1999a, p. 102).

[25] ' "Points in time" are physical entities, individuated from a third-person-perspective' (Metzinger, 2003a, p. 602). See Rinofner-Kreidl (2003b), pp. 222–39. Maintaining that there is a difference between the succession of brain states and the temporality of consciousness is relevant, too, with regard to the question of whether experiments concerning neurological processes offer any evidence for denying free will. Cf. Husserl (1952a), pp. 259–60, 286–7, 291–6; Rinofner-Kreidl (2003a). See Metzinger's brief remark on his idea of freedom ('the opposite of functional rigidity') which refers to degrees of behavioural, attentional and cognitive flexibility (Metzinger, 2003a, pp. 40, 419 (fn. 25)).

[26] Arguing in favour of different phenomena, i.e. denying that a naturalization of subjectivity saves the formerly given phenomena with regard to their essential meaning contents, normally goes hand in hand with a strong interpretation of the *explanatory-gap-argument.* Cf. Petitot *et al.* (1999), pp. 1–18.

[27] See 'The phenomenal agent is a virtual agent perceiving virtual objects in a virtual world' (Metzinger, 2000, p. 300). Psychopathological cases and neurological disorders (cf. Metzinger, 2003d) are suited

idea that the world is *not* the sum total of all things, and instead an encompassing meaning-horizon without which we would be unable to encounter things. It does not suffice to consider the holistic character of reality (Metzinger, 1995), if this holism, again, is interpreted according to the functionalistic approach of Metzinger's 'bottom-up' neurophenomenology. If we proceed from the scientifically reduced, non-natural idea of the world which manifests itself in Metzinger's self-model theory, it may well be that we can describe how our brains are related to *a* virtual or real world. Nevertheless, this does not say anything about our natural experience of *the* world. It only shows that in constructing theoretical models we are free to talk about a world or certain aspects of reality. This is owing to the fact that the definition of 'world' or 'reality' depends on internal criteria of the models in question. From this point of view the main concern of the naturalism debate is how we should consider theoretical models to be related to our life-world practice. Can we really leave it to some special scientific model to determine what 'world' or 'reality' means? Or must we rely on our primordial experience which always operates on condition that we already have an understanding of world and reality? Should we not acknowledge this fundamental status of primordial experience, how, then, could we claim to critically assess *different* models of reality resulting from different theoretical approaches? Our natural understanding of the world is already involved if we are told that to 'have an ontology is to interpret a world' and that 'the brain, viewed as a representational system aimed at interpreting our world, possesses an ontology, too' (Metzinger and Gallese 2003a, p. 549). In methodical terms this amounts to a 'mathematical model describing the phenomenal ontology of the human brain — i.e. that which *exists* according to conscious experience — in a precise and empirically plausible manner' (Metzinger, 1995, p. 427).

If a phenomenologist advances the view, as I do, that representationalistic theories distort or even eliminate those phenomena they claim to explain, what then, should we think about the naturalism debate insofar as theories of this kind are concerned? We certainly cannot expect that (a) scientific methods are neutral with regard to the objects investigated, and that (b) the naturalism debate can be decided by comparing the efficiency of diverse (scientific) methods of analysing and explaining phenomena. Every statement concerning methodical efficiency tacitly implies some conception of how our theorizing is related to the world as it presents itself in everyday life. Applying methods always involves a certain structuring of its correlating objects. This being the case, it is clear that the dispute between naturalists and anti-naturalists cannot be settled at the level of describing and explaining phenomena. To describe or explain phenomena and to discuss the methodical and conceptual framework of our descriptions and explanations are quite different activities which should be clearly distinguished. However, the results of the former activity might turn out to be problematic due to

---

to making us susceptible to the experience of 'simultaneously (existing) in different parallel worlds' (Metzinger, 1995, p. 427). However, we could not even understand what 'parallel worlds' means if there were not some privileged experience of being-in-the-world. Accordingly, we could not identify disorder if there were not some privileged experience of order.

ignoring the difficulties brought to light by the latter. Both (a) and (b) suggest that if we phenomenologically challenge projects of naturalizing the human mind we have to focus on the issue of how theory and practice are interrelated. Thus, asking on what *theoretical* grounds it might be possible to adequately discuss naturalizations of subjectivity is still insufficient if it does not comprise a radical reflection on our idea of theory.

References

Dreyfus, H.L. (1985), *Grenzen künstlicher Intelligenz. Was Computer nicht können* (Königstein/Ts.: Athenäum).

Heidegger, M. (1996), *Einleitung in die Philosophie* (Frankfurt: Vittorio Klostermann) (= *Collected Works*, Vol. 27).

Heidegger, M. (2001), *Sein und Zeit* (Tübingen: Max Niemeyer).

Husserl, E. (1952a), *Ideen zu einer reinen Phänomenologie und phänomenologischen Philosophie. Zweites Buch: Phänomenologische Untersuchungen zur Konstitution*, ed. M. Biemel (Den Haag: Martinus Nijhoff) (= *Husserliana*, Vol. IV).

Husserl, E. (1952b), *Ideen zu einer reinen Phänomenologie und phänomenologischen Philosophie. Drittes Buch: Die Phänomenologie und die Fundamente der Wissenschaften*, ed. M. Biemel (Haag: Martinus Nijhoff) (= *Husserliana*, Vol. V).

Husserl, E. (1962), *Die Krisis der europäischen Wissenschaften und die transzendentale Phänomenologie*, ed. W. Biemel (Den Haag: Martinus Nijhoff) (= *Husserliana*, Vol. VI).

Husserl, E. (1985), *Erfahrung und Urteil. Untersuchungen zur Genealogie der Logik*, ed. L. Landgrebe (Hamburg: Felix Meiner).

Husserl, E. (2001), *Natur und Geist. Vorlesungen Sommersemester 1927*, ed. M. Weiler (Dordrecht/Boston/London: Kluwer Academic Publishers) (= *Husserliana*, Vol. XXXII).

Metzinger, T. (1994), 'Schimpansen, Spiegelbilder, Selbstmodelle und Subjekte', in *Geist — Gehirn — künstliche Intelligenz. Zeitgenössische Modelle des Denkens. Ringvorlesung an der Freien Universität Berlin*, ed. S. Krämer (Berlin, New York: De Gruyter), pp. 41–70.

Metzinger, T (1995), 'Faster than thought: Holism, homogeneity and temporal coding', in T. Metzinger, *Conscious Experience* (Exeter: Imprint Academic/Paderborn: Mentis), pp. 425–61.

Metzinger, T. (ed. 1996a), *Bewußtsein. Beiträge aus der Gegenwartsphilosophie* (Paderborn *et al.*: Ferdinand Schöningh).

Metzinger, T. (1996b), '*Niemand* sein. Kann man eine naturalistische Perspektive auf die Subjektivität des Mentalen einnehmen?', in *Bewußtsein. Philosophische Beiträge*, ed. S. Krämer (Frankfurt: Suhrkamp), pp. 130–54.

Metzinger, T. (1996c), 'Ganzheit, Homogenität und Zeitkodierung', in Metzinger (1996a), pp. 595–633.

Metzinger, T. (1998), 'Anthropologie und Kognitionswissenschaften', in *Der Mensch in der Perspektive der Kognitionswissenschaften*, ed. P. Gold and A.K. Engel (Frankfurt: Suhrkamp), pp. 326–72.

Metzinger, T. (1999a), *Subjekt und Selbstmodell. Die Perspektivität phänomenalen Bewußtseins vor dem Hintergrund einer naturalistischen Theorie mentaler Repräsentation* (Paderborn: Mentis).

Metzinger, T. (1999b), 'Präsentationaler Gehalt', in *Bewußtsein und Repräsentation*, ed. F. Esken and D. Heckmann (Paderborn: Mentis), pp. 377–405.

Metzinger, T. (2000), 'The Subjectivity of subjective experience: A representational analysis of the first-person perspective', in *Neural Correlates of Consciousness: Empirical and Conceptual Questions*, ed. T. Metzinger (Cambridge, MA: The MIT Press), pp. 285–306 (*http://www.philosophie.uni-mainz.de/metzinger/publikationen, 20.6.2004*).

Metzinger, T. (2003a), *Being No One. The Self-Model Theory of Subjectivity* (Cambridge, MA/ London: The MIT Press).

Metzinger, T. (2003b), 'Phenomenal transparency and cognitive self-reference', *Phenomenology and Cognitive Science*, **2**, pp. 353–93.

Metzinger, T. (2003c), 'The pre-scientific concept of a "soul": A neurophenomenological hypothesis about its origin', in *Haben Computer eine Seele? Der Begriff der Seele Bd. IV*, ed. F.-M.

Peschl and H.-D. Klein (Würzburg: Königshausen & Neumann) (forthcoming), pp. 1–36 (*http://www.philosophie.uni-mainz.de/metzinger/publikationen, 20.6.2004*).

Metzinger, T. (2003d), 'Why are identity-disorders interesting for philosophers?', in *Philosophy and Psychiatry*, ed. T. Schramme and J. Thome (Berlin: de Gruyter) (forthcoming), pp. 1–29 (*http://www.philosophie.uni-mainz.de/metzinger/publikationen*).

Metzinger, T. and Gallese, V. (2003a), 'The emergence of a shared action ontology: Building blocks for a theory, *Consciousness and Cognition*, **12**, pp. 549–71.

Metzinger, T. and Gallese, V. (2003b), 'Motor ontology: The representational reality of goals, actions and selves', *Philosophical Psychology*, **16** (3), pp. 365–88.

Metzinger, T. and Walde, B. (2000), 'Commentary on Jakab's *Ineffability of Qualia*', *Consciousness and Cognition*, **7**, pp. 353–62.

Nagel, T. (1997), 'Why we can't understand thought from the outside', in T. Nagel, *The Last Word* (New York, Oxford: Oxford University Press).

Petitot, J., Varela, F.J., Pachoud, B. and Roy, J.-M. (ed. 1999), *Naturalizing Phenomenology: Issues in Contemporary Phenomenology and Cognitive Science* (Stanford CA: Stanford University Press).

Ricoeur, P. (1996), *Das Selbst als ein Anderer* (Munich: Wilhelm Fink).

Rinofner-Kreidl, S. (2000), *Edmund Husserl. Zeitlichkeit und Intentionalität* (Freiburg, Munich: Karl Alber).

Rinofner-Kreidl, S. (2003a), 'Do cognitive scientists succeed in naturalizing free will?', in *Persons. An Interdisciplinary Approach/Personen. Ein interdisziplinärer Dialog*, ed. C. Kanzian, J. Quitterer and E. Runggaldier (Vienna: Österreichischer Bundesverlag), pp. 222–31.

Rinofner-Kreidl, S. (2003b), *Mediane Phänomenologie. Subjektivität im Spannungsfeld von Naturalität und Kulturalität* (Würzburg: Königshausen & Neumann).

Rinofner-Kreidl, S. (2004), 'Das "Gehirn-Selbst". Ist die Erste-Person-Perspektive naturalisierbar?', *Phänomenologische Forschungen* (forthcoming).

Varela, F.J., Thompson, E. and Rosch, E. (1993), *The Embodied Mind: Cognitive Science and Human Experience* (Cambridge and London: The MIT Press).

Thompson, E., Lutz, A. and Cosmelli, D. (2004), 'Neurophenomenology: An introduction for neurophilosophers', in *Cognition and the Brain: The Philosophy and Neuroscience Movement*, ed. A. Brook and K. Akins (New York and Cambridge: Cambridge University Press) (forthcoming).

John J. Drummond

'Cognitive Impenetrability' and the Complex Intentionality of the Emotions

I

When a young boy playing in a wooded area, I tripped over exposed roots extending from the trunk of a tree. I threw my arms out in front of me to break my fall and disturbed a nest of bees. As I lay on the ground, I was repeatedly stung by bees until I could regain my feet and run away. Frightened and in a great deal of pain — that is what I remember most vividly — I walked home. My mother took me to the doctor, who undoubtedly gave me some sort of treatment and medication, but this has been lost to memory. The part of the visit to the doctor's office that I remember is his removing any stingers remaining in me; this too I remember for its pain. The doctor counted more than seventy stings. Although the exact number escapes memory, I believe it was seventy-one. In brief, the descriptive details of the day's experiences elude memory, but the affective dimension — the pain and fear — does not.

To this day I am fearful of bees. If approached by a bee, I get tense and anxious, fearing that the bee will sting me. And if there is a swarm of bees, my fright can grow into a mild panic. I know that my chances of being stung are slight. Indeed, I know that if I let the bees go about their business undisturbed, they will most likely just move on and I will emerge unharmed. While I have over the years learned to restrain my response to some degree, I still move away or try to chase the bee or bees away with somewhat frenzied motions. It can appear to observers that my fear is out of proportion to the situation I face when one or more bees approach. Indeed, this is how the situation appears even to myself.

Peter Goldie (2000) refers to this phenomenon as the 'cognitive impenetrability' of some emotions. Goldie uses examples involving cognitive impenetrability to stress the role that feelings play in the emotions and thereby to reveal the inadequacies of the belief-desire account of the emotions. The belief-desire account holds that the emotions are a conjunction of beliefs grounding a desire and that only the believing and desiring aspects of an emotion have intentional content (Kenny, 1963; Alston, 1967; Davidson, 1976; Taylor, 1976; 1985). On the belief-desire view, the feelings are non-essential to the intentionality of the emotions, mere supplements to emotional episodes that do not bear directly upon their intentional content. According to Goldie, such 'add-on views' (Goldie, 2000, p. 4) fail to capture the important role that feelings play in the emotions and their intentionality (Goldie, 2000, pp. 18–28, 37–47, 72–81).

Goldie distinguishes two kinds of feelings in an emotional episode: bodily feelings (intentionally related to the body) and 'feeling towards' (intentionally related to an object) (Goldie, 2000, pp. 19, 51–62; Goldie 2002, pp. 236–42). He by no means reduces emotions to feelings. Feeling towards is a 'thinking with feeling' (Goldie, 2000, 19, 71) that displays an object in a particular manner and involves perception, imagination or memory (Goldie, 2000, pp. 19–20, 72–4). An emotion, in other words, involves thoughts that are non-contingently related to the emotion, and certain kinds of determinate and determinable properties are related to particular emotions (Goldie, 2000, pp. 20–1). In fearing bees, for example, I believe that there is some determinate feature that bees possess — having a stinger — that makes them dangerous and objects of fear. On Goldie's account, it is possible for someone to have feelings towards something, say, fearing bees, and yet not believe that the affective property, say, dangerous, is a property ordinarily attributed to bees (Goldie, 2000, p. 74). Even while fearing bees, in other words, I believe that although they have stingers, they are unlikely to use them against me except in special circumstances.

My fear of bees is not irrational. It is intelligible insofar as it is motivated by past experience; there are reasons for my fear of bees, and these reasons coexist with *true* beliefs. There is neither false belief nor a conflict of beliefs. Hence, such an experience is not irrational, although everyone, even I, can recognize that it is, as Goldie puts it, 'inappropriate or disproportionate' (Goldie, 2000, pp. 23, 74). It is in this light that Goldie uses the expression 'cognitively impenetrable.' 'Someone's emotion or emotional experience is cognitively penetrable,' he says, 'only if it can be affected by his relevant beliefs' (Goldie, 2000, p. 76); hence, it is cognitively impenetrable when it cannot be affected by relevant beliefs.

Goldie's carefully nuanced and sensitive account of the emotions is largely descriptive in character, and as such, invites reflection from a phenomenological point of view. Phenomenology is also descriptive, but its descriptions are not, as Goldie's are, psychological and causal. To discern the causalities operative in the world, including the causalities operative between objects and subjects as particular entities in the world, presupposes a certain kind of experience of the world on the basis of which we posit causal relations between worldly existents. Psychology with its causal explanations cannot give an account of that world that is always already present to us before we begin to frame our causal explanations. Psychological explanations, in other words, account for the subject that is an entity among other entities *in* the world, but psychological explanations alone cannot reveal the subject *of* the world, the subject whose intentional experience first brings a world to disclosure. Intentionality is the proper theme of phenomenology, and intentionality is puzzling precisely because in intending objects the subject is not in a causal relation with them, but is instead directed to them in their significance for us, i.e., *as* something.

Phenomenology, then, involves a particular kind of non-psychological reflection that describes the intentional correlation between (a) the subjective performances in which objects are disclosed as having a certain significance and (b) these objects precisely as disclosed. It thereby identifies the conditions that make it possible for objects and a world to be experienced — to disclose themselves — as having the significance they have for us. Phenomenology explores the internal unity of subject and object as experienced rather than taking subject and object as externally, i.e., causally, related entities. This does not mean that phenomenological reflection is introspective; it is concerned not to identify the features of the reflecting subject's experience, but to identify the *essential* structures of experience and of objects as disclosed by the intentionalities at work in different kinds of experience as lived by any experiencing subject, not just the reflecting subject. The phenomenologist must describe how a world filled with physical, affective, practical, and cultural significance is disclosed by consciousness without presupposing psychological explanations that cannot get off the ground apart from the more fundamental experience of the world that psychology takes for granted.

In what follows I shall present an account of the emotions that is rooted in the phenomenological tradition, in particular the work of Edmund Husserl and Adolf Reinach. This account will in many ways be similar to Goldie's, but the phenomenological approach provides resources that supplement and complement Goldie's account. I shall elaborate the intentionality involved in emotional experience (a) by providing in section II a more detailed account of the affective dimension of the emotions, (b) by considering in section III the pre-reflective self-awareness that belongs to our object-directed emotional experiences, and (c) by exploring in section IV the temporality of the emotions. Finally, I shall in section V sketch an account of how this more robust account of the intentionality of emotional experience allows us to understand the phenomenon of cognitive impenetrability as well as one's own awareness that a cognitively impenetrable emotional response is inappropriate to the circumstances.

II

Husserl's phenomenology of the emotions is rooted in Brentano's claim that emotive acts are founded in 'presentations' (Brentano, 1995, pp. 45, 80, 276). To say that B is founded upon A means (1) that B presupposes A as necessary for it and (2) that B builds itself upon A so as to form a unity with it. However, the term 'presentation' is ambiguous (Husserl, 1984, pp. 496–515; 1970, pp. 636–48). A presentation can be a complete experience — a perceiving, remembering, imagining, or judging — that presents an object with a particular set of descriptive properties. Husserl calls such experiences 'objectifying acts' (Husserl, 1984, pp. 500–1; 1970, p. 639). For example, I see the growling dog or judge that the dog is growling. Presentations of this sort can be analysed into their type — perceiving or judging — and their material content. But the term 'presentation' can also refer more narrowly just to the material content that accounts for the object's being presented in the determinate way that it is (Husserl, 1984, pp. 474–6, 514; 1970, pp. 620–1, 648). The significance of this narrower sense of 'presentation' for the foundational claim is that experiences that are not themselves objectifying acts must be founded not on another *act*, but on a matter — a presentational or descriptive content — of the sort that belongs to an objectifying act. Put another way, the foundational claim states that any act founded on a presentation — e.g., fearing — comprises a matter (the dog's growling) identical to that of the objectifying intention (the hearing) that presents the merely descriptive features of the object in just that determinate manner present in the founded act as well. In the case of the emotions, the founded emotional experience then discloses additional determinations of the object — say, the growling dog's being dangerous — determinations related to the affective dimension of experience.

Husserl's later reinterprets the material content of a presentation as the 'sense' belonging to the intentional correlate of the experience (Husserl, 1976, p. 298; 1983, p. 310). The more precise foundational claim stated above can then be restated as follows: the presentational sense, i.e., the sense-content presenting the merely 'descriptive' properties of the thing (the dog as growling), founds a sense-content presenting the affective characteristics of the thing (the growling dog as dangerous), and these senses can in turn found a motivational sense-content. The concrete experience takes its name from the highest, founded levels of sense within the complete sense the object has for us in that experience, i.e., when the affective sense is the highest, the experience is emotional and evaluative, and when the motivational sense is highest, the experience is volitional and practical (Husserl, 1976, pp. 220–1; 1983, pp. 231–2; 1988, pp. 252–7). It is possible, of course, to put our feelings and desires aside such that we experience the object purely cognitively. We would then experience it in an objectifying act as a thing without worth for us.

A merely objectifying act, however, is an abstraction. As Husserl puts it:

> All life is an incessant striving; all gratification a transitory gratification. Mere sensation-data and, at a higher level, sensory objects, as things that are there for the subject but there 'value-free' are abstractions. There can be nothing that does not affect the feelings, and the indifferent is merely an intermediate phase between attraction and aversion; something is neither attractive nor aversive in the same sense that an object is neither warm nor cold, neither large nor small, and so forth.'[1]

---

[1] Unpublished Ms. A VI 26, 42a. The text is difficult to date. Ullrich Melle of the Husserl-Archief in Leuven guesses, based on the content of the manuscript and the context of the folio in which it is found, that it is from the early 1920s, but perhaps, given a brief note written on the back of the page, as early as 1918. But no certainty as to the date is possible. I thank Professor Melle for his assistance in attempting to date the manuscript, and I thank Professor Rudolf Bernet, the director of the Husserl-Archief in Leuven, for permission to quote the manuscript.

Similarly, he says, 'Everything that is touches our feelings; every existent is apperceived in a value-apperception and thereby awakens desirous attitudes (*begehrende Stellungnahmen*)' (Husserl, 1973, pp. 404–5). Things and circumstances *from the beginning* appear to us as likeable or not, useful or not, pleasurable or not, safe or dangerous, joyous or sad, and so on. Actions and agents *from the beginning* appear as noble, virtuous, generous, honest, just, compassionate, hospitable, friendly, base, vicious, rancorous, spiteful, mean-spirited, treacherous, and so on.

My cognitively impenetrable fear of bees (example A) is an example of an experience comprising presentational, affective, and motivational moments.[2] I at once see the bee approaching, fear it, and am motivated to move myself away or to wave it away. So too does a cognitively penetrable experience comprise presentational, affective, and motivational moments. Consider, for example, the case (example B) in which I turn a corner only to find an apparently angered Doberman Pinscher in front of me. This very large, powerful dog pulls its ears back, bares its teeth, and starts to growl. In a single, complex experience I see the large and powerful dog with its ears pulled back and its teeth bared, hear the dog growl, feel the tensing of my muscles, negatively value what produces this affect, experience fear, and am motivated to flee or to stand perfectly still hoping the dog will ignore me. In both these examples, the presentational sense is highly determined, i.e., I clearly recognize the descriptive features underlying my response, the affective moment is vivid, and the motivational moment has a certain urgency to it.

Not all our immediate experiences need have this balance among the three moments. It is possible that the motivational moment disappears or, perhaps better, approaches the vanishing point. I might simply enjoy the moment when (example C) I am witnessing a spectacular sunset. The most we can say, perhaps, is that I am motivated only to continue in the experience. There is also a sense — albeit counterintuitive — in which the presentational sense disappears from the experience. I think, however, that this is a misleading way to view a particular kind of example. Suppose (example D) I am at a reception and am introduced to someone to whom I take an immediate and strong dislike. It is just this feature of some affective responses that can suggest to us that the emotions can present the value or disvalue of an object prior to cognition (Scheler, 1980, p. 40; 1973a, p. 18; Goldie, 2000, p. 45).[3] In one way, this is true; I do not explicitly know and cannot tell you exactly why I dislike this person. What I am suggesting, however,

---

[2] The term 'moment' refers throughout the paper to a part that is non-independent relative to the whole of which it is a part. A moment, in other words, is an abstract part or abstract content that cannot exist apart from other parts with which it forms a concrete whole. Moments are non-independent, therefore, in relation both to one another and to the whole that they compose. Moments supplement one another necessarily, and it is this notion of necessary supplementation that defines Husserl's notion of their non-independence.

[3] Scheler also claims that emotional intentionality has a cognitive content and that the logic of value is independent of the logic of reason. But it is hard to understand how the priority of the experience of value allows for cognitive content and how the logic of value would apply to the cognitive content of our evaluations and to the rational criticism and guidance of our actions. It is difficult, in other words,

is that this is only apparently the case, because the presentational sense is highly indeterminate and vague but not absent. While the features to which I am affectively responding have not been raised to the level of explicit cognition, I am nevertheless aware of the person in certain ways; I am reacting or responding to something. When the person 'just' strikes me in an unpleasant way, there is something about the way he carries himself or his manner in responding to the introduction that affects me. I am indeterminately aware of what I *could* — but do not in this case — determine to be a haughty air about the person, and it is just this air that motivates my response. The *determination* in the presentational sense can vary considerably, even to the point of approaching the vanishing point, but it does not actually vanish.

If we abstract from the motivational moment, the basic — but still overly simplified — view is, in Husserl's terms, that the sense of an object as disclosed by an emotion comprises presentational (cognitive) and affective (evaluative) senses with the former grounding the latter, a structure to which Goldie refers as the tie between recognition and response (Goldie, 2000, pp. 45–7). However, we must more precisely analyse the affective moment. As previously mentioned, Goldie distinguishes two kinds of feelings in the response: bodily feelings, especially our feeling the visceral changes that occur in the body when experiencing an emotion, and feeling towards, the thinking with feeling that is directed toward the object. This distinction parallels Husserl's distinction between feeling-sensations and feeling-acts (Husserl, 1984, pp. 406–9; 1970, pp. 572–5). Feeling-sensations are those sensory experiences, e.g., the feelings that accompany visceral changes, that we locate in the body and that belong to our prereflective bodily self-awareness, although Husserl does not consider them intentional even in relation to presentations of the body. In some cases, of course, as in the case of the pain we feel when we burn ourselves, they can become involved in an intentional relatedness to our own bodies taken as the object of a reflective regard, but they can be felt in the body without our attention turning to our bodies. Such is the case in examples A and B when I feel the tensing of my muscles when the bee approaches or I come upon the Doberman. But I do not attend to my body; my attention remains fixed on the bees or the dog. The feeling- sensations or bodily feelings are not *as such* presentations of the *object* that arouses them. Feeling-sensations can be characterized primarily in terms of *my* pleasure and pain. Feeling-acts, on the other hand, have an intentional direction to the object. The object that gives us pleasure we find likeable and value positively; the object that gives us pain we find unlikeable and value negatively.

I shall use the term 'intentional' in a narrower sense of 'directed to *an object*' (intentional$_o$) and a broader sense of 'tending toward' or 'directed to' that involves a non-thematized and non-objectifying awareness (intentional$_d$). Hence, we can reinterpret Husserl's claim to mean that feeling-sensations are non-intentional$_o$ and that feeling-acts are intentional$_o$. There are, then, in the

to see how on Scheler's view a cognitive content *effectively* enters our evaluations (cf. Scheler, 1980, pp. 68–101; 1973a, pp. 48–81; 1973b, p. 117; 1979, p. 362).

emotive experience both (a) a set of $intentional_d$ feelings of our own bodily states, i.e., feelings that are not intentionally referred *to the object,* although they are involved in our pre-reflective, non-thematic bodily self-awareness (which can be thematized in turning my attention to the body in grasping it, say, as injured), and (b) an $intentional_o$ feeling (a feeling towards or feeling-act) aimed at the object whose affection of the self motivates the $intentional_d$ feelings. Husserl leaves open the inference that the feeling-act completes the emotional experience, and Goldie seems to believe that the feeling towards, the thinking with feeling, completes what he calls the emotional episode. The episode is distinguished from the emotion proper. Whereas the episode is just that — episodic and transitory — the emotion is complex, dynamic and enduring, involving many different episodes, periods of intensity and of dormancy, different perceptions, beliefs, images, and feelings (Goldie, 2000, pp. 12–13, 68–9).

The $intentional_o$ feeling, however, even when considered as inclusive of its underlying presentational content, should be distinguished from both the emotional episode and the emotion proper. For the moment I shall focus on the emotional episode. Following Reinach (1989, I, p. 295), I shall call (b) the $intentional_o$ feeling an 'apprehending feeling' *(erfassende Fühlen).* Apprehending feelings typically lack specific names but are, as we have seen, most broadly characterized as like or dislike; we apprehend the object as likeable or not. Apprehending feelings are directed back to the object, grasping it as valuable or not on the basis of its descriptive properties and the pleasurable or painful character of our felt, bodily reaction thereto. In example B, the presentational content of the large, powerful, toothy, and growling Doberman, along with the (unpleasant) tensing of the muscles underlies my dislike, my negative evaluation, of the situation. This dislike is $intentional_o$; it discloses the situation as unlikeable. But we do not yet have the emotion, the fear, itself.

Before turning to the complete emotional episode, I must emphasize that we must be careful not to distinguish these different kinds of feelings too sharply; they are intertwined with one another in complex and various ways. Indeed, they are the same feelings considered in two different relations, once in relation to the body and once in relation to the object. They are, in other words, feelings that are at work simultaneously in bodily self-awareness ($intentional_d$) and in object-awareness ($intentional_o$), and this is why we name them differently — pleasure or pain in the former relation and like or dislike (of the object) in the latter relation.

The bodily, $intentional_d$ feelings are likely insufficient to determine any particular emotional episode, since different emotions can share the same bodily feelings. For example, in both anger and fear I experience the tightening of the muscles around the stomach. More generally, the range of bodily feelings directed to visceral changes in the body seems much narrower than the range of emotions. More importantly, however, the bodily feelings with their $intentionality_d$ cannot alone account for the more specific $intentionality_o$ of the emotion. For a particular emotion to arise, cognitive and contextual factors must come into play such that I experience anger at the cognized wrongdoing I have suffered at someone's hands or I experience fear in the cognized situation I encounter. Similarly, the apprehending feeling is insufficient to determine the emotional episode, since liking and disliking are characteristic of the whole class of emotions.

There is, therefore, in the emotional experience (c) a third affective aspect in addition to (a) the bodily feelings and (b) the apprehending feeling. Again following Reinach, I call this third aspect an 'emotional condition' *(zuständliches Gefühl)*. The emotional condition is a condition of the subject, and again one that is intentional$_o$. Emotional conditions do have specific names, and these names tell us not simply about how we are valuing the object, but also something new about both the object of our experience and ourselves. The emotional condition intends the particular affective properties of the situation beyond its merely being likeable or dislikeable, valued or disvalued. In examples A and B, the emotional condition is fear, and the situation is disclosed not merely as negative, as unlikeable, but, more particularly, as dangerous; I do not merely dislike the displeasing situation, but am fearful of the danger. In example C, the emotional condition is (contemplative) joy, and the sunset is disclosed as beautiful, whereas in example D, the emotional condition is antipathy and the person is disclosed as disfavoured.

Once again we must be careful not to separate the apprehending feeling and the emotional condition too sharply. It is, nevertheless, worthwhile distinguishing them, since it is possible to have an apprehending feeling without the arousal of a full-blown emotion. If, for example, I cook myself a dinner that I find satiating and pleasing, and therefore positively value the dinner, I need not move beyond finding the meal pleasing and likeable. I need not, in other words, experience joy or elation in the meal.

Damasio (1994) has argued that feelings are an integral part of practical reasoning, a view that is consonant with the view presented here, since, I have claimed, the motivational moment of experience is founded on the affective and evaluative. The emotions display the value or disvalue of things and situations, and underlie the desires that motivate us to act for certain ends. But I must note important differences between the views presented here and Damasio's. In the first place, there are significant terminological differences. Damasio claims that the emotion is the underlying phenomenon, a set of primarily visceral bodily changes, and that feelings are our awareness of the emotions. But for both Goldie and myself the emotion is neither the bodily changes themselves nor feelings of those changes, but is grounded in those feelings. Moreover, Damasio's view is reminiscent of William James's view (James, 1950, II, p. 449), although again the terminology is reversed. For Damasio, feelings — or at least some feelings — originate in emotions and are our not yet self-conscious feeling (intentional$_d$?) of the originating emotion (Damasio 1994, chap. 7; 1999, pp. 8, 36–8, 279ff,; 2003, pp. 29–30). However, even if Damasio provides an account of pre-reflective bodily awareness, his account of feelings leaves unclear both the exact relation between body and mind (which is distinguished from the brain but, nevertheless, always spoken of in neurophysiological terms) and, even more importantly from my perspective, the intentionality$_o$ of the emotions.

III

The involvement of feelings within an emotional experience means that the emotions necessarily involve a first-person perspective. Goldie (2000, pp. 1–2, 41, 82–3) insists on this point, and it is also an essential aspect of the phenomenological perspective that considers objects in relation to the experiences in which objects are disclosed in determinate ways. There are two aspects of this first-personal perspective in emotional experiences that warrant further consideration. The first concerns the kind of self-awareness that arises with emotional experience, and we shall consider this issue in this section. The second concerns the fact that any emotional experience takes its place within the history of a particular subject's experience, and this requires that in the next section we briefly consider the temporality of emotional experience.

In examples A and B the affective disclosure of the situation as dangerous cannot be understood apart from the fact that the situation is dangerous *to me*. While Goldie recognizes this, he underestimates its significance. Goldie claims that feeling towards, thinking of something with feeling, is directed toward objects (intentional$_o$) and 'is part of one's consciousness of the world with which one is emotionally engaged' (Goldie, 2000, p. 64). It is, he says, an 'unreflective emotional engagement with the world beyond the body; it is not a consciousness of oneself, either of one's bodily condition or of oneself *as* experiencing an emotion' (Goldie, 2002, p. 241). He distinguishes this unreflective object-directed consciousness from what he calls reflective consciousness. As examples of reflective consciousness he cites: 'being aware that I feel afraid; being aware that I feel afraid of the oncoming vehicle; and being aware that I am thinking of the oncoming vehicle as out of control; and as something to be avoided — that I am thinking of it in that special emotionally engaged way which is feeling fear of it' (Goldie, 2000, p. 64). For Goldie our self-awareness as experiencing an emotion is an intentional$_o$, reflective self-consciousness.

Goldie's concern, I take it, is to stress the fact that our emotional encounters are often focused exclusively on the object and that I do not thematize my own condition. This is true. Nevertheless, in fearing the bee or the dog, I am pre-reflectively and non-thematically aware of *my* fearing the dog; otherwise, *I* would not be fearing it. This claim simply specifies the general phenomenological claim that object-awareness (intentional$_o$) always and necessarily involves pre-reflective self-awareness (intentional$_d$) (Zahavi, 1999, pp. 19, 23–4). In fearing the bee or the dog, I feel the tensing of *my* muscles, and I am aware of *my* fearing the bee or dog without my attention being turned explicitly either to my bodily feelings or to my fear. Goldie is correct that we can be unreflectively engaged with the world without reflective self-awareness, but we cannot be unreflectively engaged with the world without a pre-reflective awareness of that engagement. Otherwise, *I* am simply not engaged. I cannot fear the bees without being pre-reflectively aware of *my fearing* them.

This first-personal relation of emotional experiences and the pre-reflective self-awareness that attaches to them should not be taken to suggest that the experience of fear is purely subjective. The disclosure of the situation as dangerous to me is available not only to me. It is objective in its own way. The situation's being dangerous and my being fearful of the danger are characteristics of the worldly situation for anyone experiencing my encounter with bees or with the Doberman. You see me duck away from the approaching bee and taking actions to avoid it or chase it away; you see my body stiffen and my muscles tense in my reaction to the presence of the Doberman. You recognize, in other words, that I encounter these situations as dangerous and that they are fearful for me. This is perfectly consonant with your not fearing the hovering bee or with your not fearing the Doberman that cannot see, reach, and harm you.

Along with this objectivity comes an appropriate normativity. The rootedness of fear in certain descriptive properties and the correlation between fear and something's being dangerous means that at one and the same time I learn both certain features of the world and the appropriate emotional responses and evaluations (Goldie, 2000, pp. 30–1). I thereby become habituated to have certain emotions upon encountering certain objects or situations. These habituated emotional conditions are emotional states, and they shape new encounters we have. Emotional states inform our experiences such that we immediately recognize what is evaluatively salient in the object or situation. When I round that corner and encounter the Doberman in its agitated state, I immediately experience fear and recognize the danger. But I not only *do* fear the Doberman in its agitated state, I *ought* to recognize the danger and experience fear. If I do not, I am impervious to the 'true' character of the situation. This normativity of the emotions is tied to our awareness of the correctness or appropriateness of our emotional responses, and I shall return to this issue in section V.

IV

To say that an emotional experience is first-personal is to say that it is related to a particular person with determinate instincts, interests, personal history, communal traditions, and so forth. The importance of this point is obvious, for without reference to the subject's instincts, interests, history, traditions, etc., the structural characteristics of emotional experiences outlined in the preceding sections do not allow us to distinguish the cognitively impenetrable example A from the cognitively penetrable example B. The cognitively impenetrable emotion is one I *should not* feel given the objective circumstances, and something in *my* experience must account for the impenetrability of *my* emotion.

Goldie recognizes the importance of the temporality of the emotions in the importance he places on the notion of narrative. Narrative is central to Goldie's account of how we understand the emotions of ourselves and others. The emotions, for Goldie, take their place in a narrative unity that ties together the individual episodes of emotional experience, and we understand different emotional episodes or emotions in terms of their place in this unity (Goldie, 2000, pp. 4–5, 33). To understand and explain an emotional experience, including cognitively impenetrable emotions, requires not only that we recognize that a person is experiencing a particular emotion — by, for example, noting their bodily reactions (Goldie, 2000, p. 182) — but that we provide an account that places the experience in the context of that person's life-narrative (Goldie, 2000, pp. 5, 35, 181–9).

Goldie's appeal to narrative, however, is problematic. Narratives are reflective selections and organizations of a life. In this sense the narrative captures less than an individual's life, for not all of a life as pre-reflectively lived can be fitted into a narrative, which best suits goal-directed action.[4] From the opposite perspective, narratives, by virtue of their selectivity, impose more unity than life itself has manifested. The narrative makes sense of emotional experiences and emotional states, but only *ex post facto* and in reflection. But we should not confuse the reflective, narrative grasp of a life with an account of the pre-reflective experience that makes up that life prior to that experience being organized into a narrative. The narrative account is inadequate to identify the structures and conditions that make possible our emotions, including those that irrupt our ongoing narratives and are subsequently captured in new narratives. Narratives fall short of clarifying the emotional experience *as lived,* and in particular, they fall short of differentiating the cognitively penetrable from the cognitively impenetrable *as lived.*

Accounting for the richness and spontaneity of emotional conditions and states as lived requires an expanded sense of the intentionality$_d$ involved in emotional conditions. This expansion leads us to Husserl's accounts of the temporality of experience and of association, which Husserl regards as an extension of his account of temporality (Husserl, 1966, p. 118; 2001, p. 163). It should be noted in passing, that this account also makes clear how the life-narratives to which Goldie turns are themselves possible.

In experiencing an object, I am conscious of an object that has temporal determinations (processive or enduring) and of an experience that also has an enduring temporality. Husserl distinguishes in the momentary phase of consciousness three intentional moments that make possible this experience of succession.[5] The first is the primal impression in which consciousness is affected, in which it turns toward that which affects it, and is pre-reflectively aware of its turning. In primal impression, therefore, we find an intentional$_d$ aspect in which consciousness is aware of itself as experiencing the affecting object and an intentional$_o$ aspect in which it directs itself to an object. There must, however, be more to any phase of consciousness than the impressional moment in which affection occurs, otherwise the awareness of temporal objects would not be possible, for there would be

[4] Blattner (2000) argues against the adequacy of narrative, even multiple narratives, as accounting for the kind of lives that humans lead.

[5] Brough (1972; 1989; 1991) provides excellent accounts of the development and details of Husserl's views of time-consciousness.

simply a succession of awarenesses and not the awareness of succession. Hence, the momentary phase of consciousness must also include intentional references to elapsed and yet-to-come phases of experiences in the intentional$_d$ moments that Husserl calls 'retention' and 'protention'. The second moment of any momentary phase of consciousness is, therefore, retention in which consciousness is directed to (intends$_d$) elapsed phases of experience, and the third moment is protention in which the momentary phase intends$_d$ yet-to-come phases of experience. Retention holds on to past phases of experience that themselves have this tri-partite structure, and the retention of retentions ensures therefore that we preserve these phases in their experiential order. Protention, on the other, tends forward to yet-to-come phases and, influenced both by what has been retained and by practical interests, desires, and moods, anticipates new appearances. Because retention and protention intend$_d$ experiential phases having this same tri-partite structure including primal impression, retention and protention indirectly contribute to the intending$_o$ of the object. Hearing the opening bars of Beethoven's Fifth Symphony provides a clear example of how, several bars into the piece, what we have already heard forms a unity in the present with what we actually hear now and with what we know is to come. We are perceptually directed to the whole of the piece, even though we have not yet actually and presently heard the whole.

Primal impression, retention, and protention are not three temporally distinct moments, but three unified moments of a whole that, while not itself temporal, temporalizes our experience and makes possible both our self-awareness as a temporal being and the awareness of objects having temporal characteristics.[6] There are, in other words, two different kinds of intentionality present: an object-intentionality that involves a certain alterity affecting consciousness and to which consciousness explicitly directs itself as the accusative of consciousness, and a non-intentional$_o$, self-directed-intentionality$_d$. I am non-thematically and pre-reflectively aware of temporally individuated experiences of objects as *mine*, and I am pre-reflectively aware of my experiences as forming a synthetic unity, i.e., I am non-thematically aware of *myself* as a flowing unity of experiences. I am aware of myself not as a reflectively focused accusative of consciousness but, so to speak, as the genitive of consciousness. It is, then, this structure of the momentary phase of consciousness that underlies the pre-reflective self-awareness that belongs to our object-directed experiences and that was discussed in the previous section.

------

[6] The Husserlian account of what he calls 'absolute consciousness' (cf. Brough, 1972) as a non-temporal, but temporalizing form underlies Heidegger's account of the *ek-stases* of time; cf. Heidegger (1967), pp. 328–9; (1962), pp. 376–8. Whereas Husserl in accounting for our awareness of temporal objects focuses most of his attention on the retentional moment, Heidegger in accounting for the temporality of care emphasizes the futural moment. In addition, by explicitly introducing mood and care as fundamental, Heidegger unfolds the direction to the future as something more than the projection of past patterns of experience into the future. Husserl's discussions of temporality only occasionally explicitly acknowledge the role of interests and emotions in temporal and associative syntheses, but if we return to his claim that nothing fails to affect the emotions, there is room to build such an account into his thinking.

The same structure underlies Husserl's account of association. Retention and protention operate not only over just elapsed and immediately yet-to-come phases of experience. What is given in primal impression can motivate the recollection — better, re-collection — of past phases of experience into the present so that these past experiences inform and shape the present experience. But re-collection is not memory, which indexes the object of its attention as past. Present experiences can trigger memories, but in the associative re-collection of past experiences as informing my present experience, my attention does not turn away from the present object or state of affairs to the past. I do not actively remember; I passively re-collect. What is re-collected, along with my interests, attitudes, and volitions, shapes my sense of what it is I experience and, again without a change of temporal index to the future, shapes my sense of how my present experience will unfold.

It is a mistake to think of these associative processes as mechanical; they are a matter of intentionality. It is a mistake also to think of them exclusively in terms of contiguity and resemblance; patterns of intentional association can also involve, for example, analogy and metaphor, or they can weave together only loosely related experiences that lead me to see the present object or situation in a new light. The affection in the present, the re-collection into the present, and the tending in the present toward what is yet to come form a unity in which an object or situation is presented to me all at once — an intentionally woven fabric — without any explicit awareness or thematizing of the various parts that make up the concrete experience. My attention remains fixed on the object or situation with its unitary meaning and not on the experiences re-collectively and anticipatorily woven together.

This sketch of the importance of temporality and association in Husserl illuminates the distinction between cognitively penetrable and cognitively impenetrable emotions. When a bee approaches me, I do not need to remember that I was once stung over seventy times in order for fear to arise in me. The sight of the bee passively re-collects that previous experience into the present and informs my present encounter of the bee. Upon seeing the bee, the vivid painfulness of the retained and re-collected experience affects me anew and regenerates the bodily feelings, the apprehending feeling tied thereto, and the emotion — fear — appropriate to that apprehending feeling and my present situation. My present experience of bees is so marked by that re-collected experience that I respond emotionally in the present in a manner suitable to the re-collected experience rather than to the cognitive content of the present experience.

These passive associations arise not only in relation to our own, personal stream of experience. They arise as well in relation to passively received social and cultural beliefs and traditions handed down to us in our upbringing and education. The manner in which I am raised within my familial, social, and cultural contexts affects my manner of experiencing the world and my manner of thinking. Hence, as we have seen, my learning certain features of the world is tied to my learning what my culture considers appropriate emotional responses to those same features. In learning about the world, I learn which situations merit fear and which do not, which situations merit anger and which do not, which situations merit compassion and which do not, and so forth. And in the case of example A, the education of the emotions I received conflicts with what my own emotional experience tells me. This conflict helps us to understand how cognitive impenetrability arises. I learn — in part on the basis of this education — what I should fear and when, but the primary associations at work in my re-calling my awful encounter with bees as a young boy conflict with this. The primary associations produce the kind of bodily feelings and apprehending feeling appropriate to fear despite my having the correct, culturally transmitted beliefs about fear.

V

We have previously noted that in experiencing a cognitively impenetrable emotion, I can be aware of its 'inappropriateness'. The analyses presented so far account for the possibility of the cognitively impenetrable experience, but they do not account for my own awareness of its inappropriateness at the moment in which the experience is lived. For this, we must turn to a discussion of the normativity of the emotions. How is it that I recognize that the emotion I experience does not satisfy the norm for a particular emotion? What are the grounds *in the lived experience itself,* i.e., prior to reflection, for distinguishing between warranted and unwarranted responses? Or, to put the matter differently, what constitutes the 'truthfulness' of the emotions?

Husserl thinks that there is a special kind of evidence that confirms the 'truthfulness' or 'rationality' or 'appropriateness' of our emotional experiences (Husserl, 1952, p. 9; 1989, p. 10). However, we must distinguish two senses of 'evidence'. The first is the ordinary sense of a datum that counts for a belief and thus provides a reason for accepting that belief as true. The second, more fundamental sense is the intentional experience that takes something *as* such a datum. This means that evidential experiences are always paired with mere intendings, say, judging (without evidence) that S is p. The evidencing experience then directly grasps the fact that S is actually p and thereby confirms the judgment, or it directly grasps that S is r — a disconfirming experience. In the case of emotional experiences, the case is similar. An emotive evidence directly grasps that S is actually, say, dangerous or not; the direct experience confirms or disconfirms the apprehension of the affective property of the object.

Insofar as emotional experiences involve presentational and affective moments, we must in considering the 'evidence' for the 'truthtfulness', 'rationality' or 'appropriateness' of our emotional responses consider not only the presentational dimension but the affective. In confirming our emotional experiences, we evidentially encounter at the presentational level the veridicality of our grasp of the thing's descriptive properties or the truth of the cognitions underlying the emotion and we evidentially experience at the affective level the appropriateness of our emotional grasp of the thing's affective properties.

The simplest case in which an emotion might be 'irrational' or unwarranted is when the presentational moment is non-veridical. For example, if Joe is angry at

Mary for spreading false rumours about him behind his back, it can turn out that Joe's belief that Mary was spreading false rumours is itself false. Once Joe discovers this, his anger toward Mary disappears (although he is undoubtedly still angry that someone is spreading the rumours). In this case, the course of experience — much as occurs with simple cognition — will introduce cognitive elements that are disharmonious with the cognitive content underlying the emotion, and we critically reflect on both the cognitions and the emotion rooted in them. Indeed, it is right to say that Joe *should not* be angry with Mary.

This example, however, does not help us understand our lived recognition of cognitively impenetrable emotions precisely because they are characterized by true belief. So we must consider the case wherein the presentational moment underlying the emotion is veridical, but the emotion is nevertheless an 'irrational', unwarranted, or inappropriate response. In example A, my fear is not so much cognitively irrational as just exaggerated and inappropriate, 'affectively irrational' we might say. I do feel fear, and there are reasons for my feeling fear. Nevertheless, we can still say that I *should not* feel fear, that there is really nothing to fear from the bee. What, when the beliefs underlying the emotion are true, counts as evidence against the cognitively impenetrable emotion such that I can pre-reflectively recognize the inappropriateness of the emotion in the lived emotion itself?

We can uncover this dimension of emotive evidence by appealing to our pre-reflective self-awareness, which, like our awareness of the world, is in our ordinary experience imbued with affective dimensions. We intend$_d$ our own emotional condition in a feeling of approbation or disapprobation, and along with that apprehending feeling, experience self-directed emotions: pride, embarrassment, shame, and guilt (cf. Taylor, 1985). This is why we think that the emotions ordered toward the world tell us much about ourselves and our character; they are themselves valued in these self-regarding emotions.

When I am flailing my arms in order to chase away a bee while knowing that it is unlikely that the bee will harm me, I experience a certain measure of embarrassment both about my fear of bees and my behaviour. I feel my own emotional condition unlikeable and am embarrassed. Feelings of self-disapprobation and related emotional conditions such as embarrassment, shame, and guilt disclose the fact that the underlying emotional condition is unwarranted and inappropriate; feelings of approbation and related emotional conditions such as pride, on the other hand, disclose the fact that our underlying condition is warranted.

These examples point, then, to different ways in which a critical reason can enter into our emotional experience. In short, both disharmony in the presentational dimension of the original emotional disclosure (as in Joe's anger at Mary) and a negatively affective dimension of my self-awareness (as in my embarrassment about my fear of bees) can motivate reflection on the object-directed emotion that originally discloses the situation in which the subject is involved. The normative character of certain emotional responses is revealed in these critical reflections upon our emotional experiences and our intersubjective working out of what emotions are appropriate for what circumstances.[7]

In summary, we can identify three points where reason — understood in the broad, Husserlian sense as the achievement of evidencing experiences — enters our experience of the emotions. Reason enters, first, in confirming the presentational content of the emotional experience; we evidentially experience the veridicality of the presentations or beliefs underlying the affective response. Reason enters, second, in our evidentially experiencing the fitness of the emotional condition experienced to the underlying descriptive properties. This experience of fitness is, as we have seen, related to the context in which we experience the value and to the education of the emotions handed down to us by the traditions in which we were raised. Reason enters for a third time in our evidentially experiencing our own emotional condition in a feeling of approbation or disapprobation. In example A, I feel my own emotional condition unlikeable and experience embarrassment. This second emotional condition of embarrassment discloses the fact that my first emotional condition, i.e., my fearing bees as dangerous, is inappropriate. These self-approbative and self-disapprobative experiences of our own emotional conditions themselves have intersubjective contexts. Our sense of what is embarrassing or shameful is formed in part by received traditions and is constantly renewed and revised by new experiences as our sense of the propriety of emotional responses is challenged, subjected to critical reflection, and developed or revised.

This paper has claimed that the phenomenon of cognitive impenetrability requires a consideration of how it is possible to have true presentations but a 'mistaken' emotion grounded therein. While psychological explanations and narratives such as Goldie's provide one kind of understanding of our emotions, including cognitively impenetrable ones, they do not, I believe, provide a full account of emotional experiences as lived. In particular, the phenomenological account provided herein has clarified the relations among bodily feelings, apprehending feelings, and emotional conditions. The emotional episode is more that the feeling-towards or the apprehending feeling, since these characterize the whole class of emotions and do not distinguish particular emotions.

More importantly, however, the account presented herein surpasses Goldie's account in its discussion of the temporality of the emotions and the role of association in the lived experience of cognitively impenetrable emotions. For Goldie, our understanding of such emotions is revealed in narratives that are grasped in intentional$_o$ reflections. But this means that our understanding of the emotion is necessarily after the fact. Nor does the narrative clarify the conditions that make possible cognitively impenetrable experiences. The phenomenological analyses of temporality and association identify the intentional$_d$ conditions that must be satisfied in order for a cognitively impenetrable emotion to be possible at all.

---

[7]   I have elsewhere suggested, but did not develop, this idea of axiological intuitions as complex experiences involving both cognitive and emotional legitimation and as confirming value-judgments in the moral sphere; cf. Drummond (2002a), p. 40; an earlier statement of the idea can be found in Drummond (2002b), pp. 184–6.

Finally, while narratives might help us to achieve an *explicit* understanding of the cognitively impenetrable emotion, it is also the case that in the experience itself I can evidentially recognize that my emotion is inappropriate. The phenomenological account of the affective dimension of our intentional$_d$ self-awareness provides the account of the *lived* experience of the recognition of the inappropriateness of my emotion. In addition, along with the account of association, it underlies the possibility of providing a narrative that clarifies this inappropriateness. It is these analyses of the intentionality$_d$, temporality, association, and self-awareness at work in our emotional experience that provide the supplements and complements to Goldie's account of the emotions.

References

Alston, W.P. (1967), 'Emotion and feeling', in *The Encyclopedia of Philosophy,* Vol. 2 (New York: Macmillan).

Blattner, W.D. (2000), 'Life is not literature', in *The Many Faces of Time,* ed. J. Brough and L.Embree (Dordrecht: Kluwer Academic Publishers).

Brentano, F. (1995), *Psychology from an Empirical Standpoint,* trans. A.C. Rancurello, D.B. Terrell, and L. L. McAlister, 2nd ed. (London: Routledge & Kegan Paul).

Brough, J. (1972), 'The emergence of an absolute consciousness in Husserl's early writings on time-consciousness', *Man and World,* **5**, pp. 298–326.

Brough, J. (1989), 'Husserl's phenomenology of time-consciousness', in *Husserl's Phenomenology,* ed. J.N. Mohanty and W.R. McKenna (Lanham: University Press of America).

Brough, J. (1991), 'Translator's introduction', in Husserl (1991).

Damasio, A.R. (1994), *Descartes' Error* (New York: Quill).

Damasio, A.R. (1999), *The Feeling of what Happens* (New York: Harvest Books).

Damasio, A.R. (2003), *Looking for Spinoza* (Orlando, FL: Harcourt).

Davidson, D. (1976), 'Hume's cognitive theory of pride', in *Essays on Actions and Events* (Oxford: Oxford University Press).

Drummond, J.J. (2002a), 'Aristotelianism and phenomenology', in *Phenomenological Approaches to Moral Philosophy,* ed. J.J. Drummond and L. Embree (Dordrecht: Kluwer).

Drummond, J.J. (2002b), 'Complicating the emotions' (in Spanish translation by M. Oyata), *Areté: Revista de Filosofía,* **14**, pp. 175–89.

Goldie, P. (2000), *The Emotions: A Philosophical Exploration* (Oxford: Clarendon Press).

Goldie, P. (2002), 'Emotions, feelings, and intentionality', *Phenomenology and the Cognitive Sciences,* **1**, pp. 235–54.

Heidegger, M. (1962), *Being and Time,* trans. J. Macquarrie and E. Robinson (New York: Harper & Row).

Heidegger, M. (1967), *Sein und Zeit* (Tübingen: Max Niemeyer).

Husserl, E. (1952), *Ideen zu einer reinen Phänomenologie und phänomenologische Philosophie, zweites Buch: Phänomenologische Untersuchungen zur Konstitution,* ed. M. Biemel, Husserliana 4 (The Hague: Martinus Nijhoff).

Husserl, E. (1966), *Analysen zur passiven Synthesis: Aus Vorlesungs- und Forschungsmanuskripten 1918–1926,* ed. M. Fleischer, Husserliana 11 (The Hague: Martinus Nijhoff).

Husserl, E. (1970), *Logical Investigations,* trans. J.N. Findlay (London: Routledge and Kegan Paul).

Husserl, E. (1973), *Zur Phänomenologie der Intersubjektivität, Texte aus dem Nachlass, dritter Teil: 1929–1935,* ed. I. Kern, Husserliana 15 (The Hague: Martinus Nijhoff).

Husserl, E. (1976), *Ideen zu einer reinen Phänomenologie und phänomenologischen Philosophie, erstes Buch: Allgemeine Einführung in die reine Phänomenologie,* ed. K. Schuhmann, Husserliana 3/1 (The Hague: Martinus Nijhoff).

Husserl, E. (1983), *Ideas Pertaining to a Pure Phenomenology and to a Phenomenological Philosophy, First Book: General Introduction to a Pure Phenomenology,* trans. F. Kersten (The Hague: Martinus Nijhoff).

Husserl, E. (1984), *Logische Untersuchungen, zweiter Band, erster Teil: Untersuchungen zur Phänomenologie und Theorie der Erkenntnis*, ed. Ursula Panzer, Husserliana 19/1 (The Hague: Martinus Nijhoff).

Husserl, E. (1988), *Vorlesungen über Ethik und Wertlehre 1908–1914*, ed. U. Melle, Husserliana 28 (Dordrecht: Kluwer).

Husserl, E. (1989), *Ideas Pertaining to a Pure Phenomenology and to a Phenomenological Philosophy, Second Book: Studies in the Phenomenology of Constitution*, trans. R. Rojcewicz and A. Schuwer (Dordrecht: Kluwer).

Husserl, E. (1991), *On the Phenomenology of the Consciousness of Internal Time (1893–1917)*, trans. J. Brough (Dordrecht: Kluwer).

Husserl, E. (2001), *Analyses Concerning Passive and Active Synthesis*, trans. A. Steinbock. (Dordrecht: Kluwer).

James, W. (1950), *The Principles of Psychology*, 2 volumes (New York: Dover).

Kenny, A. (1963), *Action, Emotion, and Will* (London: Routledge).

Reinach, A. (1989), Die Überlegung. Ihre ethische und rechtliche Bedeutung. In *Sämtliche Werke. Textkritische Ausgabe in 2 Bänden*, ed. K. Schuhmann and B. Smith (Munich: Philosophia Verlag).

Scheler, M. (1973a), *Formalism in Ethics and Non-Formal Ethics of Values*, trans. M.S. Frings and R.L. Funk (Evanston, IL: Northwestern University Press).

Scheler, M. (1973b), 'Ordo amoris', in *Selected Philosophical Essays*, trans. David R. Lachterman (Evanston, IL: Northwestern University Press).

Scheler, M. (1979), 'Ordo amoris', in *Schriften aus dem Nachlaß. Gesammelte Werke,* vol. 10 (Bern: Francke).

Scheler, M. (1980), *Der Formalismus in der Ethik und die Materiale Wertethik. Gesammelte Werke,* vol. 2, ed. M. Scheler and M.S. Frings (Bern: Francke).

Taylor, G. (1976), 'Love', *Proceedings of the Aristotelian Society*, **76**, pp. 147–64.

Taylor, G. (1985), *Pride, shame, and Guilt: Emotions of Self-Assessment* (Oxford: Oxford University Press).

Zahavi, D. (1999), *Self-awareness and Alterity* (Evanston, IL: Northwestern University Press).

Louis A. Sass

Affectivity in Schizophrenia

A Phenomenological View

Schizophrenia involves profound but enigmatic disturbances of affective or emotional life. The affective responses as well as expression of many patients in the schizophrenia spectrum can seem odd, incongruent, inadequate, or otherwise off-the-mark. Such patients are, in fact, often described in rather contradictory terms: as being prone both to exaggerated and to diminished levels of emotional or affective response. According to Ernst Kretschmer, they actually tend to have both kinds of experience at the same time. This paper attempts to explain what might be termed this 'Kretschmerian paradox'. Some relevant concepts and vocabulary for affect and emotion are discussed (including the notions of 'affect', 'emotion', 'mood' and 'the passions'). The need for a phenomenological approach focusing on subjective experience is suggested. Three modes of abnormal experience in schizophrenia are investigated in light of their implications for affect or emotion: (1) alienation of the lived body (Bodily Alienation); (2) fragmented perception and loss of affordances (Unworlding); and (3) preoccupation with a quasi-delusional world created by the self (Subjectivization).

Introduction

Schizophrenia — often conceptualized as a disorder of thinking and reality-testing — also involves profound disturbances of the affective or emotional dimensions of life (Slater and Roth, 1969, pp. 269 f). It could be argued, in fact, that affective abnormalities are among the most *central* features of the schizophrenic condition, for they seem closely bound up with the alterations of personhood or self-experience, and of the sense of reality, that are so distinctive of this psychiatric illness (Mellor, 1970; Sass and Parnas, 2003).[1] Schizophrenic

---

[1] Affectivity, argue the philosophers Michel Henry (1973) and Ferdinand Alquie (1979), 'is the very essence of the self' (Alquie quoted in Tallon, 1997, p. 147). It is what provides the core sense of vital existence as a subject of experience.

affectivity is, in any case, certainly one of the most mysterious aspects of this generally enigmatic form of mental disorder.

For normal individuals, affectivity often provides a medium of connectedness, a realm of emotional resonance that both presupposes and supports the sense of sympathy or fellow feeling (Scheler, 1954). By contrast, many schizophrenic patients seem neither to feel nor to evoke a natural sense of emotional rapport. Both the affective response and the affective expression of these patients frequently seem odd, incongruent, inadequate, or otherwise off-the-mark. (This is especially true of *nonparanoid* forms of schizophrenia (Tsuang and Winokur, 1974), which will be my focus in this paper.) As a result, the affective lives of these patients often seem profoundly impenetrable; and this impenetrability is easily confused with a straightforward *absence* of underlying affective life or responsivity (Ey, 1955, p. 187). In this paper, I shall concentrate on one especially important and especially mysterious feature of schizophrenic affectivity: the fact that — contradictory though it may seem — such individuals often seem prone both to exaggerated *and* to diminished levels of emotional or affective response.

One classic symptom (or sign) of such persons is 'flat affect', a paucity of emotional expression (of bodily gesture, facial expression, variation in tone of voice, and orientation toward other people) that has frequently been assumed to indicate diminished emotional response on the subjective plane (Blanchard and Panzarella, 1998). A patient's response to provocative events will, for example, often seem blunted or weak, suggestive perhaps of a kind of affective indifference or lack of concern (Kaplan and Sadock, 1998, p. 480) — as when a patient merely shrugs at news of the death of his mother or his child, or even responds with levity. In autobiographical accounts, persons who have suffered from schizophrenia often describe a deadening of emotional vitality. At times this apparent indifference may be accompanied by forms of negativism, both active and passive. The patient's behaviour may, for example, have a manneristic quality, suggestive of disdain; or one may sense that he or she is somehow flaunting his or her detachment and indifference. The patient's whole existence may, in fact, seem to be somehow saturated with irony and a sense of distance (Ey, 1955, p. 189).

Persons with schizophrenia are, however, also portrayed as having abnormally *intense* emotional responses and as *hyper*sensitive to emotional stimuli (Cutting, 1985, p. 235; Kaplan and Sadock, 1998, p. 480; Kring, 1999). Persons with schizophrenia do sometimes respond in what appear to be excessive, or otherwise strikingly peculiar, ways. Intense affective reactions can be inspired by stimuli that seem trivial, inconsistent with the response, or just totally enigmatic. A schizophrenic patient may laugh or shed tears over some minor event, or may seem awestruck by some banal feature of the environment. He or she may experience generalized states of ecstasy or elation, of desolation or dread; and these feelings may occur 'side by side with emotional blunting and the absence of warm human feelings'. The fluctuations between these differing states may be rapid and seemingly unmotivated (Slater and Roth, 1969, p. 269). Eugen Bleuler went so far as to speak of a 'veritable dis-aggregation of the affective sphere which comes apart in contradictory and disharmonious systems' (quoted in Ey, 1955, p. 187).

Sigmund and Mundt (1999) consider the following 'structural deformations of emotional expression and affect' to be characteristic of core schizophrenia:

- Stereotypic, monotonic speech.
- A rigid look with eyes fixed in a middle position, with limited scanning of the environment or other persons; or, more rarely, a restless, wandering gaze that does not come to rest on any object.
- Incongruity between thought content and situation, or else between experienced emotion and emotional expression.
- Decreased intensity and frequency of affect, but with a fairly steady mood, which can be joyless or joyless-morose, cheerful-serene or cheerful-silly [i.e., flat, serene or silly].

It is very likely that persons with schizophrenia are heterogeneous with respect to many of the above-mentioned aspects of affective experience and expression. Not only individual patients, but distinct stages of the schizophrenic illness (acute versus chronic; prodromal versus advanced) have, for example, been found to differ from one another in terms of their characteristic levels of emotional or affective response (Zahn *et al.*, 1991). Another factor is that patients with schizophrenia often seem to *manifest* emotionality in ways that are at odds with their underlying experience. Recent research on flat affect shows, for example, that patients with this symptom may be more affectively alive than has usually been assumed. According to subjective reports from patients as well as electrodermal measures of arousal, flat-affect patients actually manifest the same or even a *higher* level of affective response that do normal individuals (Kring and Neale, 1996). It has been suggested that this discrepancy between experience and expression of emotion ('affective incongruence') may result from neuromuscular abnormalities that prevent *normal* (or even abnormally intense) emotions from being expressed in normal ways (Dworkin *et al.*, 1996).

The appearance of contradiction in accounts of schizophrenia can, then, often be resolved by distinguishing between subtypes of patients, between stages of the illness, or between experience and expression of emotion. In this paper, however, I would like to pursue the stranger and more intriguing possibility that the affective lives of persons with schizophrenia often *do* have certain contradictory qualities — that is, that such patients can, *at the very same moment* and *on the subjective plane*, experience *both* diminishment *and* exaggeration of emotional or affective response.

Early in the twentieth century, the German psychiatrist Ernst Kretschmer offered an account of 'schizothymia' — the temperament characteristic of schizoid and schizophrenic individuals — that emphasized the presence of two, opposite aspects or tendencies: on the one hand, hypersensitivity, tenderness, nervousness or vulnerability; on the other hand, insensitivity, coldness, numbness or indifference. According to Kretschmer, an 'indefinite number of individual temperamental shades emerge from . . . the manner in which in the same type of temperament the polar opponents *displace* one another, *overlay* one another, or *relieve* one another in alteration' (Kretschmer, 1936, p. 265, italics added).

But it is not only a matter of *shifting* from the hyper- to the hypo-sensitive mode. In Kretschmer's view, there is a deeper sense in which schizothymic persons *always* contain both extremes: 'As soon as we come into close personal contact with such schizoids, we find very frequently, behind the affectless, numbed exterior, in the innermost sanctuary, a tender personality-nucleus with the most vulnerable nervous sensitivity which has withdrawn into itself and lies there contorted' (Kretschmer, 1925, p. 153). Nor is this merely a matter of expression versus experience. Both aspects are *always* present, in some way, even on the plane of subjective or felt reaction: 'He alone, however, has the key to the schizoid temperament who has clearly recognized that the majority of schizoids are not either over-sensitive or cold, but that they are over-sensitive and cold *at the same time*, and that in quite different relative proportions' (Kretschmer, 1936, p. 156, emphasis added). The 'autism of the majority of schizoids and schizophrenics . . . is based on mixtures, in the most varied proportions, of the two temperamental aspects . . .' (*ibid.*, p. 162). They are people 'full of antitheses, always containing extremes, and only missing out on the means' (the middle positions) (Kretschmer, 1925, p. 245). Kretschmer quotes August Strindberg, a distinctly schizothymic, perhaps schizophrenic, individual who experienced psychotic episodes: 'I am hard as ice and yet so full of feeling that I am almost sentimental' (Kretschmer, 1936, p. 157). Strindberg's line captures what Henri Ey (1955, pp. 193 f) — one of the great French psychiatrists of the twentieth century — spoke of as 'the most paradoxical of all [the] affective paradoxes' of schizophrenia: namely, that such patients appear to be devoid of affective response yet also, somehow, affectively very alive.

Despite the odd, even contradictory, nature of Kretschmer's account, I think that he puts his finger on a key aspect of schizophrenia, and one that may be especially central in accounting for the famous '*praecox*-feeling' — the feeling of strangeness or remoteness, of encountering something beyond normal emotional contact or rapport, that normal persons may have in the presence of a person with schizophrenia. Emotion is often thought of as the realm of experience that is most refractory to verbal description or conceptual analysis. The contradictory qualities of schizophrenic emotionality make it especially difficult for patients to describe and also for psychiatrists and psychologists either to empathize with or to conceptualize. These qualities therefore contribute to the sense of alienation felt both by patients and by those who treat them.

But how is it possible to account for what might be termed the Kretschmerian paradox? Isn't it simply *nonsensical* — logically contradictory — to say that a person is at the very same moment, both hypo- *and* hyper-sensitive, both emotionally flattened and also, somehow, affectively hyper-alive? This paper draws on the resources of phenomenology in order to illuminate what may seem this ineffable domain, and thereby help to make sense of this seeming paradox. It offers phenomenologically oriented accounts of three distinct modes of schizophrenic experience — pertaining to the lived body, perceptual experience and the life of the imagination — and discusses how each of these is consistent with the Kretschmerian paradox. (I do not claim that these are the *only* modes of schizophrenic experience consistent with the Kretschmerian paradox; they do, however, represent three relevant, and highly characteristic, modes of schizophrenic experience.) The first two modes will be dealt with very briefly, the third (imagination) in more detail, largely through analysing a single case example. Before proceeding, however, it is first necessary to say a few words about the general concept of emotion and related terminology, with emphasis on the subjective dimension. At the end of the next section, I will state my overall thesis in very general terms.

Concepts of Emotion

In his comprehensive survey of psychological research and theorizing about emotion, Nico Frijda (1986, p. 256 and *passim*) lists three crucial components of emotion: a bodily or physiological component (usually involving arousal), a particular way of viewing one's situation or worldly context (sometimes described as the 'cognitive' or 'evaluative' component), and a particular mode of relational 'action readiness'. Action readiness can, but need not, involve a direct motivation to act or to change a situation. It may involve 'action tendencies', which are propensities 'to establish, maintain, or disrupt a relationship' with either environmental or mental objects (e.g., turning toward or away from a person — whether in physical action or memory, in desire or fear, with interest, disgust or indifference, etc.). Or it may simply involve 'activation modes', which are ongoing 'mode[s] of relational readiness [or unreadiness] as such' and may vary from apathy to vigour, from placidity to tenseness (Frijda, 1986, pp. 57, 71, 88, 238).

In addition to these three components, Frijda (1986, pp. 205 f) lists several features of the experienced situation that must be present for something truly to count *as* an emotion, and that, when present in high degree, will serve to intensify the emotion in question. To elicit emotion, a given object or situation cannot be experienced as a mere figment of imagination; it must have some quality of *objective* reality. This does not rule out mental objects, such as memories. It means that the subject must not experience himself as merely *conferring* meaning; rather the emotional situation '*imposes* its meaning upon the subject' (*ibid.*, p. 205, emphasis added). The object or situation must also be experienced as having *relevance* for oneself, and this relevance must have a quality of both *urgency* and *seriousness*. Underlying all of this is the more general quality of '*concern*'. Experiences having emotional significance always touch upon issues that matter to us, and that matter in an ongoing way, such as our desire for survival, for intimate human contact, or for respect from others. Emotions, as the philosopher Martha Nussbaum (2001) puts it, are not 'unthinking energies that simply push the person around, without being hooked up to the ways in which [the person] perceives or thinks about the world'. They are, rather, 'forms of evaluative judgment that ascribe to certain things and persons outside a person's own control great importance for the person's own flourishing' (*ibid.*, pp. 4, 24 f).

A related set of points is made in Martin Heidegger's (1962) classic existential-phenomenological study, *Being and Time* (orig. publ. 1927), where the concept of *Sorge* — usually translated as 'care' — and the role of temporality, have a central place. Like Nussbaum, Heidegger thinks of emotions (and moods) as profoundly evaluative; but unlike Nussbaum, he does not conceive these evaluations as involving explicit cognitive beliefs or judgments — they may be 'pre-predicative'. Like Frijda on 'concern', Heidegger conceives of 'care' as a precondition and source of emotional experience; but unlike Frijda's 'concern', *Sorge* is not to be conceived as a component of a natural process, but as a kind of transcendental ground, clearing, or source of illumination through which or by means of which phenomena can manifest themselves. For Heidegger, emotions and moods are directly bound up with the way the world presents itself to us. He describes such emotions as fear and such moods as anxiety as 'disclosing' the world in certain ways. In fear, for example, some specific — though perhaps not yet identifiable — feature of the world is revealed as being detrimental; further, this something is experienced as drawing near, but in a way that is not yet inevitable and may still be avoided (otherwise the fear would become resignation); and finally, that which is threatened is the very being who is afraid — *Dasein*, or oneself (Heidegger, 1962, pp. 179–82).[2]

According to Heidegger, the analysis of 'care' reveals the indispensable role of our experience of and in the medium of time: care 'is possible only through temporality' (Heidegger, 1962, p. 375), for 'care' is precisely a form of future-directedness, of 'being ahead-of-oneself' in the sense of being concerned about where and how one will be in the next moment or period of time (*ibid.*, p. 237). It is a form of 'anticipation' that is lived in the present, and in which *Dasein* confronts its own possibilities for being — in which, in Heidegger's words, '*Dasein*, in its ownmost potentiality-for-Being comes towards itself' (*ibid.*, p. 373). Care, however, is grounded in 'the character of "having been" ' (*ibid.*, p. 376), and in a 'specious present' (William James, 1981, p. 573) that is infused with a sense of emerging out of a past and projecting toward a future.

In another phenomenological study, *Phenomenology of Feeling* (1977, pp. 204–9), Stephan Strasser describes three key elements of the psychological acts underlying emotional feelings, each of which has a 'determinate temporal structure' (*ibid.*, p. 205):

1. 'the experience of one's own neediness', in which there is, from the very beginning, an at least inchoate sense of directedness toward or away from an object.
2. 'the experience of being-underway', in which, for example, approaching a desired object heightens the impulse to attain it, whereas moving away from a feared or repellent object gradually diminishes one's impulse to avoid.

---

[2] In *Being and Time*, Heidegger (1962, p. 178) complains that research on affectivity has hardly progressed since Aristotle. The point is echoed by Ricoeur in 1977 (in Strasser, 1977, p. xii). Emotion and affectivity continue to be relatively neglected topics in the phenomenological tradition: Note, for example, the minimal treatment of these issues in the introductory surveys by Moran (2000) and Sokolowski (2000).

3. 'the experience of termination', in which, as Strasser puts it, one 'live[s] completely in the exulting or depressing present' (Strasser, 1977, p. 209).

So far I have used the terms 'emotions', 'affect' and 'mood'. Related terms in this general semantic domain include 'feelings' and 'the passions'. Although there is no clear and universally accepted understanding of the distinctions among these terms (Strasser, 1977, p. 264), a few generalizations can safely be made (see Frijda, 1986; also Berrios, 1985).

'**Affect**' — which the Random House Dictionary of the English Language defines as meaning 'feeling' or 'emotion' — is perhaps the most general word, and the one best suited (along with such phrases as 'affective response' or 'affective reaction') to serve as a generic term that can subsume all the above-mentioned concepts. Usually we understand '**mood**' to refer to a state of mind that is more pervasive and less focused than is an 'emotion'. Whereas an '**emotion**' is typically about some *particular* object, person or situation, a mood is less targeted and more all-encompassing. The term '**feelings**' has a more subjective focus: unlike emotion, it refers not so much to an attitude toward the world as to a state of or within the self, one that does not elicit any action tendency or sense of urgency.

Turning to the '**passions**', we might say that these are the *quintessential* emotions. Not surprisingly, they tend to focus on some particular object in the world (e.g., someone loved or feared), to involve the desire to *change* a situation in some way, and to have the qualities of immediacy, relevance, seriousness and objectivity in high degree. In a recent, phenomenologically oriented, literary account, Philip Fisher (2002) describes the passions as typically bound up with either the imminent future (in the case of fear and greed, for example) or the immediate past (in the case of shame, grief and anger); as he shows, the passions are deeply embedded in a temporal dynamism that is clearly illustrated by the trepidations of fear or the feverish anticipation of greed. I have said that the passions are the *quintessential* emotions. One might say as well that, to the extent that an emotion *lacks* the qualities of the passions, it is in a sense less *emotional* in nature — and should perhaps be referred to as only a *quasi*-emotion, or with the more generic or neutral term, 'affect'. I do not suggest that there is a sharp line between emotion and quasi-emotion. These phenomena differ on a number of dimensions (e.g., role of temporality, focus on particular objects versus on overall atmosphere); on each of these dimensions, the difference would be a matter of degree.[3]

This summary of concepts about affect and emotion allows me to state my claims in summary fashion. In this article I will consider three modes of experience that are common in schizophrenia: certain disturbances of the lived-body (Bodily Alienation), alterations of perceptual meaning (Unworlding) and types of inner fantasy (Subjectivization). Each of these three forms of experience or lived-worlds involves a distinct form of temporality, and each involves or

---

[3] Strasser emphasizes neediness and concerns about changing a situation; this suggests that his account of emotional feelings is slanted towards the passions or paradigmatic emotions.

engenders a diminishment of some of the defining features of the concept 'emotion' — especially the targeted and temporal nature of 'concern', with its assumption of urgency, relevance, objectivity or seriousness. I believe, therefore, that there is a measure of truth in the traditional view of flat affect: schizophrenia often *does* involve a diminishment of specifically *emotional* forms of vitality or response. But as a phenomenological account can show, this need *not* mean that *all* forms of affective life are attenuated. To understand the Kretschmerian paradox is to realize that, in schizophrenia, diminished emotional response may be accompanied by forms of *quasi*-emotion that may be no less intense than the emotions they replace.

Bodily Alienation

The role of bodily experience in emotional life, which has been recognized since ancient times, was perhaps best expressed by William James in 1890: 'If we fancy some strong emotion and then try to abstract from our consciousness of it all the feelings of its bodily symptoms,' writes James (1981) in his *Principles of Psychology*, 'we find we have nothing left behind, no "mind-stuff" out of which the emotion can be constituted and that a cold and neutral state of intellectual perception is all that remains.' 'Can one,' he asks, 'fancy the state of rage and picture no ebullition in the chest, no flushing of the face, no dilation of the nostrils, no clenching of the teeth, no impulse to vigorous action . . . A purely disembodied human emotion is a non-entity' (*ibid.*, pp. 1067 f).

In his recent reformulation of this classic view, Damasio (1994, p. 173 and *passim*) argues that affective experience is generally rooted in what he terms 'representations' or 'images of the body' that have come to be associated as 'somatic markers' with particular contexts or stimulus situations. A point Damasio neglects, however, is that normal emotional experience involves, in large measure, not representations of the objectified or objectifiable body *image* so much as implicitly felt experiences involving the body *subject*. These would be experiences in which the somatic markers, patterns or tension states of our bodily self-awareness are not experienced as objects in themselves, but as the tacitly inhabited medium of an attitude — such as fear, desire or disgust — that is directed towards some object in the world. Such experiences (of the implicit corporeal self) could be described as the subjective correlates of the emotional affordances of the world. In this sense, we might say that the 'somatic markers' of emotion are not normally experienced as focal *objects* but, rather, as a *medium* of awareness — or perhaps one should say, as a kind of orienting vector that joins an implicit sense of self with a focal object in the world (Merleau-Ponty, 1962; Sass and Parnas, 2003).

This point is crucial for grasping some of the distinctive features of emotional or affective experience in schizophrenia. In such persons, a fragmented and alienated sense of the lived body tends to disrupt the world-directedness as well as the normal fluidity and flow of affective experience and expression, leading to a sense of disharmony, artificiality and distance, both in the patient's own experience of emotion and in the expression visible to others. One might describe this condition as involving a diminishment of emotion in favour of other forms of affective life.

Bodily self-alienation is obvious in certain classic, first-rank symptoms in which patients feel that their own body or actions are somehow under the control or in the possession of some distant being or force. Analogous but milder experiences of corporeal alienation have been demonstrated by German research on the 'basic symptoms', which occur in all the various subtypes of schizophrenia as well as in the prodromal and residual phases (Klosterkoetter, 1992). One important group of basic symptoms consists in the cenesthesias: sensations of movement or of pulling or pressure inside the body or on its surfaces; electric or migrating sensations; awareness of kinesthetic, vestibular or thermic sensations; and sensations of diminution or enlargement of the body or its parts. Generally unpleasant, and frequently accompanied by feelings of decline of vital energy, these experiences are combined with blockage or disruption of automatic skills and the smooth flow of motor activity. The basic symptom experiences are not typically found in normal individuals; they are, however, strikingly similar to what is reported by normal subjects who adopt a special, introspective stance towards their own experiences (Sass, 1994, pp. 90, 94, 161).

It is hardly surprising that such mutations affect both the experience and expression of emotion. Schizophrenia patients often feel that there is something odd, unsatisfying or awry about their facial expression or bodily gestures — that these are not fully under their control, or that they do not harmoniously or accurately conform to or convey an underlying state of feeling or emotion (Carr and Wale, 1986, p. 144; Koehler and Sauer, 1984). When experiences that normally exist in the tacit dimension come to be the objects of a more focal and objectifying awareness, one would expect profound transformations in the felt quality of the affective life. Rather than serving as an attitude *towards* the world, certain affectively charged configurations of bodily tension do not feel genuine, natural or appropriate to the context; instead they are experienced at a subjective distance, almost as objects in themselves.

It is not, in fact, clear that 'emotion' is even the appropriate term for these quasi-affective sensations that are dissociated from the ongoing sense of self that gives normal emotions a compelling quality of intimacy and personal relevance (re this ongoing sense of self, see Sass and Parnas, 2003, re '*ipseity*'). When bodily states and processes replace persons and situations as the *focus* of awareness, the affective experiences in question are deprived of an essential component of normal, targeted emotional meaning. They cannot be part and parcel of a coherent and meaningful state of directedness towards the world — the kind that normally involves a sense of neediness, of being-underway, and of eventual termination and surcease (Strasser, 1977). Instead they exist in a kind of free-floating space. This need not, however, imply a general dampening of *all* forms of affective life.

Withdrawal from worldly emotional directedness can sometimes serve defensive needs, providing a haven of escape from the unpredictability of external circumstances and the feelings linked to them. Research shows, however, that states of arousal that cannot be identified cognitively tend to be experienced as disruptive and dysphoric (Maslach, 1979), so it is not surprising that these free-floating, objectlike, states of tension that are common in schizophrenia *are* often associated with a general sense of indefinable anxious perturbation.

Unworlding

It is not uncommon for persons with schizophrenia to experience a certain fragmentation of the cognitive or perceptual world. This may take the form of an analytic, bottom-up approach to understanding scenes that normal individuals are more likely to approach in a holistic or even impressionistic way. '[O]bjects seemed altered from the usual', said one patient with schizophrenia. 'They did not stand together in an overall context, and I saw them as meaningless details' (Matussek, 1987, p. 92).

In a related manifestation, people, things or actions are perceived as lacking not basic geometric unity but their recognizable affordances (Gibson, 1979) — the qualities of human relevance or practical significance that, for example, make a chair a thing-to-sit-on, a hammer something-to-pound-with, or a human body something to be approached, feared or caressed. Renee, author of the famous *Autobiography of a Schizophrenic Girl*, is unusually articulate in describing experiences in which, as she puts it, 'objects are stage trappings, placed here and there, geometric cubes without meaning' (Sechehaye, 1970, p. 33).

> When, for example, I looked at a chair or a jug, I thought not of their use or function — a jug not as something to hold water and milk, a chair not as something to sit in — but as having lost their names, their functions and meanings; they became 'things' and began to take on life, to exist. This existence accounted for my great fear. In the unreal scene, in the murky quiet of my perception, suddenly 'the thing' sprang up. The stone jar, decorated with blue flowers, was there facing me, defying me with its presence, with its existence. (Sechehaye, 1970, pp. 40 f)

If we understand 'world' in the Heideggerian sense — as a complex unity held together by a set of instrumental meanings and relationships (Heidegger, 1962, pp. 91–149) — it is clear that these experiences of fragmentation and loss of affordances can be termed a kind of *un-worlding* of the world; and if one accepts the emotionally *constitutive* role of the 'situation', then it is obvious that both fragmentation and loss of affordances have clear implications for affective life. As noted earlier, paradigm emotions target specific objects and situations that play a necessary role in *constituting* the emotion in question; and it is, of course, the *affordance*-aspect of whole objects and situations that are normally relevant. To see eyes, nose, mouth and ears as distinct objects is not to experience a *face*, let alone one capable of the expressive significance appropriate for reacting with love, admiration, envy or the like. To see a human body, or a chair, as pure three-dimensional geometry, is to forfeit the potential for reacting with lust, loathing or a yearning for peaceful repose. The un-worlding of the world is therefore synonymous with the disappearance or attenuation of many common forms of emotionality, and of the normal forms of engaged temporality that emotions usually imply.

This attenuation of emotional response should not, however, be confused with a straightforward dimming of the intensity of subjective life, nor even with a general disappearance of all forms of affective reactivity. Descriptions by such patients as Renee show that the fragmentation and loss of affordances tends *itself* to arouse a variety of feelings, including consternation and anxiety but also, at times, feelings of wonderment or awe. The unfocused, often persistent quality of these affective states gives them a moodlike or atmospheric quality. They should not, however, be confused with mere physiological 'intensities', for they *are* linked with a distinct experience of the worldly situation (fragmentation and loss of affordances), albeit not with specific objects that are likely to have strong action-implications for the subject in question.[4]

We cannot say that such a person's overall experience of affect is either more *or* less intense than that of normal individuals. In circumstances such as these, the paradigmatic emotions (targeted, with strong implications for action-readiness) are likely to be diminished. But, in these conditions involving contemplation and withdrawal, there may well be a heightening of *other* forms of affectivity that are more present-oriented and mood-like, keyed not to action but to the spectacle of unworlding. Phenomenological analysis makes it understandable, then, that the patient may experience generalized affective states such as awe or desolation, and that these may occur, as Slater and Roth (1969, p. 269) note, 'side by side with emotional blunting and the absence of warm human feelings'.

In this and the previous section, I have argued that the blunted emotionality and apparent contradictions of affective response found in schizophrenia, are understandable in the light of certain alterations in the experience of both body and world. One might be tempted to interpret this as implying that the peculiarities of schizophrenic affectivity are entirely *secondary* to supposedly more basic disturbances in cognitive, perceptual or perhaps kinesthetic/proprioceptive dimensions of psychological life — that is, to see these affective peculiarities as *sequelae*, perhaps as rational or reasonable responses, to the cognitive/perceptual/kinesthetic changes. It is not my purpose here to provide an overall account of the full range and possible interrelationships of schizophrenic symptomatology. I will say, however, that my inclination would be to resist the just mentioned interpretation of the affective dimension as merely secondary. In fact, the alterations of cognitive/perceptual and kinesthetic/proprioceptive dimensions can *themselves* be seen as manifestations of a more central disturbance of *'ipseity'* — that is, of the fundamental sense of existing as a vital and directed subject of awareness that is at one with itself at any given moment (Sass and Parnas, 2003). This, in turn, involves (among other things) a diminishment of basic 'self-affection' — of the passively or automatically experienced (and

---

[4] Both Tellenbach (1968/1983) and Kimura (1995) mention the importance of atmosphere in schizophrenic experience, and note the relevance of passivity and of receptivity towards the 'world as a whole'. [Thanks to an anonymous reviewer for calling my attention to these references.]

affect-related) sense of existing as a living and unified subject of awareness (Henry, 1973).[5] (For more on disturbances of the experiential field in relationship to ipseity and self-affection, see also Sass, in press; Sass and Uhlhaas, in press.)

Subjectivization

We turn now to a third mode of schizophrenic experience. I will treat this mode at greater length, using ideas from philosophical aesthetics as well as phenomenology in order to clarify some of the complexities, and perhaps also to evoke some of the distinctive feel, of at least one particular mode of schizophrenic affective life.

This third mode of schizophrenic experience is inward in character, bound up with imagination rather than perception, and likely to occur in the chronic and withdrawn phases of the illness. One patient with schizophrenia spoke, for example, of an introversion that occurred in a condition of inaction, and that led, in turn, to a disruption of spontaneous activity:

> I was lying on my bed and reality somehow passed inwards as if my brain turned round . . . I then became more interested in memory than perceiving reality around me . . . At the beginning I had a sense of despair almost amounting to terror, later replaced by flattening . . . (Cutting, 1985, p. 390)

This sort of withdrawal often involves a turning of attention away from external or social reality in favour of a preoccupation with a delusional or quasi-delusional realm of inner fantasy. (I say 'quasi-delusional' here because the preoccupations to be described do *not* seem to involve the condition of mistaken belief that is an essential feature of standard conceptions of 'delusion' — that is, the notion that the patient takes his delusional objects as being fully real and objective. Although I will continue to use 'delusion' below, the term should not be understood in the standard 'poor-reality-testing' sense of the word.)

The experience of this kind of withdrawal has been carefully described by several phenomenologically oriented writers (e.g., Sartre, 1966; Tatossian, 1997; Sass, 1992b, 1992a chapter 9; Parnas and Sass, 2001). Sartre spoke of the 'morbid dreamer' whose wish-fulfilling delusions were an attempt to escape not the content so much as the *form* of the real. According to Sartre, the delusional objects or situations the patient experiences do not, for the patient, have the full, ontological status of 'the real'. That is, they lack one or other of those crucial characteristics — the ultimate unknowability of a realm that exceeds our grasp, the

---

[5] The term 'affection' as used here refers to a process of being affected by something or by oneself; it has nothing to do with the notion of fondness, or liking of oneself. The term 'affection' in 'self-affection' is meant to evoke the notion of both affect and passivity, as against a more active and cognitive, intentional mental process or event. Affection and intention thus form a pair of concepts, with connotations of passivity and activity, respectively. To be affected means to be touched, moved, motivated. Self-affection refers to a 'being-affected by self' or 'self-feeling of self'; this is not something we do but something that simply happens, and it is primordially linked to emotion. It is an unmediated feeling or sense of aliveness, a sense of a certain tonality or luminosity of consciousness that founds our existence and is a necessary condition for more elaborate levels of self-awareness and for our encountering of the world. See Henry (1973), Sass and Parnas (2003) and note 1, above.

recalcitrance of a realm separate from fantasy or whim — that are the marks of an objective realm independent of one's own mind and will. Such a view implies that, rather than *confusing* delusion and reality or wishing to *substitute* fantasy for reality, 'morbid dreaming' actually demands the *preservation* of this distinction; otherwise the delusional world would, for the patient, be imbued with the same potential for uncertainty, danger and potential disappointment that is characteristic of the reality he wishes to escape. A revealing example of 'morbid dreaming' and its associated forms of affect or quasi-emotion can be found in the prose texts of the schizophrenic patient and *Art Brut* artist Adolf Wölfli (Sass, 1997).

Wölfli, who resided for thirty-five years in the Waldau Asylum near Bern, Switzerland, spent most of his waking hours engaged in the creation of visual works that illustrated and prose works that described his delusional fantasies and memories. During one period of his life, the delusions (or quasi-delusions) in question mostly involved memories of amazing but curiously timeless journeys that Wölfli himself had supposedly taken through an immense cosmos ('delusional memories'). In one passage he speaks of witnessing objects and situations of overwhelming size and power, such as 'the Giant-Glacier of the Celestial-Stars-of-God-the-Father', which, he says, contains 'the greatest giant cave in the whole universe', a cave that holds a population enumerated as 5 followed by 95 zeros. In another passage Wölfli describes a walnut tree he discovered on the 'Island-of-the-Echo-of-the-Western-Sea', whose trunk has a diameter of more than twelve thousand leagues and whose crown of leaves extends 'more than two thousand leagues beyond the borders of this formidable Sea' (all quotations from Wölfli can be found in Sass, 1997, n.d.).

The world of Wölfli's delusions is best captured by the famous concept of 'the sublime' — a key aesthetic concept that dates back to the first century AD writer, Longinus, and was elaborated by Burke, Kant and Schopenhauer. *Beautiful* objects, according to Kant's classical account in the *Critique of Judgment*, have the quality of comprehensible form. By contrast, the 'sublime' always involves an experience of something so colossal in size or scope, or so powerful in force, that it beggars our mental capacities to imagine it. Instead of harmonious resonance, the associated affects are organized around a sense of tension or opposition between objects we encounter and our inadequate faculties of knowing, and involve ambivalent feelings of repulsion from as well as attraction to the same object.

There is, however, another side to this paradoxical mode of experience that is brought out by Kant and Schopenhauer — namely, an antithetical experience of the power, centrality and even superiority of one's own mind or self when faced with the looming tremendousness of the world. As I stand before Mont Blanc or the Grand Canyon, I am acutely aware of the puniness of my own body and self, of the infinitesimal irrelevance of my existence in a universe so vast. But, argues Kant, I also become aware of a comparable power contained within — namely, of my own rational faculties, including the human capacity for judgment and free will, a capacity so absolute as to amount to an infinitude that is in no way inferior to that of the external world. Schopenhauer (1928/1949) interpreted this inner infinitude in ontological terms — as involving an awareness of the mind's capacity not just to choose but, in a sense, to *create* or *constitute* the world of our experience. He describes a characteristic oscillation (or coincidence) of a sense of abjectness and omnipotence, of being overwhelmed and of feeling one's own overweening power. The feeling of the sublime, writes Schopenhauer, 'arises through the consciousness of the vanishing nothingness of our own body in the presence of a vastness which, from another point of view, itself exists only in our idea, and which we are, as knowing subject, the supporter'. '[T]he vastness of the world which disquieted us before, rests now in us; our dependence upon it is annulled by its dependence on us', on its existing 'only as our idea' (1928, pp. 172–3; 1949, pp. 242 f, 211).

Oscillation between abjectness and a quasi-solipsistic, post-Kantian assertion of the world's dependence on the knowing self, is a key feature of Wölfli's quasi-delusional fantasies. On the one hand he describes being overwhelmed by the vastness of the (imaginary) world that looms before him:

> Oh my Father, oh my sacred God, all-powerful, in your grandeur and your omnipotence. Is it possible that a son of the earth, at the spectacle of your diversity, of your beautiful and ravishing wonders, could collapse backwards, without consciousness, crushed by pure ravishment and admiration?

On the other hand, Wölfli identifies *himself* as a royal or even divine figure: the 'very highest and most superior Great-Great Majesty, Great-Great God, St. Adolf, born in Switzer-land of the Planet, Earth', or as 'Great-Great Majesty, Great-Great God, Great-Great Kaiser and Great-Great Husband, Holy St. Adolf'. Of special interest are passages in which Wölfli describes himself as equalling or even surpassing God in the quintessentially divine act of cosmic creation, as when he describes blowing into a 'Horn of Omnipotence' that was lent to him by God: 'Oh Miracle and, Ravishment: Oh Splendor, Marvelous! Not only Myriaads! [sic] No!! Many Oberons of Sstaars [sic] . . . and fragments of the Universe flew out of this horn in the direction of the South' ('Oberon' was Wölfli's neologism for the highest of all numbers). Wölfli describes specks of dust that emerge from his horn, then grow larger and larger until, finally, they coalesce into a colossal new universe that, he tells us, is eleven times larger than the previous one created by God.

Considered in one way, this occasion of world-creation is liable to seem the most absurd instance of grandiosity — almost a limit-case of a grandiose delusion that implies belief in something not only false but impossible. But from another standpoint, Wölfli's blowing of the omnipotence horn is a perfectly accurate, though allegorical, statement of the *literal* truth of his existence at the Waldau Asylum, where Adolph Wölfli spent his days immersed in his imagination, producing the worlds that he, in a sense, *aptly* terms the 'St. Adolf Creation' or 'St. Adolf Giant Creation'. Wölfli did not, of course create *actual* universes in the infinite realms of physical space; he did, however, *actually* create *virtual* universes on canvas and paper. Indeed, Wölfli seems to have devoted far more time and energy (most of his waking hours over the course of several decades) to his virtual life in these sublime, imaginary realms than to his actual life as a mental patient in the Waldau — so much so that his Waldau life may have sometimes felt to him, in some sense, less than fully real. This does not, however, mean that he confused his virtual life with an actual one; or that the colossal walnut tree on the 'island-of-the-Echo-of-the-Western-Sea' was, to him, as real (or real in the same way) as were the fir trees in the asylum grounds.

There are occasional passages in Wölfli's writings when he acknowledges his own role in creating what he seems to be recognizing as only fictional universes. In one passage, for example, Wölfli makes explicit reference to his own role as author of the text: 'But in order not to lose my way in the narrative,' he writes, 'I march right back to St Johannsen, and sit down at the table in an office decorated especially for me, take a lighted Havana to my lips and fill my jug full of beer so that I might tell the next chapter most exactly.' At times he refers to himself as a 'patient of the Waldau [clinic]' or even a 'candidate for the looney-bin' who devotes himself to the 'madman's pastime' of mere fantasizing.

One might object that Wölfli's attitude is atypical, and that *most* patients with schizophrenia do *not* have this kind of distance either from their own delusional claims or from the delusion-generating process. I would agree that, by virtue of his raw intelligence, capacity for irony, and sheer creative energy, Wölfli is hardly the most typical patient or person. I would also agree that many patients with schizophrenia lack this kind of distance from their own delusions that he sometimes shows, and that their attitude can sometimes involve something much closer to normal forms of conviction or belief — especially in some early stages of schizophrenia and in the case of many paranoid-persecutory delusions. Persecutory delusions are in fact the type of delusion that has been found most likely to be acted upon by the patient (when this acting is judged by third-party observers). This is in contrast with delusions of catastrophe or grandiosity — both highly characteristic of Wölfli — which appear to *decrease* the likelihood that a delusion (or quasi-delusion?) will be acted upon by the patient (Wessely *et al.*, 1993). According to the analysis presented in this article, affects associated with persecutory delusions would therefore be expected to be closer to normal forms of emotion. This is, in fact, consistent with Buchanan *et al.*'s (1993) finding that patient reports of acting on a delusion were positively associated with the patient's 'feeling sad, frightened or anxious as a consequence of the delusion' (p. 77).

I do believe that some kind of implicit awareness of the quasi-fictional or subjective nature of the delusional world is common enough in chronic and withdrawn patients — indeed, that retreat into a world *experienced* as merely virtual can be a key motivation for the withdrawal itself. For as Sartre and others point out, delusion can involve escape not just from the *content* of the real, but from its very form, especially from reality's way of making demands and imposing conditions on us while refusing to succumb (without manipulation) to even the most intense of our wishes. But this is not the place to debate how common this condition really is. Let us rather accept that Wölfli represents one *possibility* for schizophrenic experience and move on to ask about the affective dimension of this particular sort of 'world'.

One striking feature of Wölfli's imaginary world is the lack of any *particular* target of concern, such as a specific object of fear or desire around which any normal sort of plot, narrative energy, or temporal directedness could coalesce. Wölfli does refer to specific objects, such as the colossal walnut tree on the 'Island-of-the-Echo-of-the-Western-Sea' or the 'Giant-Glacier-of-the-Celestial-Stars-of-God-the-Father'. These, however, have an interchangeable quality — as if no object had any particular importance other than its status as an exemplar of the amazing or the tremendous. For Wölfli, one might say, the object of concern is not any specific person or thing with*in* the world, but rather the world itself, or the world as a whole. Instead of having *worldly* concerns, he is concerned with the world itself — with its reality or unreality and with the conditions of its creation. We might say, in fact, that the affective tone imbuing these realms of the amazing and the miraculous, is more a matter of 'mood' than of 'emotion' — more a pervasive state of mind or feeling than an affective charge targeting any specific object of concern. As for the particular *kinds* of mood, these, I think, are well specified by the concept of 'the sublime' discussed above: namely, the present-oriented quasi-emotions of wonderment or amazement, combined with a paradoxical mode of self-experience in which abjection and a sense of shrinking away is continually being undercut and overcome by surges of godlike grandiosity. Many of Wölfli's affective reactions are akin to what Pierre Janet, in *De L'Angoisse a L'Extase* (1928), calls *'les beatitudes'*, and distinguishes from *'les emotions'*. As Janet points out, states of beatitude have three key characteristics: a great sense of joy that is accompanied by extreme activation of internal thought processes and also by nearly complete suppression of motoric activity.

Wölfli's lack of normal, engaged temporality is reflected in the flattening and unreality of space characteristic of his quasi-delusional world. Indeed, Wölfli's work nicely illustrates the essential coupling of time and space that Heidegger (1962) has described. As Heidegger points out, a normal sense of lived space is necessarily imbued with (constituted by) the temporality of a practical being (*Dasein*) who perceives affordances and is implicitly aware of his own actual and potential movements and interactions with real objects (Heidegger, 1962, p. 419). By contrast, Wölfli exists in a sort of virtual world, a world in which objects are unreal and action is either impossible or irrelevant — a world in which (in Stephan Strasser's (1977) terms) there is no sense of neediness and no sense of being 'underway' (e.g., no quickening of desire on approaching a yearned-for object). In this sort of world, the patient is likely to experience both more *and* less affect — or perhaps we should say, affect of a different *kind*.

Consider, in this light, the fear of World-Catastrophe described in several classic accounts of schizophrenia and in many textbooks (e.g., Kaplan and Sadock, 1998, p. 480). At least in some cases, the patient's fear that the universe will explode or disappear is associated with the patient's feeling of being a kind of divine, quasi-solipsistic centre that is somehow responsible for the world's very existence. 'The world must be represented, or the world will disappear', said one patient quoted by Karl Jaspers (1963, p. 296). Patients sometimes feel it is imperative to keep their body perfectly still, lest the universe begin to tremble and collapse. From one standpoint, the dissolution of the world — which would seem to imply one's own death, and that of everyone and everything one cares about — would seem the most frightening prospect imaginable. But in another perspective, it is almost a trivial, because *virtual*, event — no more consequential than the blotting out of the world that occurs each time one blinks one's eyes. It is understandable, then, that this sense of utter desolation or panic may occur alongside a kind of emotional blunting or indifference, and in conjunction with a lack of normal fellow-feeling with other persons (Slater and Roth, 1969, p. 269).

I would suggest that many withdrawn, long-term patients are accustomed to just this sort of oscillation. The sense of safety they feel from external demands when in their virtual world is related to a *background* sense of the unreality of this world; hence they will, much of the time, maintain a residual awareness of the unreality of the world-catastrophe. One young male patient treated by a colleague of mine told the colleague that *she* had nothing to fear from the world-catastrophe he had been anticipating — the catastrophe was relevant to him and to him alone (Sass, 1992a, p. 335; see also Sechehaye, 1970, p. 27). Such a patient exists in a subjectivized, even solipsistic world; and this, obviously, alters what Frijda calls the 'situational' aspect of affective life. A catastrophe of this kind necessarily lacks several of the 'core components' of emotion (Frijda, 1986), components that *make* a situation emotional at all, and also contribute to its *intensity*: namely, 'objectivity' and 'reality level' (the sense of being affected by something external and real), 'relevance' for action, 'urgency' and 'seriousness'. By its very nature, a world-catastrophe experience is therefore incompatible with passionate emotion in the full or paradigmatic sense of the term. It may arouse a kind of intense affect, but since the affective state involves no real change in action-readiness, it is likely to be framed or surrounded with a paradoxical kind of calm. This accounts for the remarkable *sang froid* that a person with schizophrenia may display before what would seem to be the most terrifying fantasies or events; such a person is capable of experiencing horror and serenity at the very same moment.

It is worth noting that, in the case of a morbid dreamer like Wölfli, the sequence and priority of the experiences of abjection and sovereignty seem opposite to what typically occurs with the natural sublime. Kant and Schopenhauer describe situations in which one happens across a feature of the natural world (e.g. the Grand Canyon, Mont Blanc), and in which the initial experience of being overwhelmed eventually inspires an antithetical awareness of one's own centrality and power. But in the case of the morbid dreamer, the experience of one's own, godlike centrality is liable to be the prior and primordial truth. After all, the delusional world is only a *virtual* or *imaginary* world; and as such, is necessarily attended by a coefficient of subjectivity and by a residual, potentially deflationary, awareness of one's own role in *creating* this world.

It may be, in fact, that the emphasis on the colossalness of all that Wölfli perceives/creates is partially inspired by a defensive need to insist on the overwhelming, and supposedly incontrovertible, *reality* of all that he experiences — to, in a sense, *deny* the coefficient of subjectivity that may attend all that he contemplates in his virtual, quasi-delusional world. Another feature that may serve this purpose is the proliferation of irrelevant yet amazingly precise details that Wölfli sometimes provides. Consider in this light Wölfli's account of his delusional memory of a train wreck:

> Afforesaid train No. 21 of H.M. Railways (Saragossa-Granada-Cordova) of latest construction, had 2 eight-wheeled express engines, 1. With tender, 2. With luggage van, 3. With post van and 4. with 43 passenger coaches, most of them with 60 seats . . . crashed down slightly north of the center between those enormous bridge piles, holding exactly 1,431,182 cubic meters asbestos each.

There is something absurdly exaggerated about the amazing elaboration of detail concerning an event that is purely imaginary. It suggests a desperate attempt to create an *illusion* of reality — to produce what the literary theorist Roland Barthes (1986) has called the 'reality effect'. Barthes describes how novelists may include incidental details — details completely arbitrary and free of any thematic purpose — for the sole purpose of giving the *impression* of realism.

Wölfli's vanity ('Great-Great-Majesty, Great-Great God, St. Adolf') and the insistent quality of his claims, taken together with his occasional bursts of irony and self-mockery, do indicate some defensiveness or ambivalence about his own, quasi-divine status and role. Wölfli, it seems, experiences a distinctive combination of pride and amazement, of cosmic self-satisfaction and abject insecurity — the affects appropriate to a creator-god who is vain as well as insecure, and inclined at times to protest rather too insistently about the boundlessness of his power. The world Wölfli invokes is but a *virtual* world, conjured by the self, and this self is always at least residually aware of its conjuring.

Wölfli's virtual world can seem congealed, airless and inert (a mood often conveyed by his visual works). Alternatively it may seem as ephemeral or inconsequential as smoke or mist — a roiling, shape-shifting cloud that takes on one grandiose appearance after another (this is more typical of his narrative writings). In both cases, however, Wölfli's world lacks the consequentiality and the true unpredictability of 'the real'. For this reason, Wölfli's writings lack any vestige of real narrative drive. Though fascinating to sample, they can actually be quite boring to read in large amounts: Despite the emphasis on the colossal and the amazing, there seems no possibility of surprise and, hence, an utter lack of suspense; the reader is unlikely to feel gripped on an emotional level.

Crucial to the paradigmatic or passionate emotions is an intense sense of 'objectivity' — the awareness that the situation imposes its meaning rather than having it simply conferred by oneself. Also crucial are action tendencies or changes in action readiness — in 'modes of readiness for entertaining or abandoning given types of relationship with the emotional object' (Frijda, 1986, pp. 239, 263); and these, in turn, are coordinated with the person's experience of his worldly 'situation'. But to the extent that the morbid dreamer manages to live *within* his dream, there *are*, in some sense, no emotional objects. Alternatively, one might say that the *entire* virtual world is the object, not of normal emotionality, but of affectively charged concerns involving the omnipotence of the self. Such a person exists in a subjectivized or quasi-solipsistic world, and this necessarily alters the founding dimensions of affective life.

Clearly, then, the world of the 'morbid dreamer' involves a diminishment of the paradigmatic emotions, which involve such reality-oriented attitudes as fear, desire, and the like. But, at the same time, there is likely to be a concomitant heightening of other, more moodlike and ontologically oriented affects that are associated with the sublime. In place of the passions that come of being embroiled *within* the worldly, Wölfli experiences affects appropriate to a godlike source who has (in a sense) *created* the world and continues to support its ongoing existence. This includes a sense of exhilaration and of one's own incomparable grandeur, but also lingering insecurities — not only about the fragility of what one *has* created (manifest in world-catastrophe fears), but also about the reality of having created it. Such a person is therefore caught between two fears than can be viewed as either antithetical or identical: first, the fear that the universe will somehow dissolve; and second, the fear that the universe that preoccupies him, along with its imminent catastrophe, will turn out to be no more than an illusion.

Conclusion

I have described three kinds of schizophrenic experience: Bodily Alienation, Unworlding and Subjectivization. By developing phenomenological accounts of each of these kinds, I have attempted to resolve what might be called the Kretschmerian paradox — that is, to show that each mode is compatible with a diminishment of normal emotionality along with preservation, or even heightening, of *other* (*non*-emotional) forms of affective response. In this way, phenomenology can help to account for — perhaps even, in a sense, to explain (Sass and Parnas, in press) — one of the key clinical anomalies characteristic of the psychopathology of schizophrenia.

References

Alquie, F. (1979), *La Conscience Affective* (Paris: Vrin).

Barthes, R. (1986), 'The Reality Effect', in R. Barthes, *The Rustle of Language* (New York: Farrar, Straus and Giroux), pp. 141–8.

Berrios, G.E. (1985), 'The Psychopathology of Affectivity: conceptual and historical aspects', *Psychological Medicine*, **15**, pp. 745–58.

Blanchard, J.J. and Panzarella, C. (1998), 'Affect and Social Functioning in Schizophrenia', in *Handbook of Social Functioning in Schizophrenia*, ed. K.T. Mueser and N. Tarrier (Boston: Allyn & Boston), pp. 181–96.

Buchanan, A., Reed, A., Wessely, S., Garety, P., Taylor, P., Grubin, D. and Dunn, G. (1993), 'Acting on Delusions. II: the phenomenological correlates of acting on delusions', *British Journal of Psychiatry*, **163**, pp. 77–81.

Carr, V. and Wale, J. (1986), 'Schizophrenia: an information processing model', *Australian and New Zealand Journal of Psychiatry*, **20**, pp. 136–55.

Cutting, J. (1985), *The Psychology of Schizophrenia* (Edinburgh: Churchill Livingstone).

Damasio, A. (1994), *Descartes' Error: Emotion, Reason, and the Human Brain* (New York: Avon Books).

Dworkin, R. H., Clark, S. C., Amador, X. F. and Gorman, J.M. (1996), 'Does Affective Blunting in Schizophrenia Reflect Affective Deficit or Neuromotor Dysfunction?', *Schizophrenia Research*, **20**, pp. 301–6.

Ey, H. (1955), 'Description clinique de la forme typique', in *Etudes Cliniques et Psycho-pathologiques: Schizophrenie* (Paris: Synthelabo) (Collection: Les Empecheurs de Penser en Rond), pp. 165–232 (1955 is the original date of the article; the book, a reprint, is undated).

Fisher, P. (2002), *The Vehement Passions* (Princeton NJ: Princeton University Press).

Frijda, N. (1986), *The Emotions* (Cambridge UK: Cambridge University Press).

Gibson, J.J. (1979), *The Ecological Approach to Visual Perception* (Boston: Houghton Mifflin).

Heidegger, M. (1962), *Being and Time*, trans. J. Macquarrie and E. Robinson (New York: Harper & Row), translated from the German: *Sein und Zeit*, 7th edition (Tubingen: Neomarius Verlag).

Henry, M. (1973), *The Essence of Manifestation*, trans. G. Etzkorn (The Hague: Martinus Nijhoff), original in 1963: *L'Essence de la Manifestation* (Paris: PUF).

James, W. (1981), *The Principles of Psychology*, intro by G. Miller (Cambridge MA: Harvard University Press).

Janet, P. (1928), *De l'Angoisse a L'Extase* (Paris: Librairie Felix Alcan).

Jaspers, K. (1963), *General Psychopathology*, trans. J. Hoenig and M.W. Hamilton (Chicago: University of Chicago Press).

Kant, I. (1987), *Critique of Judgment*, trans. W.S. Pluhar (Indianapolis: Hackett) (orig. publ. 1790) (See Part I, Division I, Book II: 'Analytic of the Sublime').

Kaplan, H.I. and Sadock, B.J. (1998), *Synopsis of Psychiatry: Behavioral Sciences/ Clinical Psychiatry, 8th Edition* (Baltimore: Lippincott, Williams & Wilkins).

Kimura, Bin (1995), *Zwischen Mensch und Mensch* (Darmstadt: Wissenschaftliche Buchgesellschaft).

Klosterkoetter, J. (1992), 'The Meaning of Basic Symptoms for the Development of Schizo-phrenic Psychoses', *Neurology, Psychiatry and Brain Research*, **1**, pp. 30–41.

Koehler, K. and Sauer, H. (1984), 'Huber's Basic Symptoms: another approach to negative psychopathology in schizophrenia', *Comprehensive Psychiatry*, **25**, pp. 174–82.

Kretschmer, E. (1925), *Physique and Character*, trans. W.J.H. Sprott (New York: Harcourt, Brace & World).

Kretschmer, E. (1936), *Physique and Character*, 2nd revised edition, trans. W.J.H. Sprott, with appendix by E. Miller (London: Kegan Paul, Trench, Trubner).

Kring, A.M. (1999), 'Emotion in Schizophrenia: old mystery, new understanding', *Current Directions in Psychological Science*, **8**, pp. 160–3.

Kring, A. M. and Neale, J. M. (1996), 'Do Schizophrenic Patients Show a Disjunctive Relationship among Expressive, Experiential, and Psychophysiological Components of Emotion?', *Journal of Abnormal Psychology*, **105**, pp. 249–57.

Maslach, C. (1979), 'Negative Emotional Biasing of Unexplained Arousal', *Journal of Personality and Social Psychology*, **37**, pp. 953–69.

Matussek, P. (1987), 'Studies in Delusional Perception', in *The Clinical Roots of the Schizophrenia Concept*, ed. J. Cutting and M. Shepherd (Cambridge: Cambridge University Press), pp. 89–103. Excerpt from: P. Matussek (1952), *Untersuchungen uber die Wahnwahrnehmung*, *Archiv fur Psychiatrie und Zeitschrift Neurologie*, **189**, pp. 279–318.

Mellor, C.S. (1970), 'First Rank Symptoms of Schizophrenia', *British Journal of Psychiatry*, **117**, pp. 15–23.

Merleau-Ponty, M. (1962), *The Phenomenology of Perception*, trans. C. Smith (New York: Routledge & Kegan Paul).

Moran, D. (2000), *Introduction to Phenomenology* (London and New York: Routledge).

Nussbaum, M. (2001), *Upheavals of Thought: The Intelligence of the Emotions* (Cambridge University Press).

Parnas, J. and Sass, L. (2001), 'Self, Solipsism, and Schizophrenic Delusions', *Philosophy, Psychiatry, Psychology*, **8**, pp. 101–20.

Sartre, J.-P. (1966), *The Psychology of Imagination*, trans. B. Frechtman (New York: Washington Square Press).

Sass, L. (1992a), *Madness and Modernism: Insanity in the Light of Modern Art, Literature, and Thought* (New York: Basic Books) (Harvard University Press Paperback, 1994).

Sass, L. (1992b), 'Heidegger, Schizophrenia, and the Ontological Difference', *Philosophical Psychology*, **5**, pp. 109–32.

Sass, L. (1994), *The Paradoxes of Delusion* (Ithaca NY: Cornell University Press).

Sass, L. (1997), 'Adolf Wölfli, Spatiality, and the Sublime', in *Adolf Wölfli: Draftsman, Poet, Composer*, ed. E. Spoerri (Ithaca NY and London: Cornell University Press), pp. 136–45. German version: Sass, L. (n.d.), 'Adolf Wölfli, das Raumliche und das Erhabene', in *Adolf Wölfli: Schreiber, Dichter, Zeichner, Componist*, ed. E. Spoerri (Basel: Wiese Verlag), pp. 136–45.

Sass, L. (in press), 'Schizophrenia: a disturbance of the thematic field', in *Gurwitsch's Relevancy for the Cognitive Sciences*, ed. L. Embree (Dordrecth, Holland: Kluwer).

Sass, L. and Parnas, J. (2003), 'Schizophrenia, Consciousness, and the Self', *Schizophrenia Bulletin*, **29** (3), pp. 427–44.

Sass, L. and Parnas, J. (in press), 'Explaining Schizophrenia: the relevance of phenomenology', in *The Philosophical Understanding of Schizophrenia*, ed. M. Chung, W. Fulford and G. Graham (Oxford University Press).

Sass, L. and Uhlhaas, P. (in press), 'Phenomenology, Context, and Self-Experience in Schizophrenia', *Behavioral and Brain Sciences*.

Scheler, M. (1954), *The Nature of Sympathy*, trans. P. Heath (New Haven, CN: Yale University Press).

Schopenhauer, A. (1928), 'The World as Will and Idea', in *The Philosophy of Schopenhauer*, ed. Irwin Edman (New York: Modern Library), German edition: Schopenhauer, A. (1949), *Die Welt as Wille und Vorstellung*, erster Band, drittes Buch, in *Samtliche Werke*, Bd. 2 (Wiesbaden).

Sechehaye, M. (ed. 1970), *Autobiography of a Schizophrenic Girl*, trans. G. Rubin-Rabson (New York: New American Library).

Sigmund, D. and Mundt, C. (1999), 'The cycloid type and its differentiation from core schizophrenia: A phenomenological approach', *Comprehensive Psychiatry*, **40**, pp. 4–18.

Slater, E. and Roth, M. (1969), *Mayer-Gross, Slater, and Roth: Clinical Psychiatry*, 3rd edn. (London: Balliere, Tindall & Cassell).

Sokolowski, R. (2000), *Introduction to Phenomenology* (Cambridge: Cambridge University Press).

Strasser, S. (1977), *Phenomenology of Feeling* (with Foreword by Paul Ricoeur), trans. R.E. Wood (Pittsburgh PA: Duquesne University Press).

Tallon, A. (1997), *Head and Heart: Affection, Cognition, Volition as Triune Consciousness* (New York: Fordham University Press).

Tatossian, A. (1997), *La Phenomenologie des Psychoses* (Paris: L'Art du Comprendre (July 1997, Numero double, hors serie).

Tellenbach, H. (1968/1983), *Goût et atmosphère* (Paris: Presses Universitaires Françaises).

Tsuang, M. and Winokur, G. (1974), 'Criteria for Subtyping Schizophrenia: clinical differentiation of hebephrenic and paranoid schizophrenia', *Archives of General Psychiatry*, **31**, pp. 43–7.

Wessely, S., Buchanan, A., Reed, A., Cutting, J., Everitt, B., Garety, P. and Taylor, P.J. (1993), 'Acting on Delusions: I: Prevalence', *British Journal of Psychiatry*, **163**, pp, 69–76.

Zahn, T., Frith, J. and Steinhauer, S (1991), 'Autonomic Functioning in Schizophrenia', in *Handbook of Schizophrenia, Vol 5: Neuropsychology, Psychophysiology and Information Processing*, ed. S. Steinhauer, J. Gruzelier and J. Zubin (Amsterdam: Elsevier), pp. 185–226.

Josef Parnas

Belief and Pathology of Self-awareness

A Phenomenological Contribution to the Classification of Delusions

Delusions are usually defined as false beliefs about the state of affairs in the public world. Taking this premise as unquestionable, the debate in cognitive science tends to oscillate between the so-called 'rationalist approach'— proposing some breakdown in the central intellective modules embodying human rationality — and the 'empiricist approach' — proposing a primary peripheral deficit (e.g., in perception), followed by explanatory efforts in the form of delusions. In this article the foundational assumption about delusion is questioned. Especially in the case of schizophrenia, delusions are not epistemic statements about external world but metaphorical reports of altered structure of experiencing ('autistic-solipsistic delusions'). Delusions as epistemic statements or beliefs ('empirical delusions') occur paradigmatically in delusional disorder (paranoia). These two types of delusions are compared from a primarily phenomenological stance.

'So you are saying that human agreement decides what is true and what is false?' —
It is what human beings say that is true and false; and they agree in the *language* they use. That is not an agreement in opinions but in form of life.
— Wittgenstein, *Philosophical Investigations*, § 241.

This article provides a new proposal for classifying delusions; a proposal derived from phenomenologically guided clinical explorations of the characteristic features of delusions and the clinical features that occur prior to a psychotic episode. The quote from Wittgenstein reminds us that the notions of truth and falsehood are not only based on cognitive or linguistic inclinations but are embedded in a more overarching perspective — form of life — or life-world, to use a similar phenomenological term. This insight will play an essential role in this essay on classification of delusions. Delusion, the cardinal feature of madness, is perhaps also the most important psychopathological concept. Understanding of delusion was always considered as a 'royal road' to the notions of reality, reality aware-ness and related questions of mental pathology, normality and normativity, with intellectual impacts reaching outside the confines of psychiatry as a medical dis-cipline (Rigoli, 2001). Delusion — typically defined as a *strongly held false belief* — is a phenomenon that never ceases to fascinate a clinician, intrigued by intelligent, smart people, who nonetheless entertain the most bizarre, mad and implausible ideas. The novel conceptualization of delusion proposed here accounts partly for this paradoxical coexistence of madness and rationality. The adjective 'novel' is strictly speaking, a self-promoting exaggeration, because many other authors published clinical observations and theoretical reflections that contained elements, more or less similar to this proposal, a point to which I will later return.

Biology of Delusion

In biological psychiatry, delusions — as well as other psychiatric symptoms — are typically considered as signaling an underlying brain lesion or morbid pro-cess. The latter is usually envisaged in focal or modular terms.

It does not appear as if biological psychiatry has contributed a noticeable understanding of delusion that has proved its theoretical worth or turned out to be pragmatically and clinically useful.[1] In a rarely and admirably explicit quasi-biological model (Villagrán and Berrios, 1996), it is proposed that a pathologi-cal, 'irritative' neural signal that is sufficiently strong to penetrate the threshold of awareness enters into the so-called 'primordial soup'. 'Primordial soup' is construed as a proto-phenomenal recess of the mind, filled with amorphous affections and sensations. Only certain signals from the soup succeed in under-going additional transformations into explicitly accessible and reportable phe-nomenal *symptoms*. These transformations are due to 'conceptualizing processes' realizing formations of specific symptoms (e.g. delusions, hallucina-tions or obsessions). Delusions have, according to this model, no meaning, they are 'empty speech acts',[2] i.e. a sheer nonsense.

The most fundamental problem in empirical biological psychiatric research is that we have no idea of how a neural process, no matter how meticulously described, translates itself into a phenomenal, conscious level of experience. The conscious phenomena, through human suffering, attain an ontological suprem-acy that no other metaphysical approach is able to override. Conscious phenom-ena, as symptoms and distress, constitute clinical and social reality. Psychiatric

---

[1] We have known for some time that delusions are often partly responsive to treatment with antipsychotic drugs, influencing metabolism of neurotransmitters (of which the dopamine seems to be most important). In other words, dopamine, a neurotransmitter, must be somehow involved in the pathogenesis of delusions.

[2] Berrios claims that delusions do not fulfil any of the performative linguistic functions described by Austin (1962).

research is therefore in a very concrete manner rendered incomplete by Descartes' psychophysical problem or Chalmers' (1995) 'hard problem'.

The Approach to Delusions Found in Cognitive Science

The studies of this rapidly expanding group combine philosophical, neuro-cognitive and experimental approaches. The notion of belief is quite central in the neuro-cognitive literature, and it may be helpful to define this term explicitly as it is used in a standard way:

> To have a belief is to commit oneself in thought to a certain state of affairs holding in the world. The belief is true just if that state of affairs does hold, false otherwise. Belief itself is a psychological state, not a part of the thought but rather a relation to the thought. The thought itself is a postulate. To have the attitude of belief to that thought is to endorse the postulate (Bermúdez, 2003, p. 15).

Believing is portrayed here as consisting of two relata between subjectivity and its world: first, there is an inner *representation* of something in the world (state of affairs) and, second, there is a psychological attitude, designated as belief, directed towards this particular representation (also called doxic attitude, from 'doxa' = belief). This stage-wise schematisation of mentation is nicely congruent with the existence of other hypothetical mental faculties, which are assumed to be defective in the case of delusion: 'reality testing' — defined as ability to *distinguish* ongoing *perception* from ongoing *imagination* and 'reality monitoring' — defined as ability to distinguish self-generated from perceptually-derived 'mental data', including memories (Johnson, 1988).[3]

There are basically two approaches (and a mixed one) addressing delusion in the neuro-cognitive terms. Delusion formation is *either* seen as starting with the deformation of experience at 'the input end' (mainly perceptual),[4] leading to a cascade of delusional constructions as explanatory efforts, *or* delusion is seen as indicating a breakdown of rationality, caused by malfunctioning of various central intellective modules (the 'rationalist' view) — such as inferential or probabilistic reasoning, abstraction, logical failures, attribution styles or proclivities to 'jumping to conclusions', or, most recently, deficient capacities for 'meta-representation'. This latter, heavily polysemic, term designates our abilities to reflect upon our representations of the world, to introspect our thoughts, ability of 'central monitoring' (e.g. as a part of the executive processes), 'ability to

---

[3] However, an inherent problem in the neuro-cognitive models is an impenetrable mixture of phenomenal and sub-personal levels of description and explanation, rendering their evaluation and potential critique nearly impossible. This is for example the case with reality *testing* and *monitoring*. There are perhaps sub-personal processes that correspond to these functions. Phenomenologically speaking, however, there is no such thing as reality testing under normal conditions. *I do not compare my perceptions and imagination* in order to know in which state I am. Normally, I am aware of the identity of my mental states not through inference or some metacognitive move but through an immediate familiarity with the experience itself. Thus my awareness of the experience (e.g. am I imagining or perceiving?) is not given through reflection but is part of the intentional act in question; it is a question of an immediate pre-reflective self-awareness (*ipseity* [Zahavi and Parnas, 1998]).

[4] Primarily proposed by a famous German psychiatrist and neurologist, Wernicke in 1905, for whom delusions played an explanatory role, later held and elaborated by numerous other authors (e.g. De Clerambault, 1942; Klosterkötter, 1988; Maher, 1988).

represent our own mental states, including our intentions' (i.e. 'mentalizing'). Here belong the notions of defective self-monitoring and reality testing mentioned and defined above (Johnson, 1988). In summary, meta-representation appears to be a sort of a higher-level capacity for self-awareness — corresponding perhaps to the notions of the 'abstract attitude' by the neurologist Kurt Goldstein or of the 'formal operations' by the developmental psychologist Jean Piaget.

The overinclusiveness of the concept of meta-representation makes it almost trivial: so defined, metarepresentational deficit may account for just about *any kind* of disturbance in cognition or interpersonal understanding. To say, for example, that a deluded person is unable to make a cognitive meta-move (self-monitoring) in order to realize that he is, in fact, deluded, does not add much to our understanding of delusional processes.

What Is a Delusion?

In the race to make research progress, we tend to forget or circumvent unresolved basic conceptual issues, which were once causes of the headaches of our predecessors. Delusion is a good example. Twentieth-century psychiatry witnessed many fascinating and intellectually brilliant debates, often based, however, on rather scarce *systematic* research data (Schmidt, 1940). Unfortunately, psychopathological debates have come to a complete standstill after the introduction of the so-called operational criteria, based on a lay descriptive approach, simplified vocabulary, and strong bias towards behaviourism, shunning subjectivity as one of its core dogmas (Parnas and Bovet, 1995). The data available today are nearly exclusively of a quantitative kind, operating with crude distinctions, and therefore not suitable for theoretical analysis. Yet, it seems that the conclusion reached by Schmidt in his seminal review from 1940 is still relevant: definition and classification of delusion cannot avoid reference to the subjective aspects, to delusion's mode of constitution. It is therefore impossible to define delusion without being concerned with the patient's experience.

It is here that phenomenology has an important role to play today (Parnas and Zahavi, 2002). Contemporary psychopathology, after more than 20 years of behaviouristic dominance, acutely needs a conceptual *framework* where consciousness is not only considered as a thing, but also as a constitutive dimension of phenomenality. There is an urgent need of detailed descriptions of and renewed emphasis on anomalous experience and expression. Moreover, since the majority of psychopathological conditions are defined in a contrastive way, it is necessary that psychiatrists have some theoretical knowledge of the workings and structures of normal consciousness. In other words, in order to investigate subjectivity, certain familiarity is needed with distinctions and methodological approaches that phenomenology is able to offer.

All modern descriptive criteria of delusion are the descendants of the influential proposal of Karl Jaspers (1963):[5] a belief is delusional if (a) its content is false and/or impossible [there is a separate debate about which aspect Jaspers

---

[5] That is not to say that Jaspers was the sole original contributor: other and earlier French and German authors had proposed similar criteria.

actually emphasized], (b) it is held with unshakable conviction and (c) it is incorrigible by any rational argument (resistant to correction). Here (b) and (c) are two descriptive facets of the same feature rather than two independent criteria. According to a contemporary American psychiatric manual, DSM-IV (APA, 1994), delusion is 'a false, personal belief based upon incorrect inference about external reality, firmly sustained despite incontrovertible proof to the contrary, and to what almost everybody else [in that subculture] believes'. All such criteria have been 'deconstructed' by several authors (Spitzer, 1990; Parnas & Bovet, 1995; Bovet & Parnas, 1993). The attempts to improve the reliability of the definition by adding extraneous criteria such as distress, loss of function, etc. (see Oltmanns, 1988) could not compensate for the original lack of conceptual clarity.

German psychiatrists were well aware, prior to World War II, that providing a formal definition of delusion was an impossible task (Schmidt, 1940). In other words, one can always imagine (or encounter) a patient in whose case a certain criterion of the definition is not fulfilled, yet the delusion, according to clinical judgement, is nonetheless present. E.g. a patient suffering from delusional jealousy may be right — empirically speaking — in suspecting infidelity of his spouse. In this case, potential veracity of the propositional content does not rule out the possibility of that content being delusional (clinicians typically reach such conclusion because of the *way* the patient argues for his belief). Jaspers was of course well aware of these problems and therefore modestly called his own criteria 'external indicators' of delusion (*Merkmale*), in order to emphasize that the latter did not capture the essence of *what a delusion is*.

The available empirical evidence tells us that delusion, in terms of aetiology, *is not a homogenous phenomenon*. Delusions occur in many types of mental and neurological disease and in many somatic, especially endocrine disorders (Oepen *et al.*, 1988). Yet, the delusions that are the topic of this article represent the vast majority of delusional states in non-organic psychosis.[6] Delusions vary in many respects, and appear to arise and evolve following different routes. Delusion, as already noted, is not a category that may be clearly defined by the boundaries determinable in a simple operational manner. Already at the beginning of the twentieth century, several types of delusion were described with respect to content and formal characteristics such as logical coherence. Thus delusion was considered 'multi-dimensional', in so far as its concrete descriptive aspects (e.g. degree of conviction on the part of the patient, logical cohesion, or extent of enactment) could vary, often semi-independently from each other.

Clinicians are sometimes able to diagnose delusions that are overlooked by formal, criteria-based diagnostic definitions. Diagnostically essential aspects may sometimes elude explicit formalization, [7] because they refer more to the

---

[6]   Which means 90 % of all clinically relevant delusions.

[7]   A special category are 'crazy actions' (Conrad, 1958; [Unsinnige Handlung]) or 'délire en acte' (Minkowski, 1927) — slightly strange or apparently entirely normal acts, whose justification, however, is typically highly idiosyncratic, suggesting an inchoate delusional world.

context than to the propositional content as such (e.g. the patient's way of reasoning, style of being and hierarchy of values).

A hotly debated issue concerns a potential diagnostic specificity of certain delusions: do their presence indicate the diagnosis of schizophrenia rather than of another psychosis? Most researchers realized quite early that delusional content taken at face value (e.g., persecution vs. jealousy) could not be used reliably for differential diagnosis (Schmidt, 1940) and attention turned towards studying the formal aspects of delusion. Jasper proposed that a characteristic component of schizophrenic psychosis was the so-called *primary delusion*, a delusion endowed with a quite specific mode of formation. In the primary delusion, the experiential content — a percept, a thought, or reminiscence — becomes *directly* imbued with delusional significance, i.e. in a manner un-mediated by reflection. Such a delusional experience was called 'apophantic' — referring to its revelation-like character (Conrad, 1958). A paradigmatic example of primary delusion is *delusional* perception: e.g., a patient seeing a dog lift its paw becomes convinced of an impending world disaster (Schneider, 1959). Seeing the world cataclysm in the paw being lifted is a revelation of new meaning, directly grasped (apperceptively) in the perceptual act — and *not* mediated by reflective acts (such as: Why is this dog lifting its paw? Isn't it strange? I have never seen that dog around here!). Jaspers writes that primary delusions are recalcitrant to psychological empathic understanding — partly because their content is peculiar and strange ('static un-understandability'; e.g. a patient claims that his thoughts are regulated by electro-magnetic influences by extraterrestrials from another planet or his eyes are replaced by cameras) and partly because of their *incomprehensibly irruptive* character. Apparently, there is no rational or emotionally comprehensible transition between the patient's antecedent state of mind and the content and form of the emerging (primary) delusion ('genetic un-understandability'). The content aspect is allocated important diagnostic status in the DSM-IV and the ICD-10. Both systems stipulate that the presence of 'bizarre' delusions[8] (i.e. with the content that appears to be 'empirically or physically impossible') indicates the diagnosis of schizophrenia. It was hoped that the concept of bizarre delusion might in a simplified way condense Jaspers' considerations on the issue of understandability and an apparently unmotivated upsurge of primary delusional content.

Proposal of a New Distinction

The core of the standard definition of delusion is that *it is a belief about the world*, i.e., an epistemic statement about the world. Delusions are thus false claims of knowledge, neither amenable to correction by other people nor by a self-generated criticism. It is here that theories diverge: we are looking for the *causes or mechanisms* of such erroneous epistemic contents and their

---

[8] The description of what type of content is bizarre and why this might be indicative of schizophrenia is based on a very superficial reading of Jaspers and other classic authors during the preparation of recent editions of the DSM and the ICD. Equating bizarre and empirically impossible appears to be mainly dictated by reliability concerns.

incorrigibility. Incorrigibility is usually ascribed to a hypothetical lack of 'reality testing' or 'reality monitoring'. Yet the view of the delusion as a false epistemic statement has been questioned since the early days of modern psychopathology. For example, Charles Blondel (1914) explicitly raised the question of whether we can unproblematically assume that the structure of delusion corresponds to the structure of an ordinary epistemic statement such as 'I believe that Paris is the capital of France'. Blondel's negative answer is followed by a proposal that is close to the one presented here. In the more recent literature, Louis Sass (1992), basing his approach on the Heideggerian 'ontological difference' between Being — as an unnoticed framework or structure of the lived world — and beings (extant entities), noted that schizophrenic delusions tend to take the underlying metaphysical dimension of Being as their theme. Bovet and Parnas (1993) (likewise influenced by Heidegger) suggested in a similar vein that schizophrenic delusions typically thematise the ontological framework rather than the 'ontic' (i.e. concrete mundane) states of affairs and should be understood as expressive of profoundly changed subjectivity. Manfred Spitzer (1990) suggested along similar lines that the so-called Schneider's 'first rank' symptoms of schizophrenia (especially phenomena of external influence) should be considered as reports about inner states and not as epistemic opinions on the factual matters in the public world.

The widespread view of delusion as a false statement about the world — called in the DSM-IV as the 'external world' — seems to fit un-problematically to many delusions; yet it does not work invariably well, and especially not so in the case of schizophrenia. In the latter case, many delusions have nothing to do with the factualities of the public world and seem more like idiosyncratic or private self-descriptions.

'Primary' or 'true' delusion (Karl Jaspers; see text)	'Secondary' delusions or wahnhafte Idéen ('secondary' means following more primary phenomena: e.g. a delusion of poverty as a consequence of a melancholic mood change)
Delusional atmosphere/delusional mood/'eidetic cognitive feelings' (considered as inchoate primary delusional phenomena)	**???**
Delusional perception or delusional memory (Kurt Schneider; see text): variants of primary delusions	Perceptually or memory *triggered* delusion (e.g. a specific perception evokes a new delusional content in an *already paranoid* patient)
Bizarre delusions (content considered as empirically or physically impossible, and resistant to empathic understanding)	Non-bizarre delusions (DSM-IV; ICD-10) The so-called 'understandable' delusions such as mood-congruent delusions in depression
Autistic-solipsistic delusions	**Empirical delusions**

Table 1. Divisions of Delusion:
Pathological phenomena in each column overlap conceptually

I would therefore propose to call the epistemic version of delusion (delusion as a belief, a claim of knowledge about the world) an *empirical delusion* and the non-epistemic version, an *autistic-solipsistic* delusion (ASD). The latter type of delusion is not to be seen as a statement about the world but as a metaphorical description of a profoundly altered *structure* of subjective experience. This does not mean that the empirical delusions are devoid of personal-motivational factors. Yet the personal themes and their clinical manifestation are different in these two types of delusion.

The proposed division overlaps with Jaspers' distinction between secondary delusions or delusional ideas ('wahnhafte Idéen') and primary delusions, as well as with the non-bizarre vs. bizarre distinction made by the DSM-IV and ICD-10 (see Table 1). We will now try to describe the clinical features that appear to confer clinical face validity to the proposed distinction.

The Empirical Delusion

From our primary, i.e. clinical-phenomenological point of view, empirical delusions are thematically concerned with ontic, worldly or intra-mundane matters, often with a specific pragmatic significance (e.g., fighting for a recompense payment).

Clinicians or relatives have the impression that the patient — despite his increasing isolation ensuing from the delusional condition — remains attached, in his own awkward way, to the intersubjective world. First, this attachment may be visible in the delusional content as such. For example, whereas a grandiose ASD will be concerned with universal matters, such as human guilt, global inequalities or inter-human understanding, a bipolar manic grandiosity will more clearly reflect mundane dispositions, caricaturing human desires familiar to most of us, e.g., becoming rich, starting a software company in order to compete Microsoft out of business, obtaining a high, powerful position, etc. Empirical delusions comply with a normative view of natural causality (although its workings may be portrayed in a highly idiosyncratic way) and typically do not involve extra-physical mechanisms to account for their content.

The patient's *attitude* also testifies to the intersubjective attachment. The patient argues for his delusion and may adopt an actively confrontational attitude towards his family or his treating psychiatrist. He may enact the content through a behaviour *rationally congruent* with the delusion, and will perhaps try to find an 'empirical proof' for his claims (e.g. a patient comes to a session with his psychiatrist with a match-box, filled with dirt and skin debris, proving in the patient's opinion that he has skin parasites, so far undetected by countless physicians), exactly like someone strongly believing in something about which other people are sceptical or indifferent. There is often a very strong affective component in the empirical delusion.

Case 1. A 60-year old woman was hospitalised due to suicidal intentions. Her husband shared her delusional system. Approximately 15 years ago, when the couple lived in a small house, she became convinced that some small insects, which she tried to get rid of by applying various cleaning regimes, infested the furniture. She contacted relevant authorities, and the house was examined by several technical commissions — all examinations failed to detect any parasites or insects. The couple changed apartment a few times, each times burning old, and buying brand new furniture, in order to prevent a contagion of the new residence. Alas, each time they failed: once it was a carpet that was not thrown away, etc. The patient had ongoing battles or confrontations with the municipality whose employees she suspected to be in collusion with the Technical Institute and a local general practitioner. Finally, the patient attracted media interest and was interviewed by a local radio station and a TV company, portrayed as a helpless citizen, victimized by insensitive and corrupt bureaucracy. The financial conditions of the family seriously deteriorated because of the frequent moving and formidable furniture expenses. The husband recovered from the condition of folie à deux after some weeks of separation from his wife, during which period he participated in a few psychotherapeutic sessions.

We clearly see in this case the essential features of the empirical delusion in the course of delusional disorder (paranoia). The content of delusion and the patient's attitude may in a straightforward fashion be considered as a false, yet incorrigible belief about the state of affairs in the public world. It is a dispute over epistemic issue in the shared world. It is so much an epistemic debate that the patient succeeds in implicating her husband, municipal authorities, technical experts and mass media, all as the actors playing in her show. She remains actively attached to the world, enacting her belief in a seemingly rational (relevant) way, defending it to the point of needing auxiliary evidence, which is here constructed in the form of persecutory ideas (collusion between municipality, Technical Institute and a GP).

Some of the motivational, causally relevant factors in the formation of empirical delusions have roots in the patient's insecure 'self-image' or 'self-esteem' and her fragile sense of autonomy (Shapiro, 1965). We observe in these cases, the projective mechanisms described in detail by the classic psychoanalytic literature.

The Autistic-Solipsistic Delusion (ASD)

The ASD is in a sense quite different, perhaps a sort of opposite to the empirical delusion. I will first present some clinical descriptive evidence in support of the face validity of this distinction. Pierre Janet (1926), in a fascinating book on anxiety and ecstasy, subtitled as 'Analysis of the concept of belief', makes the following insightful observation:

> A *belief is ultimately a promise of action*. To believe in the Arc of Triumph [in Paris] implies being able to show it to a visitor, to drive him there, and to experience a profound disappointment, should it turn out not be there. On the other hand, [the patient's delusional belief] is totally different; it belongs to verbal acts than cannot be transformed into actions (p. 95; my italics).

Case 2. Madeleine, a patient described in detail by Janet, had a habit of walking on her tiptoes, as a part of her experience of 'divine ascension'. Janet once provokingly commented that if her 'divine ascension' was really true, then her feet should be at least 10 centimeters above the floor. Madeleine responded: 'What a strange idea, applying metric measures to divine matters!' (pp. 146–7).[9]

This case illustrates well the proposed empirical vs. autistic-solipsistic distinction. It is clear that although the patient seems to claim certain state of affairs, she does not make these claims in order to seek intersubjective agreement. A patient experiencing his thoughts being manipulated by a machine outside his head typically *does not expect* that his fellow humans will be *correspondingly affected* (whereas this may be very well the case in empirical delusions, especially in paranoia). In other words, there is something strikingly *subjective* in such apparent epistemic claims. Some patients allude more or less directly to the subjective nature of their predicament. Louis Sass (1993, p. 27) describes this phenomenon in detail in the famous case of the judge Paul Schreber:[10] all of Schreber's abnormal experiences and delusional statements retained a certain 'coefficient of subjectivity'. As an example, Schreber claimed that his body, when he inspected it carefully in the mirror, tended to acquire feminine contours. Moreover, Schreber claimed that *anyone* could see these changes as well, provided that this person was spatially located as to have exactly the same visual perspective on the mirror as Schreber himself! The term 'coefficient of subjectivity' refers to the ability of the patient to see his delusion as a subjective, *personal* construction, existing in a parallel fashion with the rest of his ordinary mundane convictions.

Yet, it is perhaps misleading to use the term 'coefficient of subjectivity', because it appears to trivialize the difference between the autistic and the empirical to a matter of degree only. Thus, Madeleine's delusion appears as a subjective revelation that needs no evidence from the shared empirical world in order to become valid. In the ASD, the validity is given through the first-person access to experience, as something directly lived through in an un-mediated fashion and not acquired originally by reflective or inferential processes.[11] The solipsistic character of these delusions is visible in the patient's attitudes towards the world and his fellow humans. A delusion nearly always isolates its holder. Yet, the delusional loneliness is qualitatively different in the case of empirical vs. solipsistic delusion. Rümke, a famous Dutch psychiatrist formulated it very nicely:

> The sufferers from [empirical] delusion become lonely, the communicative relations with the ordinary being in the world cease to exist, remain unfulfilled, but the patients remain orientated in the *common world*. It is a privative change. The

---

[9] A recent biography of Madeleine describes in detail her life, religious beliefs and mystic experiences (Maître, 1993).

[10] A famous paranoid schizophrenic patient, whose memoirs have been most meticulously studied, among others, by Freud.

[11] Yet, we cannot exclude the possibility of reflection contributing to the details and complexity of the ASD.

schizophrenic also becomes lonely during the beginning of his illness, but in such a way that loneliness so to say grows up within him as the way of being in a new *changed world* which has become adequate to him. It is not a privative loneliness, but a *determining constitutive moment* [non-independent part] of his *own world, in itself radically lonely* (Rümke, 1950, p. 186 [my addition in brackets]).

In the case of empirical delusions, social isolation is due to a progressive shrinking or loss of contacts and rejection from others due to the socio-dystonic consequences of the delusional state. In the autistic-solipsistic position, the isolation emerges *from within*, alongside the constitution of a new subjective world.

We have already noted that the patient does not make claims of the intersubjective validity of his ASD and rarely engages in arguing about its veracity in a way that we saw in Case 1. In fact, the patient may even be puzzled by the need for any justification. His delusion is given for him originally with experiential evidence (normally, we have no need to strengthen an exclamation of pain by additional data).

In other words, what appears to be characteristic of the ASD is that these, in crucial aspects, do not fit the concepts of belief and knowledge. Believing or knowing is a personally engaged, intersubjectively relevant epistemic attitude, claiming veracity of a certain state of affairs in the public world. It presupposes related background notions such as truth, proof, consensus, disagreement, doubt, etc. In the case of ASD the notion of erroneous belief is inadequate or even misleading.[12] The ASD are intersubjectively disengaged in various ways:[13] they are detached due to their idiosyncratic affective valence, the themes are not really about the common world, and the patient does not expect similar tribulations to affect his fellow humans. It is for these reasons that the schizophrenic patients never construct a true 'societas schizophrenica' (Jaspers, 1963).[14] The 'subjectivity coefficient' is here high — pointing to a metaphorical description of inner states; more precisely, to a self-description of structurally changed subjectivity, expressed here in a public language and mistaken for a kind of belief.

Case 3. A 40-year old patient participates in a research-training interview. He is an unmarried cab driver, treated continuously at a psychiatric out-patient clinic. He suffers from life-long social isolation. In his late twenties, he was hospitalized a few times because of psychotic episodes, with agitation, hallucinations and delusions of being Jesus Christ.

The patient is now considered to be in remission and he is part time working.

During the interview, he said that he still felt that he was Jesus, but he never mentioned it to the treating personnel. He dated the origin of this feeling or thought to his late adolescence. He was then extremely insecure, with a sense of inner void, as if

---

[12] Unless we abandon Bermúdez's definition and opt for a very loose concept of belief — as for instance proposed by Needham (1972): 'Ordinary discourse and common sense psychology … tend to induce us into two capital errors; first that there must be something in common to all instances of believing; second, the assumption that there must be a mental counterpart to the expression of belief' (p. 122).

[13] 'The apathy and the lack of interest extend to the delusion not only in the "end-states", but quite often even from their onset' (Bleuler, 1911, p. 129).

[14] This is not to say that the patients do not care about each other.

'not having any soul', confused about his own feelings and not knowing which attitude he should adopt versus other people (e.g. friendly, thoughtful, angry, etc.). In a certain way, he felt himself a kind of anonymous being — he did not feel that any predicates really applied to his void (he was 'without predicates'). He became overwhelmed by a feeling of being Jesus and it has persisted ever since. In retrospect, he pointed out that Jesus was also without predicates, because God cannot be said to have mundane features or predicates. This similarity apparently contributed to his own feeling of being Jesus (here we also see an example of the schizophrenic formal thought disorder, 'pars-pro-toto', where the identity between two items is established because of a shared insignificant detail).

An interesting manifestation of the subjective colouring of these delusional constructions is what Bleuler called as 'double book-keeping' and Jaspers as 'inconsequential attitudes': e.g., a patient, claiming that he is the last Roman emperor, picks up the trash in the hospital yard without any protest and without noting any existential inconsistency.

It seems therefore that 'double book-keeping' is an unavoidable existential condition in the following sense: first, the solipsistic and the mundane-epistemic orientations are — in Thomas Kuhn's (1970) terminology — 'incommensurable', i.e. operating within two different paradigms that cannot be mutually negotiated and which therefore do not appear as contradictory for the patient. Second, both paradigms are in a certain sense given: the autistic-solipsistic is the result of a morbid self-transformation, and the mundane is a condition of the real world. The destiny of the solipsistic orientation is to be enacted in the common world, resulting in a specific profile of coexistence between the private and the public.

The patient figures out when to talk and when to keep silent about his ideas. The autistic-solipsistic delusion — more a report of a particular configuration of lived subjectivity rather than an occurrent belief about the world — may have a tendency to persist albeit in a rudimentary way. Bleuler gives two examples of this peculiar persistence:

> One of our patients, who for many years [considered himself as] the Lord of the universe, [subsequently recovered] and had corrected this idea, [but] nevertheless continued to sign 'The Lord' after his name.

> [Another, apparently cured patient], a professor, dedicated an outstanding scientific work to his delusional mistress (Bleuler, 1911, p. 138; translation slightly modified).

Occasionally, in certain patients, delusions may appear to be relatively well integrated with the patient's overall 'world-view' and daily life.

The content of the autistic-solipsistic delusions is often coloured by major, universal or metaphysical themes of humanity (Müller-Suur, 1950; 1954; Bovet & Parnas, 1993). Kepinski (1974) identified here three major thematic dimensions: *ontological* (e.g., the essence of Being and existence), *charismatic* (e.g., human mission in life), and *eschatological* issues ('eschatos' means ultimate; e.g., end of the world). The contemporary DSM-IV or ICD-10 classification describes delusions in schizophrenia as being 'bizarre', in the sense of being causally or physically impossible, which fits the solipsistic rather than the empirical nature.

The Origins of ASD: Altered Structure of Subjectivity

The ASD are proposed to be self-descriptions of structural alterations of subjectivity. In schizophrenia research, considering structural distortions of subjectivity as vulnerability traits is not new. These phenomena were in fact described in detail by two Germanophone psychiatrists, Berze (1914) and Gruhle (Berze and Gruhle, 1929). Similar evidence stems from several contemporary projects with various patient samples and with cohorts of persons at high risk for schizophrenia (Parnas *et al.*, 1989; Møller & Husby, 2000; Parnas and Handest, 2003; Sass and Parnas, 2003). All these studies demonstrate that the pre-onset phases of schizophrenia and schizotypal disorders are characterized by profound alterations of the patient's subjectivity. In the most general terms, such alteration can be described as a shrinking of the tacit, subsidiary, or pre-reflective dimension of selfhood and intentionality, leading to various transformations of the sense of self and world: feeling of inner void, anonymity or diminished sense of being a subject, continuous introspective observation, split of the 'I' and loss of the naturalness and of the *im*mediate meaning of the surrounding world (see Parnas and Handest, 2003, for clinical details; see Sass and Parnas, 2003, for theoretical considerations).

These structural alterations reflect the most elementary *phenomenal level* of the vulnerability to schizophrenia. They constitute, in the original designation, the 'trouble générateur' of schizophrenia (Minkowski, 1927). This phenomenal kernel is generative, or causally operative, in several senses: first, it constitutes the vulnerability to potential further psychotic developments; second, it keeps the symptoms meaningfully interconnected across the temporal vicissitudes of the illness; and it constrains the range of their possible manifestations.

The ASD are *metaphorical* thematizations of the patient's experience. They are not imagings. The modality of consciousness or intentionality involved in the ASD is best considered as a mixture of self-experience, thought, and reflection.

References

American Psychiatric Association (1994), *Diagnostic and Statistical Manual of Mental Disorders*, 4th ed., revised (DSM-IV) (Washington: The American Psychiatric Association).
Austin, J.L. (1962), *How To Do Things With Words* (Oxford: Clarendon Press).
Bermúdez, J.L. (2003), *Thinking Without Words* (Oxford: Oxford University Press).
Berrios, G. (1991), 'Delusions as wrong beliefs: A conceptual history', *British Journal of Psychiatry*, **159**, pp. 6–13.
Berze, J. (1914), *Die primäre Insuffizienz der psychischen Aktivität* (Leipzig: Franz Deuticke).
Berze, J. and Gruhle, H.W. (1929), *Psychologie der Schizophrenie* (Berlin: Springer Verlag).
Bleuler, E. (1950), Dementia Praecox oder Gruppe der Schizophrenien (Leipzig: Deuticke, 1911), trans. J. Zinkin and N.D.C. Lewis, *Dementia Praecox or the Group of Schizophrenias* (New York: International University Press).
Blondel, C. (1914), *La conscience morbide. Essay de psychopathologie générale* (Paris: Felix Alcan).
Bovet, P. and Parnas, J. (1993), 'Schizophrenic delusions: A phenomenological approach', *Schizophrenia Bulletin*, **19**, pp. 579–97.
Chalmers, D.J. (1995), 'Facing up the problem of consciousness', *Journal of Consciousness Studies*, **2** (4), pp. 200–19.

Conrad, K. (1958), *Die beginnende Schizophrenie. Versuch einer Gestaltanalyse des Wahns* (Stuttgart: Thieme Verlag).

De Clérambault, G. (1942) *Oeuvre psychiatrique* (Paris: Presses Universitaires de France).

Janet, P. (1929), *De l'angoisse à l'extase* (Paris: Felix Alcan)

Jaspers, K. (1963), *General Psychopathology*, 3rd. ed. (first edition in 1913) (Chicago: The University of Chicago Press).

Johnson, M.K. (1988), 'Discriminating origins of information', in *Delusional Beliefs*, ed. T.F. Oltmanns & B.A. Maher (New York: John Wiley & Sons).

Kepinski, A. (1974), *Skizofrenia* (Warszawa: Panstwowy Zaklad Wydawnictw Lekarskich).

Klosterkötter, J. (1988), *Basissymptome und Endphänomene der Schizophrenie. Eine empirische Untersuchung der psychopathologischen Übergangsreihen zwischen defizitären und produktiven Schizophreniesymptomen* (Berlin: Springer).

Kuhn, T.S.(1970), *The Structure of Scientific Revolutions* (Chicago: The University of Chicago Press).

Maher, B.A. (1988), 'Anomalous experience and delusional thinking: The logic of explanations', in *Delusional Beliefs*, ed. T.F. Oltmanns and B.A. Maher. (New York: Wiley & Sons).

Maître, J. (1993), *Un inconnu célèbre. La Madeleine Lebouc de Janet* (Paris: Anthropos).

Minkowski, E. (1927), *La schizophrènie. Psychopathologie des schizoïdes et des schizophrènes* (Paris: Payot).

Møller, P. and Husby, R. (2000), 'The initial prodrome in schizophrenia: searching for naturalistic core dimensions of experience and behavior', *Schizophrenia Bulletin*, **26**, pp. 217–32.

Müller-Suur, H. (1950), 'Das Gewissheitsbewusstsein beim schizophrenen und beim paranoischen Wahnerleben', *Fortschritte der Neurologie Psychiatrie und ihrer Grenzgebiete*, **18**, pp. 44–51.

Müller-Suur, H. (1954), 'Die Wirksamkeit allgemeiner Sinnhorizonte im schizophrenen Wahnerleben' *Fortschritte der Neurologie Psychiatrie und ihrer Grenzgebiete*, **22**, pp. 38–44.

Needham, R. (1972), *Belief, Language, and Experience* (Chicago, IL: The University Chicago Press).

Oepen, G., Harrington, A., Spitzer, M. and Fünfgeld, M. (1988), '"Feelings" of conviction: On the relation of affect and thought disorders', in *Psychopathology and Philosophy*, ed. M. Spitzer, F.A. Uehlein and G. Oepen (Berlin: Springer).

Oltmanns, T.F. (1988), 'Approaches to the definition and study of delusions', in *Delusional Beliefs*, ed. T.F. Oltmanns and B.A. Maher (New York: Wiley & Sons).

Parnas, J. and Bovet, P. (1995), 'Research in psychopathology: epistemologic issues', *Comprehensive Psychiatry*, **36**, pp. 167–81.

Parnas, J. and Handest, P. (2003), 'Phenomenology of anomalous self-experience in early schizophrenia', *Comprehensive Psychiatry*, **44**, pp. 121–34.

Parnas, J., Jansson, L., Sass, L.A. and Handest, P. (1998), 'Self-experience in the prodromal phases of schizophrenia', *Neurology, Psychiatry, and Brain Research*, **6**, pp. 97–106.

Parnas, J. and Zahavi, D. (2002), 'The role of phenomenology in psychiatric classification and diagnosis', in *Psychiatric Diagnosis and Classification*, ed. M. Maj, W. Gaebel, J.J. Lopez- Ibor, N. Sartorius; World Psychiatric Association's series in Evidence and Experience in Psychiatry (Chichester: John Wiley & Sons Ltd.).

Rigoli, J. (2001), Lire le délire. Aliénisme, rhétorique et littérature en France au XIX-e siècle. (Paris: Fayard).

Rümke, H.C. (1950), 'Significance of phenomenology for the clinical study of sufferers of delusions', in Psychopathologie des délires. *Congres International de Psychiatrie*, ed. F. Morel (Paris: Hermann & Cie).

Sass, L. (1992), 'Heidegger, schizophrenia, and the ontological difference', *Philosophical Psychology*, **5**, pp. 109–32.

Sass, L. (1993), *The Paradoxes of Delusion: Wittgenstein, Schreber, and the Schizophrenic Mind* (Ithaca, NY: Cornell University Press).

Sass, L. and Parnas, J. (2003), 'Schizophrenia, consciousness, and the self', *Schizophrenia Bulletin*, **29** (3), pp. 427–44.

Schmidt, G. (1940), Der Wahn im deutchschprahingen Schriftum der letzten 25 Jahre. *Zentralblatt für die gesamte Neurologie und Psychiatrie*, **97**, pp. 113–43.

Schneider, K. (1959), *Clinical Psychopathology*, trans. M.W. Hamilton (New York: Grune and Stratton).

Shapiro, D. (1965), *Neurotic Styles* (New York: Basic Books).

Spitzer, M. (1990), 'On defining delusions', *Comprehensive Psychiatry*, **31**, pp. 377–97.

Villagrán, J.M. and Berrios, G.E. (1996), 'A descriptive model of delusion', *Neurology, Psychiatry and Brain Research*, **4**, pp. 179-170.

WHO (1992), *International Classification of Diseases*, 10th ed. (Geneva, Switzerland).

Zahavi, D. and Parnas, J. (1998), 'Phenomenal consciousness and self-awareness: A phenomenological critique of representational theory', *Journal of Consciousness Studies*, **5** (5–6), pp. 687–705.

Shaun Gallagher

Hermeneutics and the Cognitive Sciences

Philosophical hermeneutics, understood as the theory of interpretation, investigates some questions that are also asked in the cognitive sciences. The nature of human understanding, the way that we gain and organize knowledge, the role played by language and memory in these considerations, the relations between conscious and unconscious knowledge, and how we understand other persons, are all good examples of issues that form the intersection of hermeneutics and the cognitive sciences. Although hermeneutics is most often contrasted with the natural sciences, there are some clear ways in which hermeneutics can contribute to the cognitive sciences and vice versa.

Hermeneutics is usually defined as the theory and practice of interpretation. As a discipline it involves a long and complex history, starting with concerns about the proper interpretation of literary, sacred, and legal texts. In the twentieth century, hermeneutics broadens to include the idea that humans are, in Charles Taylor's phrase, 'self-interpreting animals' (Taylor, 1985). In contrast to the narrowly prescriptive questions of textual interpretation, philosophical hermeneutics, as developed by thinkers like Heidegger, Gadamer, and Ricoeur, raises questions about the conditions of possibility for human understanding — not how we *should* interpret or understand something, but what interpretation and understanding are and how they work.

For the nineteenth-century philosopher Wilhelm Dilthey, the hermeneutical disciplines were very different from the disciplines of science, including the newly emerging science of psychology. In contrast to psychology, which, in part, attempts to *explain* the natural behaviour of human animals in causal terms, Dilthey (1926) thinks of the hermeneutical disciplines as attempting to *understand* the behaviour of human persons in terms of their experience and inner motivation. Inner life is not composed of a series of mechanistic starts and stops, but is woven together into a continuity (*Zusammenhang*) that has a structure, by which he means that any part must be understood in its relations, its intrinsic connections, to other parts of the whole. The same kind of structure can be found in texts that call for a kind of interpretation which is not just a mechanical linking of words, but a search for a meaningful coherence between the whole and the parts. In both cases, that is, in the case of the textual meaning and in the case of the human person, the whole is defined as including a dimension of history — who I am or what this text means cannot be understood simply by treating my observed actions or the meaning of words as absolutely present. Rather, the meaning and significance of these things are discovered as contextualized by the meaning of past practices and past texts. As Hans-Georg Gadamer suggests, that which is to be understood is not present in my actions or in my words in the same way that a cause is present in the effect (1989, p. 224).

This contrast between hermeneutics and psychology understood as a natural science, and more generally between hermeneutics and science, has its own complex history, both prior to and subsequent to Dilthey. Dilthey's distinction between understanding (*Verstehen*) and explanation (*Erklärung*) is a useful one to consider in this regard. Habermas (1988), for example, uses this distinction to define what he calls a 'depth hermeneutics'. By this he means a combination of a hermeneutical *understanding* of the meaning of a particular social practice (its significance to the people involved, for example) and a scientific *explanation* of why such practices exist (their hidden causes, which may be a matter of economic reality or the maintenance of a power relation).

For models of depth hermeneutics Habermas appeals to Marx's critique of ideology and Freud's model of psychoanalysis. Paul Ricoeur (1970) reads Freud in this same way. Freud wants both an interpersonal practice of psychoanalytic interpretation, and a scientific metapsychology that explains the mechanisms of the unconscious. If we were to apply this model of hermeneutics to contemporary studies of consciousness, we would seek *both* an understanding of the subject's first-person experience along with its significance for her everyday life, *and* a neuroscientific explanation of how the embodied brain generates this experience. My discussion in this paper is focussed on this model of hermeneutics, and I refer to it simply as 'hermeneutics' rather than as 'depth hermeneutics' or 'philosophical hermeneutics'.[1]

There is a clear tension in this model. On the one hand the distinction between hermeneutics and science is maintained, as we see in the distinction between understanding and explanation. On the other hand, this model requires hermeneutics and science to work together in order to generate a fuller account of consciousness, cognition, and human behaviour.

In other quarters of hermeneutical theory there is a deeper tension in the sense of a genuinely perceived opposition between hermeneutical interpretation and science, and one often gets the impression that if one is doing hermeneutics, then

---

[1] To clarify this, my interest is in a hermeneutics that is (1) *philosophical* insofar as it is concerned to raise questions about the conditions of possibility for understanding the world and other people, and about what makes us self-interpreting animals, and (2) *a depth hermeneutics* only in the sense that it includes the explanatory power of science. Habermas ties depth hermeneutics to a critical project, that is, a project that takes as its goal a liberation by means of a perfected communicative praxis. I am not opposed to a critical use of hermeneutics, but it is not essential to my concern here.

one cannot be doing science, and vice versa. I think, however, that there is no question that if you sit down with practicing scientists who are at the cutting edge of their fields, they will be the first to admit as an obvious fact what Gadamer, among others, has suggested. The practice of science is itself hermeneutical. That is, scientists make interpretations, and their interpretations are biased in a very productive way by the scientific tradition to which they belong, and the specific kinds of questions that they ask. Explanation is no less interpretation than understanding. The interpretation of quantitative data, for example, relies on certain developments in the history of science, and on *qualitative* judgments among scientists, including judgments that the way they interpret their data is important and valuable for the community of scientists and the funding agencies that constitute part of their audience.

   In this paper, I intend to explore the possible relations between hermeneutics and the cognitive sciences in a way that goes beyond any simple opposition between understanding and explanation. Specifically I want to show three things:

(1) That what hermeneutics discovers is not really in opposition to what the cognitive sciences discover — in fact these disciplines are in agreement about a number of things;

(2) That hermeneutics has something to contribute to the cognitive sciences, and to the science of consciousness; and

(3) That the cognitive sciences have something to contribute to the field of hermeneutics.

I intend to do this by considering three different questions that will act as exemplars rather than an exhaustive explication of how these disciplines are related.

- *How do we know objects?* That is, how do we learn about and come to understand the variety of objects that exist in our world? The answer to this question shows that hermeneutics and cognitive sciences are not really in opposition.
- *How do we know situations?* That is, how do we actually perform cognitively on various types of pragmatic tasks or in various situations? The answer to this question shows what hermeneutics can contribute to the cognitive sciences.
- *How do we understand other people?* The answer to this question shows what the cognitive sciences can contribute to hermeneutics.

Circles, Schemas and Prototypes

How do we learn about and know the things around us? At least one important aspect of learning about objects involves our ability to refer them to the right contexts; another involves our ability to classify them as belonging to certain types. In hermeneutical approaches, answers to these problems are worked out in terms of what is called the hermeneutical circle. One basic formulation of this notion is that all understanding has a circular structure, but one that is not logically vicious. A traditional approach is to think of this circle in terms of understanding a text. To understand the meaning of a particular passage one needs to see how it relates to the text as a whole; and to understand the whole of the text, one needs to see how each part contributes to that meaning. Numerous theorists from the eighteenth century onwards also insisted that to further understand a text, one needs to place it within a larger historical whole that includes knowledge about the author, her society, her economic position, and so on. I understand X only by putting it into the proper context; and I understand the context better when I understand X. This clearly applies to learning about any kind of object. When I endeavour to learn about something, I begin to understand it only by relating it to something I already know — that is, I put it into some context with which I am familiar.

This, of course, may mean that I am led to misunderstand the object. I am naturally biased by what I already know and I often try to fit a new object into an established framework. In the end, however, accommodation must occur if learning is to progress. As Dilthey says, 'failure shows itself when the individual parts cannot be understood by this method. This then requires that the meaning be redefined so that it will take account of these parts' (Dilthey, 1926, p. 227). By some dialectical, back-and-forth process, or with some guidance by a teacher, I should finally discover the proper context and come to some acceptable understanding. When I do so, I am able to identify the object as similar to like objects; I am able to say what kind of thing it is.

This account, as far as it goes, is perfectly consistent with accounts given in cognitive psychology under the names of 'schema theory' and 'protocol theory'. Theorists from Bartlett (1932) to Piaget (1952) to Arbib and Hesse (1986), and many others, have appealed to the notion of corrigible cognitive schemas to explain how we come to understand an object. The concept of a schema signifies that the knowledge we already have does not consist of disconnected pieces of information but is organized into patterns that we access and use in the acquisition of new knowledge. Such patterns or schemas allow us to 'assimilate' new information into already established frameworks. Importantly, new information can also cause a change in previously established schemas; schemas can change or 'accommodate' themselves to the new object. In the give and take between schema and object, as Anderson suggests, we construct an interpretation, and expressing this explicitly in terms close to hermeneutics, he states: 'Text is gobbledygook unless the reader possesses an interpretive framework to breathe meaning into it' (Anderson, 1977, p. 423). Objects are meaningless unless we have recourse to some interpretive framework that will to some degree facilitate understanding.

Schemas play a conservative role in the assimilation of new meaning; but the fact that they are relatively plastic means that we can adjust to information that has a high degree of novelty — and one could here speak about the importance of imagination, a subject to which I will return in the next section. In the cognitive sciences there are interesting debates about how schemas are generated, and how best to explain them. Is the underlying structure of schemas computational? Is the plasticity of schemas best explained in terms of the plasticity of the brain? Should we rather consider schemas as generated within the framework of embodied actions? However you might answer these questions, they are questions that address the underlying mechanisms which allow us, as human seekers of understanding, to enter into hermeneutical circles that enable learning.[2]

Objects are different, yet in some sense they may share common features. Such differences and common features help us to interpret and understand objects. One theory developed in the cognitive sciences, prototype theory (e.g., Rosch, 1973; Lakoff, 1987), is quite consistent with hermeneutical approaches.

Some objects are prototypical — we know them very well; they contain clear and relatively well-demarcated instances of typical or defining features. Consider, for example, birds. One might think that a pigeon is an example of a typical bird. In this respect it operates as a useful prototype of the concept bird. But there are birds that are so unlike pigeons (e.g., chickens) that use of pigeon as a prototype doesn't capture everything there is to know about birds or operate as a definitive example. A prototype helps to map out the territory; to clarify what's different and/or the same in situations. A prototype is not simply one good example; rather it defines a cluster of phenomena, some of which are central and some peripheral.

A prototype is a pathway into a hermeneutical circle. If one thinks of schemas as a finite set of well-ordered (perhaps hierarchically ordered) categories, prototypes are more like radial organizations of meaning (Lakoff) — rather than a perfect fit, they are more a matter of degree. They also allow for a certain relativity. In some cultures, for example, pigeons are more prototypical for birds than chickens or penguins. But one can think of how that would be different where chickens or penguins constitute the majority of the bird population. Consistent with the hermeneutics of Gadamer (more so than with the hermeneutics of Dilthey or Schleiermacher) prototype theory suggests that interpretation will be more ambiguous, less objective, more a matter of degree than of complete and full understanding. The meaning of an object will be harder to pin down, and it will be more dependent on the situation. It is more about what Wittgenstein would call 'family resemblance' than about pigeon holes.

There is no opposition here between the cognitive sciences and hermeneutics. The accounts given by schema theory and protocol theory are perfectly in tune with accounts given of the hermeneutical circle. One account would enrich the other and indeed there would be a mutual enrichment and a deeper understanding of cognition if we put these two kinds of accounts together.

In the cognitive sciences, of course, there are unsettled debates about how prototypes are generated, and how best to explain them. Should we think of prototypes as metaphorical structures generated in what Lakoff and Johnson (2003) call 'kinaesthetic image schemas'. Is it possible to develop a computational

---

[2] Arbib and Hesse (1986) are among the very few to make a direct connection between the cognitive scientific schema theory and hermeneutics. For them, schema theory 'provides a model for all controlled interpretation of texts, and schemas themselves constitute the perspectives (or in Gadamer's terms, the preunderstanding) within which such interpretation takes place' (p. 181). More generally they are in agreement with philosophical hermeneutics that 'cognitive science is itself a human interpretive science (that is, a hermeneutic science) so what we have said about hermeneutics should apply to it also' (p. 182).

model of prototypically organized knowledge? Such questions about schemas and prototypes are parts of a larger whole — a larger question: is it possible to explain the ambiguity and relativity of human understanding in strictly objective computational terms? It is in respect to this question that I think hermeneutics has something to offer the cognitive sciences.

Computation and Understanding

Computational models, even if not strictly closed or complete in logical terms, are meant to be strict, precise and predictable. The human cognitive system, however, is not designed to work with strict and definitive categories, but with corrigible schemas and flexible prototypes. This suggests an important difference between human understanding and computational models. Here I can appeal to Hubert Dreyfus's analysis of what computers can and cannot do (Dreyfus, 1992). He argues that computers are quite good in contexts that are well-defined, narrowly circumscribed, and rule-governed. A good example of this is playing the game of chess. In contrast, computers are not very good at solving problems in circumstances that are ill-defined, ambiguous and without clear-cut rules to follow.

Computers are good at memory games, maze problems, word-by-word translation, responding to rigid patterns. In such activities mechanical association is important but meaning and context are irrelevant. Such activities can be handled by decision trees, list searches or templates. Computers are also good at simple formal activities, such as computable games (like tic-tac-toe), combinational problems (straightforward means-ends), mechanical proofs in mathematics. In such cases the meaning is completely explicit and context-independent. Complex computers may even be good at complex formal activities, such as games like chess, but also planning, and recognition of complex patterns in noise. In such cases meaning is still explicit but quantitatively complex. Such activities require, for example, 'search-pruning' heuristics (see Dreyfus, 1992).

Computational models, however, are inadequate for cases that involve non-formal everyday activities. Ill-defined games (e.g., riddles), open-structured problems that require insight which is not reducible simply to organizing a quantity of information, translation of natural language, recognition of varied or distorted patterns. In such cases there are implicit meanings that are highly context-dependent. These are cases in which there are no clear-cut rules to follow. Dreyfus appeals to the phenomenological tradition, especially Merleau-Ponty and Heidegger, to define such ambiguous, embodied, pragmatically contextualized situations. One could also appeal to the cognitive sciences themselves to find distinctions between non-contextualized and either pragmatically or socially contextualized situations — especially studies informed by neuropsychology (see Gallagher & Marcel, 1999).

I want to suggest that hermeneutics also offers a good model for understanding just those contexts that define the limits of computational approaches. Computational models fail in what Gadamer calls 'hermeneutical situations'. These are precisely situations that are ill-defined, ambiguous, and not open to rule-following or methodological solutions. Interpretation in such contexts, as Gadamer points out, is not accomplished simply by proceeding in a methodical fashion. Gadamer reaches back to Aristotle to find a way to describe this. Aristotle, in his *Nicomachean Ethics*, outlines a concept of *phronesis* — usually translated as 'practical wisdom' or sometimes, as 'prudence' in its original sense — that is, an ability to know the right thing to do and how to do it. *Phronesis,* rather than computation, is precisely what is needed in situations where there are no rules, but where decisions have to be made. In such situations we face a diversity of possible meanings, and there is no ultimate principle for their rank ordering.

Aristotle makes an important distinction between *phronesis* and cleverness. In the ethical context, an immoral person, a criminal, for example, can be very clever but does not have *phronesis*. Cleverness or quick wittedness can be a natural talent; *phronesis,* however, depends entirely on education or enculturation in the most basic sense. Specifically, it is something that can only be developed within the right social and educational setting. One gets *phronesis*, according to Aristotle, by hanging out with the right kind of people and by learning to act by following the example of good people. Without this informal educational backdrop, one can still be clever, but not necessarily a good person.

This moral concept of *phronesis* undergoes some important modifications in hermeneutical theory, and in this respect, I think it constitutes an important contribution that hermeneutics can make to the cognitive sciences. First, Gadamer takes it as a model for the act of interpretation, not only in moral contexts, but more generally in messy and ambiguous hermeneutical situations where there are no rules and where there exists more than one right answer (Gadamer, 1989, pp. 21–22, 312ff). More recent discussions of *phronesis* (found in the radical hermeneutical writings of Lyotard (Lyotard & Thébaud, 1985); Caputo, 1987; and others)), emphasize the idea that *phronesis*, while not reducible to cleverness, includes the use of a quick imagination. *Phronesis* depends on the use of imaginative or intuitive insight to arrive at solutions to problems that develop in the indefinite milieu of human life. In any of these cases the sought-for decision or action cannot be arrived at by precise solution through a process of eliminating alternatives or by following purely rational (rule-governed) computational procedures. As such, it goes beyond anything that can be modelled computationally.

This does not make *phronesis*, or the kind of understanding that is at stake in hermeneutical contexts, magical. To move away from strict and narrowly conceived computational models to the more dynamic models found in neuroscience is a challenge for the cognitive sciences. But if there are forms of cognition or understanding that belong to a realm that is simply not reducible to a sub-personal, computational level, and that involve personal and interpersonal processes, then new models that incorporate the effects of social interaction are required. In this regard, Gadamer suggests that understanding is dialogical. Here one can go back to Aristotle's idea that *phronesis* is gained in informal social and interactive contexts. There is something in second-person human social interaction that is irreducible to subpersonal computations. Second-person interactions cannot be adequately characterized as the interactions of two or more computational systems, or even as the interaction of two brains.

Dilthey and his nineteenth-century Romantic hermeneutical colleagues spoke of this in terms of *empathy* — something that transcends both first-person and third-person perspectives. If we look at how the proponents of Romantic hermeneutics talked about empathy, we find an appeal is made to a shared spiritual dimension that is universally human. An optimistic view is given in 1819 by Schleiermacher, who speaks of subjective–divinatory interpretation in textual hermeneutics, a form of interpretation that goes beyond following a set of rules.

> By leading the interpreter to transform himself, so to speak, into the author, the divinatory method seeks to gain an immediate comprehension of the author as an individual. . . . The divinatory is based on the assumption that each person is not only a unique individual in his own right, but that he has a receptivity to the uniqueness of every other person (Schleiermacher, 1977, §2.6).

Forty years later, Johann Droysen took a more pessimistic view. The genuine person who we try to understand is really inaccessible;

> [the person] is reserved in its own realm in which it communes with itself and God alone . . . this is a sanctuary which research cannot penetrate. One person may understand another person well; but this is only superficial; he apprehends his deeds, speech, and gestures as separate moments, never truly, never completely. (1988, §38).

Whatever we might think of such Romantic, transcendental, or theological ideas — and there is certainly much to think of here — none of this looks very scientific. Is this where, finally, we find an incommensurable opposition between hermeneutics and science? One way to sidestep this opposition is simply to deny the profound differences between persons and things. As Arbib and Hesse (1986) suggest,

> the hermeneutic approach does not require such dualism ['a radical distinction between things and persons'],

and they go on to argue for

> a continuity between natural and hermeneutic science based on the fact that they both have the same domain of objects (namely, bodies, including persons' bodies) carrying their properties around in space and time. . . . The choice of persons and participatory meanings as fundamental concepts in the hermeneutic sciences is not a necessary one' (p. 183).

Although choosing the right vocabulary, and the right levels of description for the analysis of understanding is important, what is at stake here is something more than vocabulary. It is not out of the question, or beyond the bounds of naturalism, that there just is a radical difference between things and persons. In the following section I want to suggest that in regard to just this issue, hermeneutics can learn from important insights that have been recently gained in the cognitive neurosciences.

Understanding Others

I suggested that second-person interactions cannot be characterized as simply the interaction of two brains — or the presence of shared representations in two brains. I do not mean that we should ignore neuroscience. Indeed, if there were not at least two brains involved, there would be no second-person interaction. Cognitive social neuroscience can contribute to our understanding of how we understand each other, as persons, and how empathy is possible. But this is also a central aim of hermeneutics. First, I want to briefly rehearse some familiar recent work in neuroscience that helps us to understand, from that scientific perspective, how we interact with other people. Second, I want to discuss how cognitive scientists interpret these findings.

The work on mirror neurons is now well known. Mirror neurons were discovered in the premotor cortex (area F5) of the Macaque monkey and, there is good evidence to suggest that they can be found in the premotor cortex and Broca's area in the human (see Fadiga *et al.*, 1995; Rizzolatti *et al.*, 1996; Grafton *et al.*, 1996). Mirror neurons respond *both* when a particular motor action is performed by the subject *and* when the same goal-directed action performed by another individual is observed. Mirror neurons thus constitute an intermodal link between the visual perception of action or dynamic expression, and the first-person, *intra*subjective, proprioceptive sense of one's own capabilities. Vittorio Gallese (2001) suggests that such neurons contribute to a cognitive neuroscience account of empathy. He suggests that empathy, or social cognition, consists of a 'resonance' existing between the observer's and the observed agent's motor systems, forming a 'shared manifold' between the observer's body schema and the agent's body schema.

Before we consider this and other interpretations, let's look at some more recent discoveries that are quite consistent with and extend the work on mirror neurons. Brain imaging studies of subjects who (1) engage in instrumental action, (2) observe another person act, (3) simulate the action of another, or (4) plan to imitate the action of another, show that brain areas activated for each of these tasks overlap (Jeannerod, 1997; Ruby & Decety, 2001; Grezes & Decety, 2001). If I see you pick up a glass to take a drink, the very same areas in my brain are activated as when I myself pick up a glass to take a drink. Here we are not talking about individual neurons, but neural systems. Moreover, when I consciously simulate or imagine myself doing a certain action, or imagine you doing that action, or prepare to imitate an action that you have just completed, the brain areas activated for my cognitive acts are the very same ones that are activated for my own actual motor behaviour.

These studies of mirror neurons and shared neural representations have directly informed debates that are central to the concerns of hermeneutics, that is, debates about the nature of understanding others and empathy. In effect, when philosophers of mind, psychologists, and neuroscientists address what is usually referred to as *theory of mind*, they are (and in most cases unknowingly) entering into the older hermeneutical debates about understanding and empathy.

Theory of mind is defined as our ability to 'mentalize' or mind-read the mental states of others in order to explain and predict their behaviour. There are ongoing debates between those who champion a theory approach to theory of mind and those who defend a simulation approach. The first group, the 'theory theorists', propose that the way we understand others involves the employment of a theoretical stance: we theorize (implicitly or explicitly) about others in order to explain or predict their behaviour. In contrast, *simulation theorists* argue that our understanding of others is based on our ability to simulate what the other person is thinking or feeling. For example, we virtually put ourselves in the other person's place, run a simulation routine in our own mind, and then infer that this is what she must be thinking.

Simulationists now appeal to the evidence from cognitive neuroscience discussed above (e.g., Gallese & Goldman, 1998; Gordon, 2002; in press). Simulation is possible because we have similar brains with mirror neurons and shared representational areas activated in the appropriate way. Theory theorists are not completely without scientific resources, however. They can appeal to false-belief tests that show that understanding the minds of other seems to involve a theoretical stance that is gained around four years of age in normal, non-autistic children. Importantly, both theory theorists and simulation theorists claim that theory of mind is the primary way we go about understanding others, not just when we're four, but throughout our life.

Interaction theory is an alternative to both theory theory and simulation theory (see Gallagher 2001; in press). This approach can also appeal to the neuroscience evidence about mirror neurons and shared neural representations, and a large body of evidence from developmental psychology concerning the abilities of infants to parse and understand the intentions of others in a non-mentalistic way.[3] This view pushes the age of *understanding*, if not of reason, back to infancy and suggests that throughout our life our primary way of *understanding*, if not of explaining or predicting, is more embodied and socially embedded than our ability to mentalize through the use of theory or simulation.

These different positions offer different interpretations of the scientific evidence — and here it is tempting to once again point out the hermeneutical nature of science itself. But my point is different. What I want to emphasize here is that in our attempts to explain how we understand others we do not have to appeal to an obscure universal human spirit, as Schleiermacher, Droysen, and Dilthey did. We now have the means to see the meaning of a universal human spirit in the behaviour of the infant and in the activation of common brain areas, and to give a hermeneutical account of empathy that is closely tied to these natural phenomena.

We can cash out Schleiermacher's notion of divinatory power in terms of the capacity of infants to detect and complete the intentions of others. With this innate capability (Baron-Cohen, 1995) infants are able to interpret bodily movement as goal-directed intentional movement, and are capable of perceiving other

---

[3] My intention here is not to provide the complete argument for this view (see Gallagher, 2001; in press). Important sources for this view can be found in the work of Trevarthen (1979) on 'primary' and 'secondary intersubjectivity', and in Hobson (2002).

persons as agents.[4] This 'divinatory power' is embodied and perceptual, and as
Scholl and Tremoulet suggest, 'fast, automatic, irresistible and highly stimu-
lus-driven' (2000, p. 299). Whether we should think of this as a capacity for
mentalizing, or as a non-mentalistic performance, is part of the ongoing debate.

Dilthey emphasized the importance of context for understanding the actions
and intentions of others.

> There is a regular relation between an action and some mental content which allows
> us to make probable inferences. But it is necessary to distinguish the state of mind
> which produced the action by which it is expressed from the circumstances of life
> by which it is conditioned. . . . So action separates itself from the background of the
> context of life and, unless accompanied by an explanation of how circumstances,
> purposes, means and context of life are linked together in it, allows no comprehen-
> sive account of the inner life from which it arose. (Dilthey, 1988, p. 153).

This emphasis is consistent with what Trevarthan shows about secondary
intersubjectivity. Around the age of one year, infants go beyond the per-
son-to-person immediacy of primary intersubjectivity, and enter into *contexts* of
shared attention — shared situations — in which they learn what things mean
and what they are for (see Trevarthan & Hubley, 1978).

> The defining feature of secondary intersubjectivity is that an object or event can
> become a focus *between* people. Objects and events can be communicated about . . .
> the infant's interactions with another person begin to have reference to the things
> that surround them' (Hobson, 2002, p. 62).

Eighteen-month-old children can understand what another person intends to do.
They are able to re-enact to completion the goal-directed behaviour that an
observed subject fails to complete. The child, seeing an adult who tries to manip-
ulate a toy in the right way and who appears frustrated about being unable to do
so, quite readily picks up the toy and shows the adult how to do it (Meltzoff 1995;
see Meltzoff & Brooks, 2001). This kind of understanding of actions depends on
shared attention and the pragmatic context. Just as we understand our own
actions on the highest pragmatic level possible (see, e.g., Gallagher & Marcel,
1999; Jeannerod, 1997), we understand the actions of others in the same way.
That is, we understand actions at the most relevant pragmatic level, and this is
always tied to contextualization.

This level of understanding is called 'elementary understanding' by Dilthey,
and he distinguishes it from higher forms of understanding, which include empathy. If, as Dilthey suggests, the logic of elementary understanding may be
expressed as an inductive process, he struggles to work out the correct account
(1988, p. 154). Inferences are not made from effect to cause in such cases. That
is, in our interpersonal relations we are not looking for a causal explanation of
why the other person is acting in a certain way (although this would be the theory
theorist's view). Rather, we are reading the other's expression (the action, the
gesture, the facial expression) for *meaning*. This is as far as Dilthey can go, however, in his account of elementary understanding. But his inclination is to turn to

---

[4] Baldwin and colleagues have shown that infants at 10–11 months are able to parse some kinds of continuous action according to intentional boundaries (Baldwin & Baird, 2001; Baldwin *et al.*, 2001).

observations of children, and he suggests that before the child learns to talk it is already immersed in socially organized contexts and the expressions that constitute the objective manifestations of the mind, all of which form a background context for understanding another person.

My point is that the scientific studies of primary and secondary intersubjectivity, and so forth, support Dilthey's intuitions about elementary understanding. Understanding others is not magical; nor do we need to appeal to a divinatory spirit to account for our capacity to communicate, to empathize, to fall in love, and so forth. Indeed, to be realistic, the same accounts are capable of shedding light on pathologies, the prejudices of racism and sexism, and the hatred that sometimes leads to war — such things that we would be hard pressed to explain as emanating from our divinatory spirit. More generally, it seems clear that studies and debates in the cognitive sciences can contribute to and make more precise the important insights about elementary and empathetic understanding found in the hermeneutic tradition.

Conclusion

I've tried to show, first, that what hermeneutics discovers is not in opposition to what cognitive science discovers — in fact they are in agreement about a number of things; second, that hermeneutics has something to contribute to the cognitive sciences; and third, that the cognitive sciences have something to contribute to the field of hermeneutics. I've done this by considering three questions: How do we know objects? How do we know situations? How do we understand other people?

Let me move to a quick conclusion by asking one more question. What does it mean to be scientific? People too often give an easy answer to this question by appealing to the objectivity of scientific procedure. Indeed, this is Dilthey's answer. If we cannot attain some degree of objectivity about a subject matter, then it cannot be the subject of a scientific study. Some people think that science is restricted to quantitative accounts, and that if something cannot be quantified, it doesn't allow for scientific study. In the cognitive sciences there are still people who will insist that the task of science is to be reductionistic: a good account is one that can be mapped out completely in sub-personal terms. I think that it is better to think of science as using any means possible to explain *what there is*. And if *what there is* includes such things that cannot be reduced to computational processes or the subpersonal activation of neurons, or cannot be quantified, or objectified without loss — such things that nonetheless have meaning for human life, and that therefore fall into the province of hermeneutics — then to turn away from them and to deny their actuality is in fact being unscientific.

References

Anderson, R.C. (1977), 'The notion of schemata and the educational enterprise' in *Schooling and the Acquisition of Knowledge*, ed. R.C. Anderson, R.J. Spiro & W.E. Montague (Hillsdale, NJ: Erlbaum).
Arbib, MA. & Hesse, M.B. (1986), *The Construction of Reality* (Cambridge: Cambridge University Press).
Baldwin, D.A. and Baird, J.A. (2001), 'Discerning intentions in dynamic human action', *Trends in Cognitive Science*, **5** (4), pp. 171–8.
Baldwin, D.A., Baird, J.A., Saylor, M.M., and Clark, M.A. (2001), 'Infants parse dynamic action', *Child Development*, **72** (3), pp. 708–17.

Baron-Cohen, S. (1995), *Mindblindness: An essay on autism and theory of mind* (Cambridge, MA: MIT Press).

Bartlett, F.C. (1932), *Remembering* (Cambridge: Cambridge University Press).

Caputo, J.D. (1987). *Radical Hermeneutics* (Bloomington: Indiana University Press).

Dilthey, W. (1926), *Gesammelte Schriften*, Vol 7 (Göttingen-Stuttgart: Vandenhoeck & Ruprecht).

Dilthey, W. (1988), 'The understanding of other persons and their life-expressions', Trans. K Mueller-Vollmer in *The Hermeneutics Reader* (pp. 152–64) (New York: Continuum).

Dreyfus, H. (1992), *What Computers Still Can't Do* (Cambridge, MA: MIT Press).

Droysen, J.G. (1988), 'The modes of interpretation', Trans. K. Mueller-Vollmer in *The Hermeneutics Reader* (pp. 126–31) (New York: Continuum. [Original: *Historik,* 1858]).

Fadiga, L., Fogassi, L. Pavesi, G. and Rizzolatti, G. (1995), 'Motor facilitation during action observation: a magnetic stimulation study', *Journal of Neurophysiology*, **73**, pp. 2608–11.

Gadamer, H-G. (1989), *Truth and Method*, Second revised edition (New York: Crossroad).

Gallagher, S. (in press), 'Understanding interpersonal problems in autism: Interaction theory as an alternative to theory of mind', *Philosophy, Psychiatry, and Psychology.*

Gallagher, S. (2001), 'The practice of mind: Theory, simulation, or interaction?', *Journal of Consciousness Studies*, **8** (5–7), p. 83–107.

Gallagher, S. and Marcel, A J. (1999), 'The Self in Contextualized Action', *Journal of Consciousness Studies* **6** (4), pp. 4–30.

Gallese, V. (2001), 'The "shared manifold" hypothesis: From mirror neurons to empathy', *Journal of Consciousness Studies*, **8** (5–7), pp. 33–50.

Gallese, V. and Goldman, A.I. (1998), 'Mirror neurons and the simulation theory of mind reading', *Trends in Cognitive Science*, **2**, pp. 493–501.

Gordon, R.M. (in press), 'Intentional Agents Like Myself', in *Perspectives on Imitation: From Mirror Neurons to Memes*, vol. II, ed. S. Hurley and N. Chater (Cambridge: MIT Press).

Gordon, R.M. (2002), 'Simulation and reason explanation: the radical view', *Philosophical Topics*, **29**(1–2).

Grafton, S.T., Arbib, M.A. , Fadiga, L. and Rizzolatti, G. (1996), 'Localization of grasp representations in humans by PET: 2. Observation compared with imagination', *Exp. Brain Research*, **112**, pp. 103–11.

Grezes, J. and Decety, J. (2001), 'Functional anatomy of execution, mental simulation, observation, and verb generation of actions: A meta-analysis', *Human Brain Mapping*, **12**, pp. 1–19.

Habermas, J. (1988), 'On hermeneutics' claim to universality', Trans. K. Mueller–Vollmer in *The Hermeneutics Reader* , ed. K. Mueller-Vollmer (New York: Continuum).

Hobson, P. (2002), *The Cradle of Thought* (London: Macmillan).

Jeannerod, M. (1997), *The Cognitive Neuroscience of Action* (Oxford: Blackwell Publishers).

Lakoff, G. (1987), 'Cognitive Models and Prototype Theory', in *Concepts: Core Readings*, ed. E. Margolis and S. Laurence. (MIT Press. 1999).

Lakoff, G. & Johnson, M. (2003), *Metaphors We Live By*. 2nd ed. (Chicago: University of Chicago Press).

Lyotard, J-F. & Thébaud, J-L. (1985), *Just Gaming* Trans. W. Godzich. (University of Minnesota Press).

Meltzoff, A.N. (1995), 'Understanding the intentions of others: Re-enactment of intended acts by 18-month-old children', *Developmental Psychology* **31** pp. 838–50.

Meltzoff, A.N. and Brooks, R. (2001), '"Like me" as a building block for understanding other minds: Bodily acts, attention, and intention' in *Intentions and Intentionality: Foundations of Social Cognition*, ed. B.F. Malle *et al.* (Cambridge, MA: MIT Press).

Piaget, J. (1952), *The Origin of Intelligence in Children* Trans. M. Cook (New York: International Universities Press).

Ricoeur, P. (1970), *Freud and Philosophy: An Essay on Interpretation*, Trans. D. Savage (New Haven: Yale University Press).

Rizzolatti, G., Fadiga, L., Gallese V. and Fogassi, L. (1996), 'Premotor cortex and the recognition of motor actions', *Cognitive Brain Research*, **3**, pp. 131–41.

Rosch, E. (1973), 'Natural categories' *Cognitive Psychology*, **4**(3), pp. 328–50.

Ruby, P. and Decety, J. (2001), 'Effect of subjective perspective taking during simulation of action: a PET investigation of agency', *Nature Neuroscience*, **4** (5), pp. 546–50.

Schleiermacher, F. (1977), *Hermeneutics: The Handwritten Manuscripts.* Trans. J. Duke and J. Forstmann. (Missoula, MT: Scholars Press. [Original: *Compendium*, 1819]).

Scholl, B.J. and Tremoulet, P.D. (2000), 'Perceptual causality and animacy', *Trends in Cognitive Science,* **4** (8), pp. 299–309.

Taylor, C. (1985), 'Self-Interpreting Animals', in *Human Agency and Language: Philosophical Papers, Volume 1* (Cambridge: Cambridge University Press).

Trevarthen, C. (1979), 'Communication and cooperation in early infancy: A description of primary intersubjectivity', in *Before Speech*, ed. M. Bullowa (Cambridge: Cambridge University Press).

Trevarthan, C. and Hubley, P. (1978), 'Secondary intersubjectivity: Confidence, confiding and acts of meaning in the first year', In *Action, Gesture and Symbol: The Emergence of Language,* ed. A. Lock (London: Academic Press).

Dieter Teichert

Narrative, Identity and the Self

The concept of narrative has come to play an important role in a bewildering variety of disciplines such as literary theory, linguistics, historiography, psychology, psychotherapy, ethnology and philosophy due to a number of recent trends in the social sciences including: the rejection of strong apriori unities of experience, the focus on intersubjectivity as the grounding level of experience, the turn to language as the focus of philosophical reflection, and the success of semiotics in articulating the rules for the generation and understanding of texts.

The first section of the paper presents the framework of Ricoeur's investigation into narrative identity, which he embeds within an encompassing reflection on time and an examination of current theories of personal identity. The second section, then, both specifies salient aspects of Ricoeur's narrative model and shows how, using that model, Ricoeur claims that the concept of narrative identity solves the paradoxes of personal identity. The third section presents Dennett's concept of a narrative self and compares Dennett's and Ricoeur's models. As we shall see, these two philosophers, who work within antagonistic traditions, have surprisingly similar ways of using narrative as a model for understanding the self.

I: Ricoeur and Narrative Identity

In the philosophy of Paul Ricoeur, the concept of narrative identity emerges in the context of an encompassing reflection on time and temporality that grounds the question of personal identity and explains the relevance of narrative to it. I shall begin with a sketch of Ricoeur's investigations into time, history, and narrative in the three volume work, *Time and Narrative* (1983–88), showing how the concept of narrative as a model for personal identity emerges in this context.

1. Time, history and narrative

Time, or more precisely, the experience of temporality, is one of the most prominent and intriguing themes of Husserlian phenomenology, Heideggerian ontology, and philosophical hermeneutics. Ricoeur himself is very close to the phenomenological tradition and his work is an elaborate effort to come to terms with this heritage. In Husserl's view philosophy had to be a rigorous scientific enterprise. Husserl's peculiar analytical approach — one of the most fascinating and intimidating aspects of his writings — is almost lost in subsequent phenomenology. His followers very often interpreted the late Husserl's statement 'Philosophie als [...] strenge Wissenschaft — *der Traum ist ausgeträumt*' ('Philosophy as [...] rigorous science — *the dream is dreamt and over*' (Husserl, 1976, p. 508) as an invitation to dispense with analysis, conceptually controlled reflection, and a systematic — not predominantly historical — orientation. Even in Ricoeur, the transcendental and systematic claims of Husserl's phenomenology are heavily toned down. Ricoeur's investigations into the notion of time and the experience of temporality in *Time and Narrative* present detailed reconstructions, comments and critique of philosophical work from Antiquity to the present. A major characteristic of Ricoeur is his unremitting effort to integrate the work done by analytical philosophers into his encompassing phenomenological-hermeneutic framework. He gives concise summaries, especially of the most important work done in the field of philosophy of language, action theory and epistemology of history.

Regarding his notion of time, however, the phenomenological inspiration clearly governs Ricoeur's focus on the structures and modalities of the subjective experience of time. He explicitly states that the philosophical tradition does not offer a solution to the question 'What is time?' His readings of Aristotle, Augustine, Kant, Husserl and Heidegger try to show how philosophical theorizing produces aporias, not solutions.

In this aporetic situation there is one aspect which deserves special attention, namely the divergence between an objective, physical or cosmological concept of time and a phenomenological notion of time (time as experienced by individuals). Following Ricoeur it is impossible to formulate a convincing, non-circular theory of time integrating both dimensions. Physical or cosmological time as such is not sufficient to explain the modes of subjective experience of time. Phenomenological time on the other hand is a concept of the experience of a single individual subject. It is simply inconceivable how subjective time could be the basis of objective, cosmological time.[1] Clearly, there is an impasse. It would be a crass misunderstanding of Ricoeur's attitude to take the diagnosis of this perplexing situation as a devastating critique of the philosophical tradition he analyses. Ricoeur himself never claims to formulate a systematic theory of time and temporality. Rather, he tries to show that the failure of systematic approaches is inevitable. The whole situation resembles in a certain way the Kantian antinomies in the *Critique of Pure Reason*. But of the unifying transcendental frame that recuperates the unity of the transcendental ego nothing

---

[1]   Cf. Ricoeur (1983), pp. 19–53 on Augustine; Ricoeur (1985b), pp. 19–144 on Augustine, Aristotle, Kant, Husserl, Heidegger; and the 'Conclusions', Ricoeur (1985b), pp. 349–92. Ricoeur articulates the first of three aporias as follows: '[...] we cannot think about cosmological time (the instant) without surreptitiously appealing to phenomenological time and vice versa.', Ricoeur (1988), p. 96.

remains. It is of upmost importance that narrative brings together both dimensions of time. Narrative is a bridge between time as an objective feature of reality and time as a form of subjective experience. If philosophical and scientific concepts cannot do the job of finding a proper solution to conceptual antinomies, we have to look for metaphors and narratives.

2. Two concepts of identity: sameness and selfhood

Ricoeur distinguishes two different concepts of identity: identity as sameness ('mêmeté') and identity as selfhood ('ipséité').

Identity as sameness ('mêmeté') is involved in questions like 'Is person x at t-1 the same person as y at t-2?' (where x and y stand for different singular terms — indexicals, definite descriptions or proper names). Re-identification is relevant with respect to entities existing through time (diachronic or transtemporal identity) and constitutes the core of identity as sameness. We have to re-identify all sorts of things at different times and places. At first sight it might seem plausible to treat problems of personal identity in the same manner as problems of artifact identity or identity of natural things. In fact, there are different models of personhood and personal identity using the concept of identity as sameness. Among these, *substance theories* occupy a prominent position. *Materialistic* substance theories identify a person with a determinate (living) body. A widely accepted theory claims (1) that persons are the bearers of physical as well as mental properties, (2) that neither class of properties can be reduced to the other (Strawson, 1959). The anti-materialist denies the identity of the person and the body. A radical form of *anti-materialism* is the concept of the person as identical with an immaterial soul or mind. *Relational models* of personal identity conceive of the life of a person as a series of diachronically ordered person-stages. To be a person existing at different times just means to be conscious and self-conscious through time. In this case it is the task of the theory of personal identity to formulate the right kind of psychic continuity linking the different person-stages. The question whether there is an identical substance which forms the basis for the required kind of continuity of self-consciousness is either displaced or answered in the negative in this approach.

So-called 'bundle theories' of the self (Hume, W. James) are examples of relational models not referring to substantial bearers of personal identity. Like substance theories they fall within the range of identity as sameness because it is in principle possible to formulate decidable identity statements. A series of particular (and identifiable) states of consciousness or person-stages constitutes one individual person.

The notion of *identity as selfhood* ('ipséité', cf. Ricoeur, 1985b, p. 356) concerns those aspects of diachronic identity which are not seized by re-identification strategies. To understand the impact of identity as selfhood it is vital to keep in mind that Ricoeur discusses personal identity as a practical category. 'To state the identity of an individual or a community is to answer the question, "Who did this?" "Who is the agent, the author?"' (Ricoeur, 1988, p. 246). Identity as selfhood is linked to a realm where actions are ascribed to agents in the light of ethical norms. The question 'Who did this?' can be answered by naming the agent with a proper name. This, of course, is just a triviality about the use of language. Ricoeur asks a more philosophically challenging question: What is the basis for this usage, why do we use one proper name as the designation of an individual that, from birth to death, undergoes many changes? What kind of unity constitutes the identity of the person if there is no single feature of identity neither on the level of physical properties nor on the level of psychic properties? According to Ricoeur, this unity is constituted by a narrative: 'To answer the question "Who?" [...] is to tell the story of a life. The story told tells about the action of the "who". And the identity of this "who" therefore itself must be a narrative identity' (Ricoeur, 1988, p. 246). Ricoeur claims that the concept of narrative identity avoids the difficulties inherent in substance theories of personal identity and their counterparts.

It is clear that Ricoeur is not an adherent of a substance model of the self either in its materialist or in its anti-materialist (Cartesian ego) version.[2] But he also distinguishes his position from the Anti-Cogito tradition in which the self and personal identity are debunked as mere illusions (Hume)[3] or denounced as ideologically suspect fictions (Nietzsche). He is sensitive to the problems and impasses which have dogged the Cartesians, while finding the therapeutic nihilism of the Anti-Cogito camp to be, ultimately, an exercise in the evasion of the problem. Ricoeur develops his theory by reviewing the concept of personal identity as it is formulated by Locke and his followers, who situated the question of personal identity in the ethical and social realm. Before discussing Ricoeur's construction of personal identity as narrative, I shall turn to Ricoeur's critique of the Neo-Lockean approach to personal identity.

3. Ricoeur's critique of Locke and the neo-Lockean conception of personal identity

Ricoeur's interest in Locke and the Neo-Lockeans is mainly motivated by two facts: First, Locke and his followers do not formulate substance theories of the self. Second, Locke discusses personal identity in the context of ethics. The ascription of actions to an agent is the central problem discussed by Locke, who

---

[2] 'What I essentially contest is the insinuation that a hermeneutic ipseity would amount to nothing more than the positing of a Cartesian ego, itself identified as a "further fact" distinct from mental states and corporeal facts. [...] The self [...] does not simply belong to the category of events and facts.' Ricoeur (1991), p. 76.

[3] Hume writes: 'For my part, when I enter most intimately into what I call myself, I always stumble on some particular perception or other, of heat or cold, light or shade, love or hatred, pain or pleasure. I never can catch myself at any time without a perception, and never can observe any thing but the perception.' (Hume, 1986, p. 252). Ricoeur points to the fact that somebody is writing this, there is a person looking into himself, a person in search of a self, an individual declaring not to have found anything. As he puts it: 'With the question "Who?" — who searches, who stumbles and who doesn't find, who perceives? — the self comes back just in the moment when the same evades.' Ricoeur (1990), p. 154 (my translation).

states explicitly that 'person' is a 'Forensick Term'.[4] The position of one of the most prominent Neo-Lockeans, Derek Parfit, is the target of Ricoeur's critical remarks. In the following I shall sketch Parfit's approach. My goal is to underline the contrast between Ricoeur's concept of identity as selfhood and Parfit's thinking.[5]

At the centre of Parfit's theory stands psychological continuity as the decisive criterion for personal identity. Following the psychological continuity thesis it is not bodily continuity as such which is responsible for personal identity but the continuity of consciousness.

Like Locke, who does not defend a substance theory of persons, Parfit's theory does not suppose a substance-ontology. He proposes an event-ontology in which persons are conceived as series of person-stages. Parfit claims: '[...] to be a person, a being must be self-conscious, aware of its identity and its continued existence over time' (Parfit, 1984, p. 202).[6] To capture what self-consciousness over time precisely means, he proposes several distinctions specifying the ways subsequent person-stages can be linked to each other. While 'psychological continuity' is a non-gradual, transitive relation between person stages, 'strong psychological connectedness' is non-transitive and gradual. On the basis of these relations Parfit formulates his *Psychological criterion of personal identity*:

> X today is one and the same person as Y at some past time if and only if (1) X is psychologically continuous with Y, (2) this continuity has the right kind of cause, and (3) it has not taken a 'branching' form. Personal Identity over time just consists in the holding of facts like (1) to (3) (cf. Parfit, 1984, p. 207).

Clause (2) is motivated by the ontological commitments of Parfit. He does not defend a materialistic substance-ontology which identifies persons with particular bodies, viz. living organisms. Parfit simply avoids the business of discussing the empirical question of the causal basis of consciousness. He gives an unabashedly reductionist account in the following sense: the identity of a person over time is determined by facts describable in an *impersonal* way, i.e., not requiring recourse to the notion of a person. The basic elements are momentary states of consciousness (person-stages). The stages are connected by *Relation R*: '[P]sychological connectedness and/or continuity, with the right kind of cause' (Parfit, 1984, p. 215).

---

[4] 'In [...] personal Identity is founded all the Right and Justice of Reward and Punishment [...] — ['Person'] is a Forensick Term appropriating Actions and their Merit; and so belongs only to intelligent Agents capable of a Law, and Happiness and Misery', Locke (1975), II, 27, §§ 18 and 26, pp. 341, 346.

[5] I shall not go into the details of the terminologically sophisticated theory of Parfit here. For a detailed reconstruction of Locke's account and a critical discussion of Parfit's position with bibliographical references to the vast literature cf. Teichert (1999), pp. 130–265.

[6] Cf. Locke's famous definition: '['Person' stands for] a thinking intelligent Being, that has reason and reflection, and can consider itself as itself, the same thinking thing in different times and places; which it does only by that consciousness, which is inseparable from thinking, and as it seems to me essential to it: It being impossible for any one to perceive, without perceiving that he does perceive', Locke (1975), II, 27, § 9, p. 335.

Why is clause (3) needed in the formulation of the psychological criterion? It's the possibility of so-called fission or fusion cases which necessitates this move. Parfit himself offers illustrations for these 'puzzle cases' (cf. Parfit, 1984, p. 199). Such scenarios are often discussed in the literature on personal identity in order to find a reliable criterion for personal identity which is impervious to counterfactuals generated by those thought experiments. In a so-called branching case (or fission) of personal identity there are two persons — $P1_{t2}$ and $P2_{t2}$ — presented as being identical with person P_{t1}. Branching-cases suggest that both to $P1_{t2}$ and $P2_{t2}$ are equally well qualified to count as identical with P_{t1}. Because the identity relation is reflexive (xRx), symmetrical (xRy → yRx), and transitive (xRy ∧ yRz → yRz) it is impossible, however, to treat both $P1_{t2}$ and $P2_{t2}$ as persons identical with P_{t1} (cf. Teichert, 1999, pp. 258–64).

Parfit's solution is to give up the logical notion of identity altogether and to accept Relation R (psychological continuity or psychological connected- ness) as the only relevant aspect for personal identity over time.

Why shouldn't everybody be happy with this solution? Ignoring the internal problems of Parfit's model, we shall look at Ricoeur's critical remarks. Ricoeur claims that identity as sameness ('idem') doesn't account for all relevant aspects of personal identity. As a complementary notion he uses the concept of identity as selfhood ('ipse'): 'The break between *ipse* and *idem* [...] expresses the more fundamental one between *Dasein* and *Vorhanden/Zuhanden*. Only Dasein is mine, and more generally a self.' (Ricoeur, 1991, p. 75). According to this concept the questions 'Who did this?' and 'Who am I?' are to be distinguished from the question 'What (kind of object) is this?' Only 'Who'-questions are specifically directed at persons. According to Ricoeur's view, Parfit treats a person as a manipulable object or artifact, thus failing to account for the 'ipse', or the possibility of the self being held responsible. Ricoeur's point is that the question of selfhood can't be segregated from the social nexus in which selfhood figures. Any account of personal identity that is radically unassimilable to the selfhood given to us by that social nexus, therefore, fails one of the tests of the definition of selfhood — that it would function in such a way as to account for responsibility. There is not only a close etymological connection between 'response' and 'responsibility'. The responsibility for an action presupposes the capability of an agent to communicate, to enter in a dialogue with others and to give a response to the question 'Who did this?' The ethical dimension of selfhood to personal identity is not contingent to what personal identity is, but is essential to it.

In giving an impersonal description of person-stages, Parfit blots out phenomenologically important ways in which the individuals are embedded in a social world and related to their own body. Finally, the concept of responsibility seems to vanish in the context of an impersonal approach that constitutes diachronic personal identity as a series of isolated person-stages. How is it possible to ascribe, in a moral perspective, actions and the consequences of actions to aggregates of conscious contents? If a promise is broken, who is to blame? Usually we would address our reproach at the person who made the promise. But does it make sense — in a world of person-stages which are ontologically independent events by themselves — to blame one person-stage for an action committed by another person-stage?

Of course, Parfit would protest and insist that he is precisely interested in handling moral problems in a justifiable way. Ricoeur, however, could reiterate his complaint that in an event-ontology the concept of a person is in danger of losing the basis needed to preserve the accountability of an agent.

II: Narrative Identity: A Solution or a Further Puzzle?

Ricoeur presents narrative identity as a solution to the problems of personal identity (Ricoeur (1991), p.76). To get clear about this claim it's necessary to see how identity as selfhood is related to narrative.

1. Narrative: structures and functions

A narrative is a semiotic, mostly linguistic presentation of at least two successive states of affairs, events or actions.[7] In contrast to (achronic or instantaneous) *descriptions* ('Left: orange squares, right: green leaves'), narrations display a temporal order. Mere succession, however, isn't a sufficient condition for narrativity. A non-narrative temporal sequence ('Yesterday Dagobert had a hard day. Today the Dow is up 2%.') doesn't necessarily display a semantic or meaningful relation between its two moments; we don't assume the Dow went up to cheer Dagobert. A narrative, in contrast, manifests patterns of coherence or semantic impact between its chronologically ordered elements. It is not a trivial task to spell out in detail which form of coherence or semantic impact is constitutive for a narrative discourse. Danto (1965) highlights the contrast of a narrative text with a chronicle. A *chronicle* is a list of sentences each of which describes an action or event and indicates the time of its occurrence. The standard structure of a chronicle is determined by the fact that events are reported in the order of their occurrence, i.e. the sentences are — explicitly or implicitly — related to each other by the connectives 'and then' or 'and later'.

> C:
> Louis XII was born 1462 in Blois.
> Louis XIII was born 1601 in Fontainebleau.
> Louis XIV was born 1638 in Saint-Germain-en-Laye.

A chronicle informs the reader about (the succession of) facts.[8] Despite its simplicity one can observe an interesting feature of historical sentences in C: it has an inherent temporal point of view. C as a whole could not have been

---

[7] It would be worthwhile to give a reconstruction of Ricoeur's own theory of narrative exposed in 'Time and narrative'. He develops a threefold concept of 'mimesis' in relation with action theory. Since it is impossible to do this exhaustively here I underline some essential features of narrative.

[8] Chronicles do not give the succession of events without gaps as is clearly visible in C. The connective is not necessarily 'and next' (which could be misunderstood as involving completeness) but 'and later'. Of course, C is not a list of successive French kings, but a list of some of the French kings named 'Louis'. Otherwise François I, Henri II, François II, Charles IX, Henri III and Henri IV would be missing.

formulated before the eldest son of Louis XIII succeeded his father as King of France under the name of Louis XIV in 1643. Of course, the inherence of a temporal standpoint is not a specific feature of C but a general structure of many sentences about past events. Names of historical periods and other historical entities obey the same principle of temporal perspective: even if there had been one single event causing World War I, no contemporary observer of this event could have known in that instant that he was participating in the beginning of World War I. This peculiar feature of historical knowing, in which the true descriptions available for an eyewitness are not absolutely interchangeable with the descriptions available to our retrospective knowing, even though in both moments, truth is preserved, is captured by semantico-logic rules pointed out by Leibniz, Russell and others. Logicians call this the problem of opaque contexts. Opacity of contexts and unsubstitutability of descriptions count as the most important features of historical sentences.

It goes without saying that in narrative texts the temporal standpoint of the speaker/writer is also of prime importance. Within the range of differences between chronicle and narrative the most striking one is the *explanatory function* of narrative texts. Whereas chronicles present a stock of brute information about putative facts of the past, narratives give explanations for certain states, events or actions. N1 shows a tripartite structure which makes the explanatory function of narrative explicit:

N1:
(1) Oedipus loves his wife at t-1
(2) Oedipus learns that his wife is his mother at t-2.
(3) Oedipus does not love his wife at t-3.

The change in Oedipus' feelings is explained by the fact that at t-2 Oedipus is informed about his wife's and thereby his own identity. He discovers that his wife is also his mother. Past actions and events are described anew and (1) — with 'love' in the sense of marital love — are now considered by Oedipus as an offence to a basic ethical norm.

The difference between chronicle and narrative is evident. N1 illustrates well the coherence between the components constituting a narrative. A remarkable feature of narrative is the under-determination of the text by the supposed state of affairs. In the case of the N1 it seems perfectly innocent to proceed to a permutation of the sequence in the following way:

N2:
(1) Oedipus didn't love his wife at t-3 any more
(2) as he had done at t-1
(3) after having learned at t-2 that his wife was his mother.

N1 and N2 are both compatible with the supposed state of affairs. There is no universal rule which organizes narratives to present states, events or actions in the temporal order of their respective occurrence. Quite to the contrary, important effects of narrative texts are realized by the well calculated order of (re) presentation as distinct from the (supposed) order of occurrence. The under-determination of narrative texts is pertinent not only to the order of representation of the facts. Other aspects of narrative texts as for example the use of certain singular terms (descriptions, names), stylistic and linguistic means (metonymies, metaphors, irony, emphasis) are not strictly determined by the represented content.

In view of the relation between narrative and identity, the fact that agents themselves are making sense of actions and events by telling stories shouldn't be underestimated. Narrative has the function of giving explanations of actions and events. This functional role of narrative is not restricted to explanations in retrospect. During the process of forming plans and projects agents themselves are using narrative concepts and schemata to specify the goals and organize the means of action. Narrativity concerns not only past actions and events but also gives shape to the future. Conceived in this way it is evident that there is narrativity even without any explicit narrative text. Narrative in this perspective is not only a way of representing past facts that are themselves in part independent of narrative modes of thought and speech, but a way of forming expectations about future events.

It may be useful to distinguish a strong and a weak version of the narrativist position. The strong narrativist claims that (1), that there is a fundamental connection between action and narrativity: acting presupposes narrative schemata; and upon that claim, she bases a further claim, (2) that the self is constituted by narratives.

The weak narrativist disputes the identity conditions supposed in both claims. Instead, she claims (3) that some actions presuppose narrative schemata. And she does not hold that the self is constituted by narratives but (4) that the self generates self-narratives. Ricoeur explicitly holds the strong position with regard to the constitution of personal identity in its full sense.

The strong narrativist has to face the question how the constitution of the personal identity or the self through narrative take place. Is the self constituted by narratives? The strong narrativist answers positively. Is it the self that generates the narratives? The strong narrativist probably will again answer positively and he will insist that he is not going to construct a non-circular, deductive theory of narrative identity. But he endorses this circularity explicitly: '[..] narrative identity is the poetic resolution of the hermeneutic circle' (Ricoeur, 1988, p. 248).

It is evident that self-narratives fulfil very different purposes besides the explanatory function just mentioned. A person may indulge in day-dreams to escape from a frustrating present or she may sketch attractive prospects for her future life to motivate herself to work hard. Even if self-narratives are formulated in an effort to achieve a better self-understanding, Ricoeur is prepared to accept a plurality of possible self-narratives.

Many readers may find the notion of narrative identity somehow opaque. Since as a matter of fact, ordinary people don't tell the story of their life very often and don't go into the business of writing an auto-biography it may seem weird to suppose that persons achieve their identity by means of self-narratives. It is important therefore to remember that Ricoeur does not claim that narrative is a necessary condition for the constitution of personhood on all levels. He is not proposing an empirical theory of what is going on in the minds of all human persons either. But he wants to draw attention to ways of living, acting and thinking which are important in the occidental tradition and its institutions. Narrative, then, is an essential means of the constitution of one's personal identity.

It might seem, however, that there is a certain tension between the claim that narrative identity highlights the ethical dimension of the individual's life on the one hand and the fact that the story of a life can be told in multiple ways. Where does this leave us with regard to the ethical aspect of narrative identity? How can one conceive of a person as a responsible agent deciding what to do according to ethical norms and, at the same time, affirm a plurality of possible stories modelling the life of this person? Are there no constraints with respect to the stories which make up the narrative identity of an individual? Can a notorious liar tell his life as the story about an honest person? One possibility, here, is to say: 'Of course, he can, and this is a telling fact about his character; he is not only lying but he wants others (and possibly himself too) believe him to be a respectable person.' But in the first place it is essential to realize that the liar does not tell stories in the sense of a reflexive exploration about the meaning of his actions in view of a better self-understanding. Not every narrative is a self-narrative and not all self-narratives are narratives exploring the ethical dimension of a life and seeking a fuller self-understanding. The explorative self-narratives are constitutive for the identity of a person. And they are open to re-interpretation and modification insofar as the orientations of the subject are modified and its situation is changed. There is no contradiction, then, between the claim that self-narratives are always variable and revisable, open to be retold in different versions and the ethical function of self-narratives. In an ethical perspective, self-narratives articulate the goals, values and loyalties of the self. As Ricoeur puts it, self-narrative is the platform where conscience plays an essential role. Self-narratives can create a form of interior accountability of the agent and give shape to her identity. Due to the conscience of the individual, various forms of obligation or loyalty are constituted, ways of projecting oneself into the future explored, and actions motivated independently from the consideration of the possibility of public sanctions are accepted as morally binding. The autonomous decision to adopt a certain norm during a particular episode of one's life seems to be a paradigm case of enacting what is meant by identity as selfhood.

2. Narrative identity and the collective

Ricoeur stresses the point that the self-understanding of groups as well as individuals is mediated by narratives which play a prominent role in the respective tradition (Ricoeur, 1985b, p. 356). Narrative identity constitutes the identity of a group, making a plurality of individuals one collective (cf. Ricoeur, 1985b, pp. 355–9 and 272–5). How does this happen? One paradigm case for Ricoeur is the Jewish people, whose collective identity is not primarily formed by genealogical relations or the simple fact that they are living together in a common territory. The collective identity is constituted by a common tradition in which two forms of remembrance mediated by narrative representations are of prime importance. On the one hand, there is the memory of the foundation of their community by its relation to God as it is articulated in the sacred texts. This is the constitutive element of the religious practice of Jewish people. Even if the Ten Commandments, imperatives and not narratives, are at the core of this religion, the biblical text transmits the Commandments by telling the story of their revelation on Mount Sinai. The prescriptive and normative element is indissolubly linked to the narration of Moses and the people of Israel.

On the other hand, the remembrance of the Nazi genocide constitutes an experience which unites the Jewish people as a collective and which in all its unforgettable negativity marks the lives even of those whose self-understanding is not determined by a religious orientation. Here, narrative identity is introduced in a moral, social and political dimension. The common history is represented in manifold attempts at narrative mediation. Actions, decisions and attitudes of the individuals and the groups as such are dependent on the self-concepts shaped by history and narrative tradition.

3. Narrative identity and the individual

The concept of identity as selfhood — in contrast to identity as sameness — is closely linked to the ethical sphere and to the first-person perspective in which the question 'Who am I?' can be asked. When I raise the question 'Who am I?' (as distinct from the question 'Who is she?'), I am not asking about my name, except in unusual contexts. Instead, by asking such a question I want to know myself better. One way of thinking about the question 'Who am I?' is an attempt to tell the story of one's life or to recall at least relevant fragments of this unfolding story. This is done in psychoanalysis: 'Subjects recognize themselves in the stories they tell about themselves' (Ricoeur, 1988, p. 247). Of course, self-recognition and self-understanding mediated by narrative are not exclusively achieved in psychoanalysis. When I ask the question 'Who am I?' I wonder whether the values I honour and the goals I pursue are the right ones. I try to see whether my feelings and my beliefs are compatible. I examine whether the reasons and desires that sustain me are sound or unhealthy. I want to know whether I am the person I want to be. The way I as a person confront the life I am living, the attitude I take to my life and the life of others defines my personal identity. In this sense personal identity is more than a question of re-identification. The question 'Who am I?' never finds a definite answer. This question again and again may pop up in the course of my life. Whereas identity as sameness may be brought under the heading 'What is x?' or 'Is x identical with y?', identity as selfhood has to be approached from a first-person perspective.

To be a person and to gain one's identity — in the sense of identity as selfhood — means to be a being which does not possess a stable, closed and fixed identity. Identity as selfhood is not simply there like an objective fact. To possess an identity as selfhood means to be the subject of dynamic experience, instability, and fragility: '[...] narrative identity is not a stable and seamless identity. Just as it is possible to compose several plots on the subject of the same incidents [...], so it is always possible to weave different, even opposed, plots about our lives.' (Ricoeur, 1988, p. 248).

The self does not exist as an isolated, autonomous entity which constitutes itself as a Cartesian ego. Nor is the self a mere passive product of a society. Ricoeur's position takes a middle path between these extreme options. Selves are built up in the process of assimilating, interpreting, and integrating contents of the cultural environment (Ricoeur, 1969).

There is an intimate connection between narrative and actions. Ricoeur, however, does not directly defend a strong narrativist position. He does not refer to narrative on the level of single actions and linear sequences of elementary actions, but distinguishes two further levels: so-called practices (Ricoeur, 1990, pp. 181–6) and plans of life (Ricoeur, 1990, pp. 186–93).

(1) Practices

Action theory conceives actions bottom-up: actions are composed out of primitive basic actions. A basic action in general is an elementary body movement (e.g. the raising of one's arm). Executing a basic action allows the performance of more complex actions (e.g. voting by raising one's arm). This approach accounts for the different levels of complexity in actions.

The concept of *practices* modifies this model by introducing an organizing scheme that gives an internal unity to all the different actions constituting a practice. Examples of practices are professions (farmer, teacher), games, and artistic activities. We would be at loss to enumerate all types of action belonging to these different practices. A farmer typically sows, plants, ploughs, mows, and harvests. But besides these peculiar actions he does many other things. Giving a complete list of the actions relevant for a practice is not only difficult but impossible, since practices are interactive processes which are often modified and transformed — to be a farmer in the eighteenth century implies different actions and tools than being a farmer in the twenty-first century. Practices are not systematically closed concepts. Participating in a practice presupposes learning and training based on a particular tradition. Ricoeur doesn't say that practices as such display narrative structure. He speaks about a pre-narrative structure of their organisation that is responsible for the fact that a practice gives meaning to the lives of the participating subjects (Ricoeur, 1990, p. 186).

(2) Plans of life

On the superior level of *plans of life* the link to narrative is more explicit. Here Ricoeur refers to A. MacIntyre's idea of a narrative unity of life and expresses doubts about this notion. He argues that life and fiction (or texts) are to be distinguished carefully (cf. Ricoeur, 1990, p. 190). Similarities of life and literary narratives are familiar to Ricoeur, of course, but he resists an easy transfer of the literary schemata to the domain of individual life. Whereas the unity of a literary narrative really comprehends beginning, middle and end, the unity of life is never given for a subject. At best it can be anticipated by an individual who forecasts the shape of his or her own life as a linear evolution from birth to death. As the author of a narrative text I may be completely autonomous and free in my decisions to fix beginning, middle and end of the story I am writing. As an individual living one's life, one is not free to choose the beginning and the unfolding story of that life due to the fact that the life is only in part determined by one's choices and decisions. The interventions of others and the contingencies of events destroy the illusion of an authorial position in real life. It seems less problematic to speak about plans of life than of the unity of life. Plans of life are global representations based on conceptions of relevant goals and values. Plans of life have an important function for the orientation and organisation of the individual's activities and are sketched in narrative form.

(3) Character and promise

Ricoeur's remarks on character and promise clarify the ways in which the notion of identity as sameness complements the notion of identity as selfhood. (Ricoeur, 1990, pp. 143–50).

Those distinctive properties of an individual which allow her re-identification constitute her character. Not all long-term properties are included in the concept of character. Acquired, stable dispositions are of prime importance, since they enduringly anchor a person through time. Habits and identifications are two essential aspects of character. Habits are not just given as 'natural' properties to the individuals; they are acquired by the repetition of actions and patterns of behaviour. In addition, a person can identify herself with certain values, norms, ideals, heroes. By doing so she modifies the concept of her self and, thanks to continued identifications, she gives stability to her life. Character, however, has a comparatively great affinity to the concept of identity as sameness since it can be described to a large extent in an impersonal way (Ricoeur, 1990, p. 146). It is important therefore to look at another way the person gives permanence to her being as a person in distinction from the concept of identity as sameness: by making a promise. In the act of promising, the person affirms herself as an individual whose identity is extended in time. In giving a promise — 'I promise you I shall do x' — I now actively identify myself with myself in the future. By keeping the promise I create a continuous self in time.

If I break the promise I don't become a different person, I don't change my personal identity but I distance myself now from the past self who stated his commitment with the intention to fulfil it. Even in the case of the broken promise I acknowledge the continuity of my life as a person. There is nothing comparable to this kind of active maintenance and permanence on the level of identity as sameness.

Narrative identity is the integration of both aspects of identity as selfhood — character and promise — into a dynamic model. To explore the concept of selfhood more fully it would be appropriate to look closer at Ricoeur's remarks on

Heidegger's concept of 'Dasein' and the Aristotelian notions 'dynamis' and 'energeia' (Ricoeur, 1990, pp. 351–65). They both are important points of reference for an attempt to elaborate a notion of the self which is not conceived in terms of a substance-ontology.

Does Ricoeur really offer a solution to the paradoxes of personal identity with his concept of narrative identity? No doubt, anybody reading Ricoeur expecting to find a definite answer comparable to Lockean and Neo-Lockean models of personal identity will be disappointed. Ricoeur's project is not to formulate a new criterion for personal identity. He widens the notion of personal identity and integrates aspects which are neglected by analytical philosophers. The gain is considerable. Ricoeur respects the semantic richness of the concept of a person and the notion of a self, and he includes certain important aspects of personhood that are neglected by models based on abstract theory building.[9] The cost of his strategy is a loss of systematic simplicity. It is not his aim to formulate a systematic theory which explains in a linear way the constitution of the phenomena. On various occasions he states explicitly circularities which are not to be considered as faults but as articulations of interdependencies on a fundamental level (Ricoeur, 1984a, pp. 71–2, 76; 1988, p. 248). It is no flaw of his notion of narrative identity, according to Ricoeur, to say: the identity of the person is constituted by a self-narrative. And: the self-narrative is told/constituted by the person.

III: Ricoeur and Dennett on Narrative Identity:
Collision or Complementarity?

In order to show that the narrative model of personal identity possesses advantages that have occurred to philosophers working in a completely different tradition than Ricoeur's, I shall briefly focus on the narrative moment in Dennett's work on personal identity.[10] A word on the general orientation of Dennett is in place, however, before looking at the notion of the narrative self. Dennett is highly suspicious — as are mainstream analytical philosophers in general — of the 'pseudo-problems' of traditional philosophy and the impasse of psychologistic conceptions in the philosophy of psychology and mind. He attacks the remnants of the Cartesian ego wherever he can track them. In addition

---

[9] Of course, abstraction as such is not a problematic aspect of theorizing. A problem arises, however, if authors do not differentiate carefully between the manifold functions 'person' plays in heterogeneous theoretical as well as pre-theoretical contexts on the one hand and their own investigation on the other hand. Replacing the sometimes bewildering variety of person-concepts by a single coherent notion may seem attractive. But it would be appropriate to show that the pre-theoretical rules governing the use of 'person' and the other theoretical concepts are ill conceived and incoherent, to eliminate them altogether. This, however, is never done. One example is the 'four-dimensional'-model of a person and the tension between its event-ontology and the pre-theoretical usage of the concept of a person. M. Johnston has articulated several arguments against the abandonment or complete revision of pre-theoretical conceptions; cf. Johnston (1987; 1989; 1992); Haslanger (1990), Runggaldier (1996), pp. 186–96.

[10] Dennett (1991; 1992). There are many other conceptions of narrative identity, of course: Mink (1970), Schapp (1976), Schafer (1980; 1992), Macintyre (1981), Carr (1986), Kerby (1986; 1991), White (1987), Polkinghorne (1988), Taylor (1989), Schechtman (1996), Worthington (1996).

to this set of analytic biases, his work is, for a philosopher, more than usually informed by close contact with empirical research on cognition and psychic processes. Indeed, the standard realistic scientific perspective coincides with Dennett's preference for causal explanations of mental phenomena. 'How can living physical bodies in the physical world produce such (i.e. conscious) phenomena? That is the mystery'(Dennett, 1991, p. 25).

Here lies the first major difference between Ricoeur and Dennett: Ricoeur attempts to give conceptual reconstructions and analysis without ever going into the business of finding or discussing causal explanations.

The second major difference becomes evident when we look at Dennett's 'heterophenomenology' and contrast it with Ricoeur's application of the phenomenological tradition.[11] Philosophy of mind and of language in the twentieth century has criticized with considerable success traditional concepts of the subject and especially of 'inner experience' and introspection as sources of knowledge. One of the most famous attacks has been that of Gilbert Ryle's critique of the Cartesian ego as the 'ghost in the machine', which casts doubt on the infallibility, immediacy and transparency of the subject's reflexive thoughts. Dennett claims that his philosophy of mind will be respectful of the phenomena of mental and psychic experience — i.e. will be a phenomenology — without falling into the traps of Cartesianism and subsequent speculative theories of subjectivity by according unwarranted privileges to the first-person perspective.

> Here is the *neutral* path leading from objective physical science and its insistence on the third-person point of view, to a method of phenomenological description that can (in principle) do justice to the most private and ineffable subjective experiences, while never abandoning the methodological scruples of science (Dennett, 1991, p. 71).

Now this is clearly a point where no consensus between Ricoeur and Dennett is possible. Ricoeur would insist on the conceptual impossibility of reducing subjectivity to an object of scientific research. On the other hand, he would largely approve of Dennett's critique of the Cartesian ego and its epistemic power. In fact, Dennett formulates his model of the mind in contrast to Descartes' which persists in contemporary thought under the veneer of materialism as a hybrid 'Cartesian materialism'. This approach clings to the idea that the mind is a unitary structure having a centre and a clear hierarchy. Dennett agrees with Ricoeur in his insistence that there is a lot of Cartesianism even in the age of science and materialism:

> Cartesian materialism is the view that there is a crucial finish line or boundary somewhere in the brain, marking a place where the order of arrival equals the order of 'presentation' in experience because *what happens there* is what you are conscious of (Dennett, 1991, p. 107).

As an alternative to the traditional notion of the mind as a unitary structure Dennett formulates his 'Multiple Drafts Model' of the mind. The mental process

---

[11] Cf. Dennett (2003). Dennett complains that continental phenomenologists are ignoring his research, not willing to enter into an exchange of arguments in Dennett (2003)

is not conceived here as a linear sequence of stable elements. The contents of consciousness are processed in a phenomenal space in which many partly independent modules are at work. Conscious content is constantly revised like parts of a narrative are permanently transformed in the process of writing. The stream of consciousness can be compared to an ongoing process of writing and revising drafts. The self is not an independent author of these scripts. It could not be identified as an immaterial entity or as a special part of the brain. Dennett's idea is that the self is like a centre of gravity, an abstract entity. It's simply a category mistake to speak of a centre of gravity as if it were a concrete empirical object. A self accordingly is a theoretical construct; it is the nucleus of the multiple narrative fragments constituting the conscious experiences of the individual.

> We try to make all of our material cohere into a single good story. And that story is our autobiography. The chief fictional character at the center of that autobiography is one's *self*. And if you still want to know what the self *really* is, you are making a category mistake (Dennett, 1992, p. 115).

Now, how is Dennett's concept of narrative gravity to be situated with respect to Ricoeur's notion of narrative identity? It comes somewhat as a surprise that there is no clear collision, not even a strong incompatibility between the two approaches despite the huge differences between the general orientation of Ricoeur and Dennett. One factor responsible for this is the similar way both take positions on the ontological status of the self. For Dennett the self is an abstract entity, a construct or fiction, surely not to be directly identified with a material entity, for example the brain. For Ricoeur the self is an entity that is neither a material nor an immaterial entity but the product of intersubjective praxis and active appropriation of the contents of the cultural environment. Both conceptions are compatible, even if they (viz. their authors) do not realize that this is the case. It is important, of course, not to misunderstand what is meant by compatibility. Compatibility is not positive agreement on all points, but absence of contradiction on important points.[12] In my view, the main point where Ricoeur's and Dennett's conceptions can be seen as compatible is the thesis that the self is not a substance. In addition, both authors are not proposing a relational model of personal identity like the Neo-Lockeans. They do not propose a new criterion for personal identity. They are both abandoning the project of building models of the self or personal identity that serve as the basis for justifiable and decidable identity statements. With respect to the further claim of Dennett that the self is a pure construct, a fiction, Ricoeur would certainly take his distance. For Ricoeur the way the self exists — despite the huge difficulty of conceptual articulation — is what is most real and most opposed to fiction. The compatibility comes to an end, of course, when we enter the domain of social interaction and ethics. Here, Ricoeur's and Dennett's theories are opposed to each other. For Dennett it is not evident that the concept of personal identity has to be developed by starting on

---

[12] Probably Dennett would react by declaring that compatibility means nothing, since he is impatient with Ricoeur who in his eyes has 'carried the art of bombastic redescription to new heights', Dennett (2003), p.1.

the level of interaction and ethics. From Ricoeur's point of view Dennett's concept of the self as a construct and fiction seems to undermine the idea that there is an accountable self that is understood by others and by herself as the author of action.[13]

References

Carr, D. (1986), *Time, Narrative, and History* (Bloomington, IN: Indiana University Press).
Danto, A. (1965), *Analytical Philosophy of History* (Cambridge: Cambridge University Press).
Dennett, D. (1991), *Consciousness Explained* (Boston, MA: Little Brown).
Dennett, D. (1992), 'The Self as the center of narrative gravity', in *Self and Consciousness: Multiple Perspectives*, ed. F.S. Kessel (Hillsdale, NJ: Erlbaum).
Dennett, D. (2003), 'Tiptoeing past the covered wagons: A response to Carr',
    http: //ase.tufts.edu/cogstud/papers/tiptoe.htm
Haslanger, S. (1990), 'Endurance and temporal intrinsics', *Analysis*, **50**, pp. 119–25.
Hume, D. (1986), *A Treatise on Human Nature* (Oxford: Clarendon)
Husserl, E. (1976), Die Krisis; der europäischen Wissenschaften und die transzendentale Phänomenologie (Gesammelte Werke VI) (Den Haag: Martinus Nijhoff).
Johnston, M. (1987), 'Human beings', *Journal of Philosophy*, **84**, pp. 57–83.
Johnston, M. (1989), 'Fission and the facts', *Philosophical Perspectives*, **3**, pp. 369–97.
Johnston, M. (1992), 'Reasons and reductionism', *The Philosophical Review*, **101**, pp. 590–618.
Kerby, P. (1986), 'The language of the self', *Philosophy Today*, **31**, pp. 210–23.
Kerby, P. (1991), *Narrative and the Self* (Bloomington, IN: Indiana University Press).
Locke, J. (1975), *An Essay Concerning Human Understanding* (Oxford: Clarendon).
Macintyre, A. (1981), *After Virtue* (Notre Dame, IN: University of Notre Dame Press).
Mink, L.O. (1970), 'History and fiction as modes of comprehension', *New Literary History*, **1**, pp. 541–58.
Parfit, D. (1984), *Reasons and Persons* (Oxford: Clarendon).
Polkinghorne, D.E. (1988), *Narrative Knowing and the Human Sciences* (Albany, NY: State University of New York Press).
Ricoeur, P. (1969), 'Existence et herméneutique', in: P. Ricoeur, Le conflit des interprétations (Paris: Seuil).
Ricoeur, P. (1983), Temps et récit I (Paris: Seuil).
Ricoeur, P. (1984a), *Time and Narrative I*, trans. K. McLaughlin and D. Pellauer (Chicago, IL: University of Chicago Press).
Ricoeur, P. (1984b), Temps et récit II – La configuration du temps dans le récit de fiction (Paris: Seuil).
Ricoeur, P. (1985a), *Time and Narrative II*, trans. K. McLaughlin and D. Pellauer (Chicago, IL: University of Chicago Press).
Ricoeur, P. (1985b), Temps et récit III – Le temps raconté (Paris: Seuil).
Ricoeur, P. (1988), *Time and Narrative III*, trans. K. Blamey and D. Pellauer (Chicago, IL: University of Chicago Press).
Ricoeur, P. (1990), Soi-même comme un autre (Paris: Seuil).
Ricoeur, P. (1991), 'Narrative identity', *Philosophy Today*, **35**, pp. 73–81.
Ricoeur, P. (2000), La mémoire, l'histoire, l'oubli (Paris: Seuil).
Runggaldier, E. (1996), Was sind Handlungen? Eine philosophische Auseinandersetzung mit dem Naturalismus (Stuttgart: Kohlhammer).
Schafer, R. (1980), 'Narration in the psychoanalytic dialogue', in *On Narrative*, ed. W.J.T. Mitchell (Chicago, IL: University of Chicago Press).
Schafer, R. (1992), *Retelling a Life: Narration and Dialogue in Psychoanalysis* (New York: Basic Books)
Schapp, W. (1976), In Geschichten verstrickt (Wiesbaden: Heymann).
Schechtman, M. (1996), 'The narrative self-constitution view', in *The Constitution of Selves* (Ithaca, NY: Cornell University Press).
Strawson, P.F. (1959), *Individuals: An Essay in Descriptive Metaphysics* (London: Methuen).
Taylor, C. (1989), *Sources of the Self: The Making of Modern Identity* (Cambridge: Cambridge University Press).
Teichert, D. (1999), Personen und Identitäten (Berlin: de Gruyter).
White, H. (1987), *The Content of the Form: Narrative Discourse and Historical Representation* (Baltimore: Johns Hopkins University Press)
Worthington, K.L. (1996), *Self as Narrative* (Oxford: Clarendon).

[13] Thanks to Delbert Barley, Jürgen Bechtold, Andris Breitling, Roger Gathman, Johanna Seibt, Dan Zahavi, and two anonymous referees for critical remarks and suggestions.